Dr. John Skull

Key Terms
in Art Craft &
Design

 **Elbrook Press**

Elbrook Press,
P.O. Box 520, 515, Brighton Road,
Adelaide, South Australia, 5048.

First published 1988

Copyright © John Skull, 1988

Designed by John Skull

ISBN 0 7316 1787 8

Typeset by The Government Printing Division, South
Australia

Printed by Singapore National Printers Ltd., Singapore

Illustrated mainly by David Malpas and also by Judith
Dawson, Lim Swee Eng and Amanda Graham

Book cover by Keith McEwan and David Lancashire
Design, Melbourne

Photographs (unless otherwise indicated)
by Gordon Burrow and Terry Carr

Acknowledgments

We are most grateful to the following people for their advice and help in the production of this book: Bruce Anderson, Ian Arcus, Ross Barnes, Doug Boughton, Alan Bundy, Christopher Burfield, John Copeland, Betty Derby, Carol Ann Fooks, Bram Fynnart, Keith Goldsworthy, Roger Green, Jeff Harris, Helen Herde, Bill Jolley ,Fred Littlejohn ,Bob Miller-Smith, Christopher Myors, Ian North, Erica Pfitzner, Jack Peake, Peter Schulz, Terry Smith and George Tetlow.

We are also grateful to the following art galleries and commercial firms for permission to use copyright material:

Australian National Gallery, Canberra, Australia; Art Gallery of South Australia, Adelaide, Australia; National Gallery of Victoria, Melbourne, Australia; Charles Brand Machinery Inc., New York, U.S.A.; Shimpo Industrial Co. Ltd., Yyoto, Japan.

Foreword

The rationale of this book is based on the following opinions:

The beginning of understanding and wisdom begins with the precise meaning of terms.

> (Confucius)

As he uses words a person notices or neglects types of relationships and phenomena; he channels his reasoning and builds the house of consciousness.

> (B.L.Whorf in *Language, Thought and Reality*)

Yes, I want to know, to know in order to feel more deeply, to feel more deeply in order to know more.

> (Paul Cézanne)

What we cannot speak about, we consign to silence.

> (L. Wittgenstein in *Tractus Logico-Philosophicus*)

For if words are not things, they are living powers by which things of most importance to mankind are activated, combined and humanified.

> (Samuel Taylor Coleridge in *Preface to Aids to Reflection*)

It seems to be one of the paradoxes of creativity that in order to think originally, we must familiarise ourselves with the ideas of others.

> (George Keller in *The Art and Science of Creativity*)

He who has imagination without learning has wings but no feet.

> (Chinese proverb)

Abstract and Abstract Art

Pronounced: AB-STRAKT (*a's as in cat*)

Origin

Abstract is from the Latin words *ab* meaning *away from* and *tract* from *trahere* meaning *to draw*. That is *to draw away* or *withdraw* from realism and naturalism. The term was first applied in art to the works of Wassily Kandinsky in 1910, and he could be called the founder of Abstract Painting. The first international exhibition of Abstract Art was by Michel Sempor in Paris in 1930.

Meaning

Abstract refers to an idea or thought that is drawn away from the ordinary normal or real and then given expression. Michel Sempor, an art critic said "*I call abstract art any art that contains no reference to, no evocation of, reality, whether or not the reality was the artist's point of departure*". In abstract art, the artist expresses not a representation of objective forms but his or her emotional or intellectual reactions to the forms - sometimes by energetic and furious line and brilliant and vehement colour; at other times through non-objective forms, strongly resembling the geometric designs of traditional Arabic art. The artists laid stress on the act of painting, considering it almost a ritual. The emphasis on formalism in Abstract Art makes it a forerunner of Modernism.

an abstract drawing by Doug Boughton

Associations

See the paintings of Wassily Kandinsky (Russian 1866-1944), Frantisek Kupka (Czech 1871-1957), Robert Delaunay (French 1885-1941), and Piet Mondrian (Dutch 1872-1944) and the sculptures of Constantin Brancusi (Romanian 1876-1957) and more recently the paintings of Jackson Pollock (USA 1912-1956) and Willen de Kooning (Dutch 1904-). The nearest opposite to Abstract Art is **representational art**, where the picture aims to represent reality.

See: **Abstract Expressionism, Fauvism, Dadaism, Cubism, Action Painting, geometric, objective, subjective, Realism, biomorphic, Hard-Edge Painting, tachisme.**

Accelerator

Pronounced: AK-SEL-A-RA-TA (*1st a as in cat, 2nd a as in ago, 3rd a as in late, 4th a as in ago, e as in bell*)

Origin

From the Latin *acceleratio* meaning *to increase speed*. The Latin word *celer* means *swift* and *celerity* in English means *swiftness*.

Meaning

An accelerator is a substance which when added to other substances speeds up the chemical reaction. If salt, for example, is added to plaster, it accelerates the setting of the plaster. An accelerator added to a photographic developer increases the rate of development.

Associations

A **Retarder** is a substance which can slow down the setting process. Keraton, for example, when added to plaster retards the setting time. An accelerator is sometimes called an **activator** or **promotor**. A **siccative** is a substance which is added to oil paint or to varnish to accelerate drying time.

Accent

Pronounced: AK-SENT (*a as in cat, e as in tent*)

Origin

From the Latin *ad* meaning *to* and *cantus* meaning *singing*. It means the way something is said, sung, interpreted or stressed.

Meaning

An accent is an emphasis given to, or stress placed on, part of an artistic composition, in order to attract attention to it. The accent may be created in painting by increased colour, tone or brightness, increased size and light or dark contrast. *To accent* something means to make it conspicuous or to intensify it.

Associations

Accentual lighting is where attention to a visual object is drawn by special lighting effects.

See: **highlight, focal point, contrast, composition.**

Acrylic

Pronounced: A-KRIL-IK (*a as in ago,i's as in ill*)

Origin

From the Latin *acer* meaning *sharp* and *olere* meaning *to smell*. Acrylic paints were developed in the 1920's from a man-made acrylic acid (which has a sharp smell) to produce a synthetic resin.

Meaning

Acrylic paints are used by some painters rather than oils, as they can be used thickly (for impasto effect) or diluted with water (for water colours) and they dry in ten minutes. Acrylic paint should not be mixed with oil paint. The colours are opaque and dry to a matt finish and tolerate most atmospheric conditions well. Because they are so versatile, these plastic emulsion paints are popular with artists.

Associations

An **emulsion** is the fine mixing of one liquid into another. **Synthetic** substances are mixed together to make a compound substance.

See: **ground, canvas, impasto, opacity, matt.**

Action Painting

Pronounced: AK-SHUN (*a as in cat, u as in bonus*), PANT-ING (*a as in late*)

Origin

Action Painting is a term first used by the American Art critic, Harold Rosenberg, in 1952 to describe the Abstract Art work of some American painters. It is also referred to as *Abstract Expressionism.*

Meaning

Action Painting is painting which is not directly controlled but tends to have a large element of chance in what is produced. The artist flings or smears or trickles paint onto a canvas, using a range of objects to create shapes and patterns. The sub-conscious is supposedly a source of inspiration for the "*event*". Jackson Pollock, a leader in this type of painting, said his intention was to "*express feelings rather than illustrate them*". It emphasised that pictures should show the various stages of the creative process in which the artist is involved in producing the work-that is **painting in action**. Similar techniques are **dip painting** and **stain painting**. **Tachisme** is the French equivalent of Action Painting. **Abstract Expressionism** was first used to describe the work of Kandinsky but is now associated with the work of Kline, Pollock and Gorky and other artists, including those who did not use Action Painting techniques.

Associations

See: **Abstract, Tachisme, Art Brut, amorphous.**

See the works of Jackson Pollock (American 1912-1956), Mark Rothko, (American 1903-1970), William de Kooning (Dutch 1904 -).

Aesthetics

Pronounced: ES-THET-IKS (*e's as in escape, i as in ink*)

Origin

From the Greek *aisthetikos* meaning *perception-noticing-* e.g. beauty. The word aesthetics was first used in Germany in about 1750 by Alexander Baumgarten and related to "*good taste*". It first appeared in English in the mid 19th century.

Meaning

Aesthetics is the study and perception of the nature and theories of art and of the characteristics of beauty and the origins of sensitivity to art form. Generally when aesthetic is used to describe something, it refers to experience through the senses rather than through the intellect. Nowadays, it also means the study of the relationship of art to other aspects of culture, such as philosophy, religion, morality, science and industry and commerce.

Associations

See: **Fine Art, harmony, perception.**

Air Brush Work

Pronounced: AR (*a as in fare*), BRUSH (*u as in bonus*), WURK (*u as in fur*)

Origin

The air brush is a device first developed by a British artist Charles Burdick in 1893.

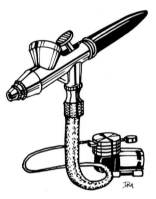

an air brush

Meaning

Air brush work is a method of painting using compressed air or an inert gas in a mechanical pump-sprayer, which can be very finely controlled (by an air-control valve and a colour-control valve) to produce delicate lines, toning and shading effects. It is used extensively in **graphics** to produce smooth, neutral finishes. It is used also in **Pop Art** and for retouching photographs and in lithography. The part of a composition not to be airbrushed is covered by a mask ,called a **frisket**.

Associations

The term **aerograph** is also used for air brush work.

See: **masking, composition, Graphic Design, Pop Art.**

Alla Prima

Pronounced: ALLA-PREEMA (*a's as in bat, ee as in meet, final a as in ago*)

Origin

From the Italian meaning *at first*.

Meaning

Alla prima is a painting which has one layer of paint, usually on a white ground without the use of an undercoat or the use of retouching. The lighter colours are usually applied first, followed by the darker ones. A painting is begun and finished during one working period and therefore there is a large element of spontaneity in the finished work. Sometimes it is called **wet-in-wet** technique.

Associations

Alla prima is also called *au premier coup* which is French for *at the first attempt.*

See the paintings of the French artists Claud Monet (1840-1926), Alfred Sisley (1839-1899), Camille Pissarro (1839-1903), Pierre Auguste Renoir (1841-1919).

Allegory

Pronounced: ALA-GORY (*first a as in bat, second as in ago, o as in pot*)

Origin

From the Greek *allas* meaning *other* and *agoria* meaning *speaking.* That is speaking otherwise than one does in a direct open manner- with a hidden meaning.

Meaning

Allegory refers to a description or expression of something under the guise of something else which resembles it in some respects. It tells a story in which the characters or events are symbols of certain truths about human life. It is an extended metaphor, or an emblem.

Associations:

See: **symbol, figurative, Surrealism, subjective.**

See Sandro Botticelli's (1444-1510) "*Birth of Venus*", Picasso's (1881-1973) "*Guernica*", which is an allegory of war, and Stanley Spencer's (1891-1959) paintings of religious allegories.

All-Over Painting

Meaning

An All-Over Painting has no figure and ground arrangement and no central point of composition or accent but gives equal emphasis to all aspects of the composition.

Associations

The term is often applied to the Action Paintings of Jackson Pollock (1912-1956) and the late works of Claude Monet (1840-1926).

See: **Action Painting, accent, composition, ground, amorphous.**

Amorphous

Pronounced: AMOR-FUS (*a as in ago, o as in port, u as in bus*)

Origin

From the Greek *a* meaning *not* and *morphe* meaning *form* or *shape. A- morphe* is *without shape.*

John Olsen, Australia born 1928
Half past six at the Fitzroy (detail)
oil on canvas 137.5 x 182.0 cm *Art Gallery of South Australia, Adelaide, South Australia*

Meaning

Amorphous means without a definite, recognizable shape.

Associations

Biomorphic refers to shapes which are irregular or resemble curves found in organic life. **Mechanomorphic** refers to forms which resemble a part of a machine (e.g. they are hard-edged) or seem to be machine-made. **Morphology** is the study of shapes.

See: **Action Painting, All-Over Painting, symmetrical.**

Animation

Pronounced: ANI-MASHUN (*a as in cat, i as in pin, ashun rhymes with station*)

Origin

From the Latin *animare* meaning *to give life to*. The Latin word *anima* means *life*.

Meaning

Animation is used mainly in cinematography. It means a process of filming people or things (animals, buildings, machines,etc.) one frame at a time in such a way that when the film is projected the people or things appear to move and to be "*alive*".

Associations

See: **movement, gradation, illusion, projection, technique.**

Annealing

Pronounced: AN-EE-LING (*a as in pan, ee as in bee, i as in sing*)

Origin

From an old English word *onaela* meaning *to burn, bake* or *set on fire* or from an Old French word *neeler* meaning *to enamel*.

Meaning

Annealing is a process of reducing the stresses caused by heating metal or glass by controlled cooling. Metal (for instance in jewellery making) or glass are softened by heat, and when slowly cooled they are less brittle and more easily worked (e.g.hammered, twisted or bent). This process toughens and tempers or glazes the materials. With silver and copper, cooling must be done quickly by quenching them in cold water. Glass must be cooled slowly in an oven (called a **lehr**) to prevent cracking. Each metal requires a different temperature for annealing.

Associations

See: **pickle, glaze, glass.**

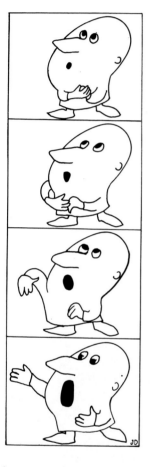

frames in an animation sequence

Appliqué

Pronounced: A-PLEE-KAY (*a as in apple, ee as in meet, ay as in say*).

Origin

From the Latin *applicare* meaning *to join* or *attach* and the French *appliquer* meaning *to apply* or *fasten to*, or *to lay something on something*. The technique dates back to the thirteenth century.

Meaning

Appliqué is a type of embroidery where a design in one material is cut out and then, using embroidery stitchery, is attached to another foundation material. This is called **overlaid appliqué**. An **inlaid appliqué** is where a design is cut out from a foundation material and the cut spaces are filled by another material, which is stitched on using embroidery stitchery. It used to be a very popular way of decorating such things as table linen, towels, and other domestic materials with bold, colourful designs. Appliqué is also used in jewellery, where decorative pieces are soldered onto a metal base and also in leatherwork, where patterns cut from leather are glued or sewn onto another piece of leather. When paper is used it is usually called **decoupage**.

Associations

See: **motif, embroidery, solder, decoupage**.

Aquarelle

Pronounced: AKWA-REL (*a's as in actor, e as in well*)

Origin

From the Italian *aquarella* meaning *water colour. Aqua* is the Latin for *water.*

Meaning

An aquarelle is a painting where transparent water colours (in contrast to *tempera* or *casein* mediums) are used. The word may also refer to the paints themselves. An artist who paints using an aquarelle technique is an **aquarellist**. The term **water-colour** is more generally used than aquarelle.

Associations

Gouache is an opaque water colour, whereas an aquarelle is transparent.

See: **tempera, watercolour, gouache**.

Aquatint

Pronounced: AKWA-TINT (*a's as in actor, i as in mint*).

Origin

The word originates from the fact that prints made with this technique resemble works produced using water-colour wash. It is from the Latin *aqua* meaning *water* and *tintus* meaning *dyeing.* Aquatint was invented by Jean-Baptiste Leprince in the second half of the 18th century.

Meaning

An aquatint is an etching technique where a copper-plate is covered with resin (or powdered asphaltum) in order to make the plate slightly granular in texture and to give it a *tooth* to hold ink. Parts which are to appear white are varnished. The plate is put in a bath of acid which *bites* (etches) into the unvarnished parts of the plate. This process is carried out a number of times to get the desired design. In **sugarlift aquatint** an image is painted onto a plate with a mixture of sugar and water. The image is varnished and dried and then the plate is placed in water. The sugar lifts off the plate but the varnish remains. The remaining image is then bitten with acid. The completed plate is inked and then printed. The technique aims to produce tones in the print similar to those in water-colour paintings.

Associations

See the aquatints of Goya (Spanish 1746-1828) and Paul Sandby (English 1725-1809).

See: **copper-plate, etching, watercolour, planograph**.

Arabesque

Pronounced: ARA-BESK (*a's as in actor, e as in best*)

Origin

From the French *arabesque* meaning *like the Arabs* or *Arabian* and *resembling the patterns and designs of the Arabs*. The Romans and Greeks used arabesque forms, which they doubtless took from oriental countries. The French term was first used at the end of the 17th century.

Meaning

Moslem artists are forbidden by their religion to represent living figures in their art. Consequently, Moslem art and Moorish art developed decoration to a high level of design, of which arabesque is one of the best known. Arabesque describes a complex design with curves, flowing lines, and intertwining leaves, branches and scrolls. It usually refers to a design which is very ornamental and elaborate. It has been used in decorative arts since Classical times as motifs in mural decorations, metalwork, ceramics, woodwork, embroidery, tapestry and bookbinding. In pottery, arabesque refers to Italian **Majolica** pottery. That is earthenware with coloured ornamentation on opaque white glaze-originally made in Majolica.

Associations

See: **Art Nouveau, Rococo, Decorative Art, cursive, curvilinear, biomorphic, earthenware**.

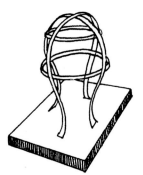

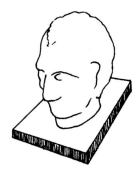

armatures

Armature

Pronounced: ARM-A-CHUR (*1st a as in farm, 2nd a as in ago, chur as in church*)

Origin

From the Latin *armatura* meaning *armour*. That is something strong to give support and protection.

Meaning

An armature is a rigid frame-work (like a skeleton) made from strong material (such as wire, metal rods or chairs, pipes etc.) to support the weight of a sculpture, structure, doll or puppet while it is being made from wax, clay, plaster or some heavy material. The armature "*protects*" (*See armour above*) the work being constructed. Armatures of heads or figures can be purchased.

Associations

See: **sculpture, papier maché.**

Art Brut

Pronounced: ART-BROO (*a as in far, oo as in root*)

Origin

From the French *brut* meaning *brutish, rough, raw, or unrefined*. The term *Art Brut* was first used by the French painter Jean Dubuffet about 1948 to express the opposite of "*Cultured Art*".

Meaning

Art Brut is the violent, tough art produced by people who are not trained in art (e.g. primitives, prisoners, graffitists), especially people who are mentally-ill (usually psychopathic) or maladjusted. It relates to concepts which are free from traditional artistic culture and which draw upon thoughts and feelings of great variety from the creators themselves. It is art of spontaneous impulse rather than art which relies to any extent on cultural processes and activities. The term has come to be associated with the work of the French artist Dubuffet, as he was the main influence in its developmenmt,but his own work is certainly not *untutored* and is not Art Brut in the true sense. Dubuffet experimented with many materials, such as vegetable matter, ashes and sand to produce rough textures on which he scrawled his imagery. Art Brut was regarded as anti-art when it first began.

Associations

See the works of: Jean Dubuffet (French 1901 -), especially "*Vache la Belle Allegre*", 1954 which is in the Cochrane Gallery, London. It is one of best-known Art

Brut works. See also the work of Scottie Wilson (Scottish 1889-1972).

See: **tachisme, Action Painting, All-Over Painting, amorphous**.

Art Deco

Pronounced: ART-DEKO (*a as in far, e as in neck, o as in go*)

Origin

Deco is from the French word *decoratif.* Art Deco is an abbreviation of *L'Exposition (exhibition) Internationale des Arts Decoratifs et Industries modernes* which opened in Paris in 1925. The movement developed in reaction to *Art Nouveau.*

Meaning

Art Deco is an architectural and decorative art style which flourished between 1905-1930. It reflected the energy and innovation of the *Jazz Age* and delighted in everything that was modern, fashionable and *avant garde*. It was sometimes referred to as **moderne**. It used a wide range of materials, including luxurious materials, such as ivory, bronze and ebony but also cheaper materials such as glass, bakelite and plastics. In its textiles and wallpaper designs, it emphasised simple forms mainly through geometric motifs and industrial images and used vivid colours such as cerise, violet and orange. It was popular in the interior decoration of hotels, ocean liners and cinemas. Probably its most conspicuous form of expression is in the huge skyscrapers in the United States. It helped to popularise **Cubism** and **Futurism** by using their geometric language to some extent.

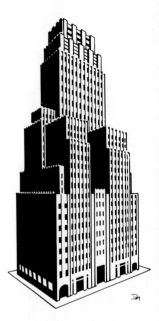

a New York skyscraper which exemplifies Art Deco

Associations

See: **motif, Cubism, Futurism, Decorative Arts, geometric**.

Artefact

Pronounced: ART-I-FACT (*1st a as in far, i as in lip, 2nd a as in act*)

Origin

From Latin *ars* meaning *art* and *fact* meaning *made*. A *fact-ory* is where things are made.

Meaning

An artefact (also spelled **artifact**) is something made with skill and art by a person rather than created by nature.

Associations

See: **technique, manipulation, hand-building**.

Art Nouveau

Pronounced: ART (*a as in far*) NOO-VO (*oo as in root, o as in go*)

Origin

Nouveau is the French for *new*. The term originates from one of two sources: either the name of an Art gallery in Paris in 1895 or a shop in Paris which sold objects of original rather than traditional style and which opened in 1895. The style was derived from various sources but the strongest influences were from Britain and Japan.

Meaning

Art Nouveau was a *"new art"* which became popular in Europe (mainly in Munich, London, Brussels, Barcelona and Vienna) and the USA in the 1890's, and lasted as a major force (Its influence is still felt.) until about 1910 and then to a lesser extent until the 1930's. It significantly influenced architecture, graphic arts, interior decoration, posters, wallpapers, decorative glass, furniture, murals, textiles and jewellery. It is particularly noted for its use of sinuous line (expressed through flames, waves, flowing human hair and especially fine tendrils) and floral and geometric decorative shapes. It was concerned with beauty, elegance and decorativeness.

Associations

See: **Rococo, Baroque, Symbolism, Expressionism, arabesque, geometric, stained-glass, Decorative Art**.

See the works of: James Ensor (Belgian 1860-1949), William Morris (English 1834-1896), Aubrey Beardsley (English 1872-1898), Henri de Toulouse-Lautrec (French 1864-1901), Oskar Kokoschka (Austrian 1886-1980), Paul Gauguin (French 1848-1903), mosaics by Antoni Gaudi (Spanish 1852-1926), glass work by Émile Gallé (French 1846-1904), René Lalique (French 1860-1945), Louis Comfort Tiffany (American 1848-1933) and designs by Auguste Delaherche (French 1857-1940), Eugene Gaillard (French 1862-1933), and George Watton (Scottish 1867-1933).

Art Nouveau designs

Assemblage

Pronounced: A-SEM-BLIGE (*a as in ago, e as in lemon, ige to rhyme with ridge*).

Origin
From the French *assembler* meaning *to bring or call together, to gather, collect, or combine.* The word was first used by the French artist Jean Dubuffet in 1953 to describe his own work which used all kinds of mixed mediums. Assemblage Art was popular in the late 1950's and early 1960's.

Meaning
Assemblage is the use of three-dimensional objects which have been found (e.g. either natural objects, such as driftwood, or man-made objects, such as bottle caps, pieces of wire etc.) and combined to create an art object. **Collage** is a two-dimensional combination in that it mounts objects; assemblage is a three-dimensional combination in that it constructs or assembles objects.

Associations
See: **objet trouvé, Cubism, collage, sculpture (Junk Art), metamorphosis.**

See the works of: Robert Rauschenberg (American 1925 -), Georges Braque (French 1882-1963), Jackson Pollock (American 1912-1956), Edward Kienholz (American 1927 -), John Chamberlain (American 1927 -), Jean Tinguely (Swiss 1925 -), Lee Bontecon (American 1931 -), Louise Nevelson (Russian/American 1900 -).

Asymmetry

Pronounced: A-SIM-I-TRY (*a as in ago, i's as in dim, y as in duty*)

Origin
From the Greek *summetria* meaning *same measurement* and *a* meaning *not.* That is *not having the same measurement.*

Meaning
Asymmetry refers either to objects which are placed on different sides of a vertical axis and which appear out of balance or unproportional because they are of different size, or to an object which has a different number of sides from a vertical axis. **Symmetrical** designs tend to give the impression of inactivity; **asymmetrical** designs tend to give the impression of activity.

Associations
See: **symmetrical, proportion, movement, distortion, Rococo.**

For asymmetry of composition see *"Cafe at Evening"* by Vincent Van Gogh (1853-1890).

symmetry

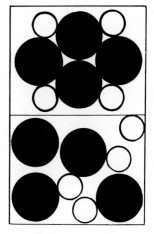

asymmetry

Bark Painting

Pronounced: BARK (*a as in far*)

Origin

Bark is from an old Icelandic word *borkr* meaning *the outer sheath of a tree trunk and branches.*

Meaning

Bark painting is paintings made on bark stripped from a tree and is an ancient art of Australian Aborigines. Pigments from plants, soil and stones are used to create pictures of the Aboriginal culture. The paintings are usually either instructive (i.e. pictures showing to hunters the position of animals' vital organs) or ritualistic and symbolic. To show that they believe that the thought of art is more important that the product, the Aboriginal people, traditionally, discard their bark paintings at the end of a ceremony.

Associations

See: **allegory, ideogram, pattern, proportion, rythm, concentric.**

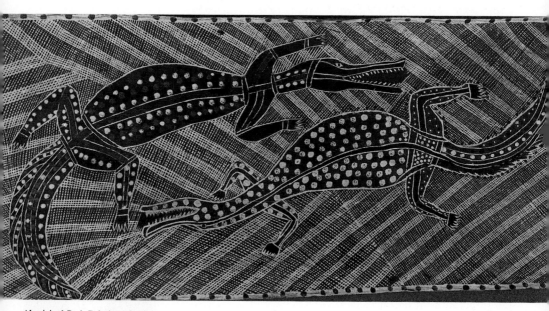

Aboriginal Bark Painting of a fight of two salt-water crocodiles by **Binyanbi Peter** of the Rembaranga tribe, Arnhem Land, Northern Australia

Baroque

Pronounced: BA-ROK (*a as in ago, o as in rock*)

Origin

Baroque is a French word from a Spanish word *barrucco* meaning *a rough (or irregularly-shaped) pearl*. It was used to describe something irregular, bizarre or odd. The first major Baroque artist is considered to be the Italian painter Caravaggio (1573-1610).

Meaning

Baroque is a style of painting and sculpture which developed in Italy around 1580 and remained strong in Europe until the beginning of the Rococo style about 1730. It developed as a reaction to **Mannerism**. The style is characterised by massive and complex design, vigorous or violent movement in figures and lively but symmetrical forms- in contrast to Rococo (which followed Baroque), which is often asymmetrical and exaggerated. Baroque delighted in the use of ornaments, such as scrolls, putti (Italian for *little boys*), acanthus and masks.

Associations

See: **symmetry, Rococo,** .

See the works of the Italian sculptor Gianlorenzo Bernini (1598-1680) and the ceramic figures made by Johann Kandler at Meissen, Germany. See also the works of: Caravaggio (1573-1610), Velasquez (1599-1660), Van Dyck (1599-1641), and Rembrandt (1606-1669).

Bat

Pronounced: BAT (*a as in cat*)

Origin

From the abbreviation of the French *bon a tirer* meaning *good to pull*; that is *to shape*.

Meaning

A bat is a slab or disc of wood or plaster on which clay can be shaped to form a ceramic object. It fits on the head of a potter's wheel. The bat allows the object to be lifted off the head of the wheel without damaging the object. It also can be used to absorb excess water. The word is also used in ceramics for a **kiln shelf**, a **pot board** and a **pot beater**.

Associations

See: **furniture, potter's wheel, kiln.**

placing a bat on a potter's wheel

Batik

Pronounced: BA-TEEK (*a as in bar, ee as in feet*)

Origin

Batik does not, as is generally thought, belong to the Javanese language. Its origin is unknown, although it is probably related to *titik*, which in Indonesian and Malaysian means *a point, dot or drop*. The ancient craft of batik dates back two thousand years. Its origins are not known but it was practised in China, Japan, India, Egypt and Persia and is now popular throughout the world, especially in Java and Bali. The term first appeared in writing in about 1600.

producing a design with a tjanting

Meaning

Batik is a resist technique of printing coloured designs onto fabrics using dyes. Most batiks in the past were, and to a large extent are today, dyed in blues and browns. Indigo is the most common colour in traditional batik. Parts of the fabric not to be dyed are covered with hot wax which resists the dyes which are used. When the wax is removed, by boiling the fabric or by using solvents, the designs appear. The process is repeated on one piece of cloth to produce variegated patterns. Nowadays, the batik effect is often produced by machines rather than being hand-made. The way to tell the difference between a hand-made batik and mass-produced material from a screen method is to examine both sides of the fabric. Hand-made batik has the pattern equally clear on both sides; mass-made batik has the pattern clear only on one side. The finest hand-made batik is called **tulis**, from the Javanese word meaning *writing*.

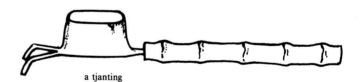

a tjanting

Associations

Tjanting (pronounced *jant-ing*) is the tool used for fine-line drawing in wax on a fabric. It is also called a **canting**. It comprises a copper crucible (a melting pot) with a spout by which wax can be applied to a fabric in continuous lines of varying thickness. It was invented in the 17th century.

See: **tie-dye, resist**.

Bauhaus

Pronounced: BOW-HOWS (*both ow's as in cow*)

Origin

The German word *bau* means *construction* and *haus* means *house*. The Bauhaus was a place (or house) of construction and creativity.

Meaning

Bauhaus refers to a School of Design and Architecture and Craft founded by a German, Walter Gropius, in Wermar, Germany, in 1919 and which closed in Berlin in 1933. The school aimed to unite the arts and to combine the ideals of skill in craft and good design with mass production and to close the gap between the creative artist and the industrial craftsperson. A new Bauhaus was opened in Chicago in 1937 by Lazlo Maholy-Nagy.

Associations

See: **Design, Graphic Design, Industrial Design.**

Associated with the Bauhaus School were famous artists, such as Wassily Kandinsky (Russian 1866-1944), Paul Klee (Swiss 1879-1940), Lyonel Feininger (American 1871-1956). Lazlo Moholy-Nagy (Hungarian 1895-1946) has probably had the greatest influence on the development of basic design principles in this century.

the Bauhaus logo

Biomorphic

Pronounced: BI-O-MOR-FIK (*i as in bicycle, first o as in go, second o as in more, i as in stick*)

Origin

From the Greek *bios* meaning *life* and *morphe* meaning *shape* or *form*.

Meaning

Biomorphic forms have the natural curves and irregular shapes of some living things. Biomorphic form or **free form** art was a branch of **Abstract Art** which developed from **Surrealism**. It drew its inspiration from living organisms rather than from man-made geometrical shapes.

Associations

See: **Abstract Art, curvilinear, Surrealism.**

Morphology is the study of living forms or the study of the formation of words. **Free-form work** is characteristic of the painting and sculpture of Hans Arp (German 1887-1966). See also the works of: Yves Tanguy (French 1900-1955), Joan Miro (Spanish 1893 -), Jackson Pollock (American 1912-1956), Mark Rothko (American/Russian 1903-1970).

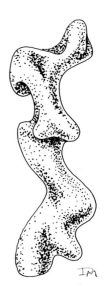

Bisque (or Bisc and Bisqueware)

Pronounced: BISK (*i as in bit*)

Origin
From the Latin *bis* meaning *twice* and *coctus* meaning *cooked* or *baked*.

Meaning
Bisque is **greenware** pottery which is fired slowly to approximately 900°c. This process evaporates the water in the clay and changes the molecular structure of the clay so that it is hardened and is ready, if necessary, for glazing and subsequent glaze-firing. Potteryware that receives only one firing and no glaze is also called **bisqueware**.
Greenware should be fired slowly to allow water to leave the clay slowly (this is often called *steaming*) and then fired to *red heat* at about 600°c. This slow, careful process prevents the ware from exploding (sometimes called *blowing*). **Biscuit** means baked to crisp, dry hardness.

Associations
See: **greenware, earthenware, glaze, pottery, grog, firing**.

Bleeding

Pronounced: BLEED-ING (*ee as in see*)

Origin
Bleed is from an old English word *bledan* with its current meaning of letting blood.

Meaning
If an image on a photograph or other art work reaches the edge of a printed page and there is no margin or border, it is said to **bleed**. Bleeding (through) also applies to the tendency of some pigments to work through coats of paint. This often occurs with dyes. To bleed also refers to a wash of water colour or other medium which runs into another area of colour. This can be intentional or accidental (e.g. in batik and tie-dyeing or wood dyeing). In metalwork, bleeding refers to the draining of gas hoses to an oxyacetylene welding tank.

The photograph above *bleeds off* this page

Associations
See: **dye, mounting, crop, space**.

Blocking in (or out)

Pronounced: BLOK-ING (*o as in got*)

Origin
From the French *bloquer* meaning *to block* or *fill up*.

Meaning
Blocking *in* or *out* is a technique used in painting where an artist draws or paints in outline only in approximately

the area of a painting where the final composition will be. In glass-making, it means the shaping of glass in wooden or metal moulds, or the removal of blemishes on the surface of an object. Blocking refers also to covering an area of a painting or drawing which is not to be worked, in order to leave the area that is. This is also called **opaquing** and **stopping out**.

Associations
Roughing in is an alternative term for blocking in.

See: **resist, sketch, masking**.

Brief

Pronounced: BREEF (*ee as in see*)

Origin
From the Latin *brevis* meaning *short* and later *breve* meaning *a dispatch*.

Meaning
Originally, a brief meant a **summary** of facts and law points for a legal case. It now refers also in design to a contract situation which governs the operational and legal relationship between the person who wants something designed and is prepared to pay for this service and the designer of a project. A brief includes a definition of the design problems to be solved and also the terms and conditions under which a designer will offer his or her services to a client. **To brief** someone means to inform them thoroughly in advance of some action to be taken.

Associations
Brief-case originally meant a case for briefs.

See: **specification, Design**.

Bromide

Pronounced: BRO-MIDE (*o as in go, i as in ride*)

Origin
From the Greek *bromos* meaning *a bad smell*, then applied to bromiate, the salt of bromic acid. The element *bromine* was discovered in salt water by Antoine Jerome Balard in 1826. Johann Heinrich Schulze, a professor of Anatomical Science at the University of Altdorf in Germany, was the first to discover that a compound of nitrate (silver nitrate) blackened when exposed to sunlight. This was the beginning of the use of light-sensitive materials, essential in photography.

Meaning
The word bromide is often used for bromide paper, which is a photographic printing paper coated with a silver

bromide emulsion which makes the paper very light-sensitive. It is the most popular form of photographic enlarging paper because it needs quite short exposure time to give good black images.

Burin

a burin

Pronounced: BUR-IN (*u as in pure, i as in win*)

Origin
From the French word for *a graving tool* or *etcher's needle*.

Meaning
The burin is probably the most useful tool in engraving. It is made of a metal rod with a pointed triangular head of tempered steel and usually has a wooden handle. It is used to scoop out wood, metal or other material. A burin is sometimes called a **graver**.

Associations
See: **copper-plate, engraving, lino-block, graver**.

Burnish

burnishing with a spoon

Pronounced: BUR-NISH (*u as in fur, i as in dish*)

Origin
From an Old French word *burnir* meaning *to brown*.

Meaning
To burnish is to polish something (e.g. clay, glass, metal) by rubbing it. A pinched pot, or coiled pot of leatherhard clay, for example, can be burnished until it is shining *brown* with a pebble, the back of a spoon, or a strip of spring steel.

Associations
Tools used to burnish are called **burnishers**.
See: **pottery, leatherhard**.

Bust

Pronounced: BUST (*u as in just*)

Origin
From the French *buste* meaning *a half-length portrait* of a person. It originated in about the seventeenth century.

Meaning
In sculpture, a bust is a model of the head, shoulders and chest of a person. The word originally referred to the upper part of a woman's body, including the bosom or bust.

Associations
See: **armature, sculpture, glyptic**.

Calligraphy

Pronounced: KALIG-RAF-Y (*a's as in ant, i as in pig, y as in duty*).

Origin

From the Greek *kallos* meaning *beautiful* and *graphos* meaning *writing*. The three most important scripts (Gothic, Roman and Italic) in calligraphy were developed between the twelfth and fifteenth centuries.

Meaning

Calligraphy means elegant handwriting which differs from ordinary handwriting by its fine craft. A type-face which is like handwriting is called a **calligraphic** typeface. The word is sometimes used to refer to the manner in which an artist applies his or her medium (i.e. freely and rhythmically) to a canvas, particularly in the use of water colour. In some traditional Chinese paintings there is little difference between painting and handwriting. In ceramics, it refers to brushwork or decorating that uses the shape of a brush for a design on potteryware.

Associations

Calligraphers use a **lettering pen** to produce their work.

See: **canvas, water-colour, pottery, Design, Graphic Design, typography.**

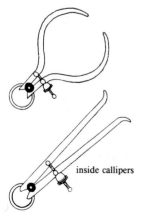

Art does not reproduce the visible, but makes visible

Paul Klee

calligraphy by Don Hatcher

Callipers

(*Callipers may also be spelled with one l*)

Pronounced: KAL-IP-AS (*a as in cat, i as in ship, a as in ago*)

Origin

Callipers are a variation of *calibre* (or *caliber*) from the Italian *calibro* which comes from the Arab word *qalib* meaning *a mould for casting metal*. Calliper compasses were used for measuring the calibre (diameter) of a bullet. Bronze outside callipers were used in Pompeii in A.D. 79. Vernier callipers wre invented in 1851 by J.R.Brown of the United States.

Meaning

Callipers are tools made of wood, metal or plastic used for measuring convex, concave or irregular-shaped objects. **Inside callipers** measure the diameter of holes and cylinders; **outside callipers** measure the outside diameter of circular objects. In ceramics, they are used to measure the inside and outside of pots on a potter's wheel. They are also used to measure the thickness of a sheet of paper or board or film in microns (millionths of a metre). They are not direct-reading tools. Calliper settings are measured using a scale or a micrometer.

outside callipers

inside callipers

Associations

A **Vernier calliper** is a precision tool which is able to measure as accurately as 0.025 mm. It is usually used where minute tolerances are required. A **hermaphrodite calliper** (also called a *morphy*), which has one sharp, pointed leg, is used for special lay-out work. **Calibrate** means to find the **calibre** of something. In animation photography, it means to mark moves on the artwork.

Cameo

Pronounced: KAM-EE-O (*a as in lamb, ee as in see, o as in go*)

cameo type

Origin

From the Latin *cammaeus* and the Italian *cammeo* of unknown derivation. Cameos were popular for portraits and crests in Roman times and also for coats of arms in the Middle Ages (up to the 15th century).

Meaning

Cameo means an engraved work on gemstones, ceramics, glass, paste, and papier-maché, where the ground is cut away so that a design stands out in relief above the surface. It refers, too, to a precious stone, usually with coloured layers (e.g. agate, onyx, sardonyx) with a carved figure in relief on the upper layers. The stone is usually set in a clasp. It is also the technique used in shell carving where different coloured layers of shell are revealed. A cameo is also a type of water mark on paper. In ceramics, it refers to very fine potteryware which is decorated with figures in colour on a different coloured ground. Cameo glass consists of layers of different coloured, laminated glass cut to reveal the layers. In typography, it refers to those typefaces in which characters are reversed white out of a solid or shaded background.

George Woodall, Great Britain 1850 - 1920, working for Thomas Webb & Sons, *Vase* cameo glass *Art Gallery of South Australia, Adelaide, South Australia*

Associations

The reverse of cameo technique is **intaglio**.
See: **ground, relief, watermark, intaglio, engrave.**

Camera Obscura

Pronounced: KAM-A-RA (*1st a as in lamb, 2nd and 3rd a as in ago*), OB-SKUR-A (*o as in lot, u as in pure, a as in ago*).

Origin

Camera is from the Greek *Kamar* meaning *anything with an arched cover*. It came to mean a *chamber*. It was used with this meaning until it was popularized in connection with photography. Obscura is Latin for *dark*. Camera obscura means, literally, *a dark chamber*. The device was used by Arab astronomers in the 9th century to plot the position of the sun throughout a year. Leonardo da Vinci (1452-1519) wrote about it, and Giovanni Battista della Porta (1543-1615) published the first description of the device in 1558.

Meaning

The camera obscura which was developed in the early sixteenth century comprised a box (a dark chamber) which lets in light through a series of lenses and mirrors. These projected a reduced image onto a flat surface (e.g. on glass or paper) from which an artist could trace a drawing with a high degree of accuracy.

Associations

The Dutch painter Jan Vermeer (1632-1675) made considerable use of a camera obscura. (See his "*The Guitar Player*"), as did Velazquez, and the Venetian painters of the 18th century-particulary Antonio Canaletto (1697-1768) and Luca Carlevaris (1665-1731)), and the landscape painters of the 17th and 18th centuries.

See: **pantograph, replica, facsimile, pointing**.

Canvas

Pronounced: KAN-VUS (*a as a in bat, u as in bonus*)

Origin

From the Middle English or Norman French *Canevas*.

Meaning

Canvas is the usual material (linen, cotton, hemp or jute) on which a painting is made. Linen is the best material as it is durable, readily accepts priming and sizing solutions and is less likely to crack when dry than most other materials. It is sold in a variety of weights and weaves. All these materials are stretched over a wooden frame and primed before they are used.

Associations

Canvas should not be confused with **canvass** (note the spelling with two s's) which means *to try to get votes in an election.*

See: **priming, size, weave, stretcher, key**.

Caricature

Pronounced: KARI-KA-TUR (*1st a as in cat, i as in ink, 2nd a as in ago, u as in pure*)

Origin

From the Italian *caricatura* from *caricare* meaning *to load* or *pile up*; that is *to exaggerate*. The technique was probably first developed by the Carracci circle in Rome in the sixteenth century.

Meaning

Caricaturists exaggerate a person's, animal's or even a machine's outstanding or noticeable physical features, sometimes grotesquely, to create a humorous or satirical effect, namely the caricature.

Associations

Some fine **caricaturists** are: William Hogarth (English 1697-1764), Francisco Goya (Spanish 1746-1828), Honoré Daumier (French 1808-1879), Gianlorenzo Bernini (Italian 1598-1680), Max Beerbohn (1872-1956) and David Low (1891-1963).

See: **distortion, accent, dominance, drawing.**

The French artist Honoré Daumier (1808 - 1879) was imprisoned for producing this caricature of King Louis Phillipe. The pear shape in France signifies an idiot.

Cartoon

Pronounced: KAR-TOON (*a as in car, oo as in soon*)

Origin

From the Italian *cartone* meaning *paper* or *card*. The meaning has changed from the material used in drawing to the drawing itself.

Meaning

Originally a cartoon meant a full-sized drawing on strong paper (See *cartone* above) in preparation for painting, a fresco, a tapestry or a stained-glass window. It was a **study**. Cartoons did not become humorous until about 1860. Nowadays, it means a humorous or satirical drawing, with or without a caption, by a cartoonist, which appears, often daily, in newspapers journals and strip comics. Usually some physical characteristics of a person, animal or thing are exaggerated.

Associations

For an example of a cartoon (as the word was originally used) see Raphael's (Italian 1483-1520) *"Draught of Fish"*. For a modern cartoon see works by Henri de Toulouse Lautrec (French 1864-1905). See also *'The World Encyclopedia of Cartoons'* edited by Maurice Hom.

See: **sketch, study, draft, accent, dominance, distortion, fresco, tapestry.**

Casting

Pronounced: KAST-ING (*a as in car*)

Origin

From the Old Norse *Kasta* meaning *to throw*.

a casting flask

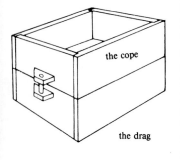
the cope

the drag

Meaning

To cast is to create an object by putting (that is to cast) molten metal into a mould (or mold), in order that it will harden into a required shape. **Crucible furnaces** are used for melting metals which are transferred in a **crucible** into a mould. In **sand mould casting**, a **moulding box** or **moulding flask** is used, whose upper half is called the **cope** and whose lower half is called **the drag**. In the moulding flask is tempered and dampened sand, into which is placed a **pattern**, usually made of wood but sometimes of styrofoam. The sand is packed around the pattern and then the pattern is removed leaving a cavity, which is the mould into which the molten metal is poured to create a metal object like the pattern.

Associations

Foundry sand is a mixture of silica and fine sand, which does not dry out and can be used constantly. It can be readily shaped to produce precise and detailed castings.

See: **cire perdu, sculpture.**

Ceramics

Pronounced: SUR-AM-IKS (*u as in fur, a as in lamb, i as in stick*)

Origin

From the Greek *keramikos* meaning *pottery* and *keramos* meaning *potter's clay*. Ceramics became a subject of study in the late 19th Century.

Meaning

Ceramics refers to products made by the process of changing materials consisting mainly of silicates by heat until they are very hard. Clay and glass are the most common ceramic materials, each of which is made by a variety of processes. Clay products are termed according to the temperature at which they are hardened, such as

A ceramic sculpture by Joyce Scott,South Australia

earthenware, terra cotta, and stoneware. Glass is classified according to the method by which it is formed; that is by a furnace method or a kiln method.

Associations

A **ceramist** is a person who works with clay and glazes. **Ceramography** is the study or the historical description of **pottery**. Ceramics is another term for pottery, but it includes also sculptural works in clay, tiles, brick, sanitary ware and anything made from clay.

See the work of Thorvald Bindesboll (Danish 1846-1908), Ernest Chaplet (French 1856-1909), Theodorus Colenbrander (Dutch 1841-1930), Taxile Doat (French 1851-1938), Bernard Leach (British 1887 -).

See: **pottery, clay, firing, earthenware, stoneware, china, kaolin, porcelain, trailing, slip, glaze.**

Chasing

Pronounced: CHAS-ING (*a as in face*).

Origin

From the French *enchasser* meaning *to mount or frame jewels etc. in a setting* and the Middle English *enchassen* meaning *to emboss*.

Meaning

Chasing is to decorate a metal object (such as a sword) by indenting its surface from the front (See **Intaglio**) with a hammer, punch, or some tool without a cutting edge to form a design. Chasing tools (e.g. hammers) have heads which can produce patterns showing ovals, squares, domes and lines. The word also applies to the removal of roughness or blemishes on metal which is being modelled, e.g. as in **cire perdu** casting.

Associations

See: **emboss, intaglio, cire perdu, die, repoussé**.

Chiaroscuro

Pronounced: KEE-A-ROS-KOO-RO (*ee as in see, a as in far, o as in loss, oo as in cool, final o as in so*)

Origin

From the Italian *chiaro* meaning *clear* and *oscuro* meaning *dark*. Its use as an effective new technique in painting began with Leonardo Da Vinci (1452-1519).

Meaning

Chiaroscuro is the blending by painters of the gradations of light and shade in a painting, not only to suggest depth but also to create atmosphere and mood. Artists realize that the eye sees brighter objects as appearing closer than

dimmer ones and use brightness and shade to create illusion of depth among figures and ground.

Associations

The French term for chiaroscuro is **clair-obscur**.

See: **gradation, illusion, ground, grisaille**.

See the paintings of: Rembrandt (Dutch 1606-1669), Caravaggio (Italian 1573-1610), Velazquez (Spanish 1599-1660), Jean-Baptiste Chardin (French 1699-1779).

Giovanni Segantini, Italy 1858-1899, **Spinning**
oil on canvas 58.3 x 89.1 cm, Art Gallery of South Australia, Adelaide, Elder Bequest Fund 1899

China

Pronounced: CHINA (*i a in line, a as in ago*)

Origin

China is an abbreviation of chinaware, which was produced in the 17th century in Europe to imitate genuine Chinese porcelain. China was known as *soft paste porcelain* (although to be accurate it is not porcelain, as porcelain is a hard paste material).

Meaning

China refers to white earthenware. It has a white body (which is sometimes translucent) covered with a glaze which has been fired at a temperature lower than that of the body. It is made mainly from china clay (See **kaolin**) which is the purest natural clay.

Associations
Bone china refers to china which contains bone-ash (oxbones burnt to ashes), kaolin and cornish stone, which makes the ware particularly translucent.

See: **porcelain, earthenware, translucent, glaze, firing, kaolin**.

Cire Perdu

Pronounced: SEAR (*ea as in fear*), PAIR-DU (*ai as in fair, u as in due*)

Origin
From the French *cire* meaning *wax* and *perdu* meaning *lost*. The cire perdu (lost wax) process of casting was used in Egypt in 2500 B.C..

Meaning
Cire perdu is a casting technique where a model is made first in wax. The wax model is covered in soft clay and plaster to form a mould when dry. The wax is melted and drained from the plaster mould and then molten metal is poured into the mould to produce a replica of the original sculpture. Another technique is where the metal is forced into the mould by centrifugal force.

Associations
Cire perdu is also called **lost wax method** or **centrifugal casting**.

See: **sculpture, replica, facsimile, cerography**.

Classical

Pronounced: KLAS-I-KAL (*a's as in cat, i as in pin*)

Origin
From the Latin *classicus* meaning *of the highest class or rank*. The term comes from the art of ancient Greece in the fourth and fifth centuries before Christ.

Meaning
Classical refers to an art form which is characterized by an approach which is intellectual, controlled, disciplined and rational and which is noted for its clarity, order, harmony and balance. It flourished in Greece in the 5th century and again in Europe in the 17th and 18 centuries (See **Neo-Classicism**), but is found to some extent in art even today.

Associations
Broadly, the opposite of classical is **Romantic**. See the works of Nicolas Poussin (French 1594-1665), Raphael (Italian 1483-1520), Baccio Bandinelli (Italian 1493-1560).

See: **Golden Section, proportion, contrapposto, Romanticism, figurative**.

a Classical ancanthus design

Clay

Pronounced: KLA (*a as in late*)

Origin

From the Old English *claeg* meaning *earth which is sticky.*

Meaning

Clay is a stiff, sticky earth found in many varieties near the surface of the ground. It is composed of partially-disintegrated rock, pebbles, sand and flint. The brownish colour is given to some clays by a variety of oxides. Clay is a plastic material, in that it will take and retain shapes made from it. When exposed to temperatures of about 1000°c, it becomes permanently hard. There are many kinds and colours of clay which are used (sometimes blended) to make ceramic ware. It is purchased in a dry or plastic state. Dry clay should be mixed with water, as needed, and be stored in air-tight bins. Plastic clay is usually transferred immediately to bins.

Associations

Ball clays are fine-grained, plastic clays which have little impurity. As they have high shrinkage, they are not used alone but combined with other clays. Often it is added to kaolin. **Bentonite** is a sticky silica which is added to other clays to increase their plasticity. **Dead clay** is clay which has lost its plasticity, owing to old age or poor storage conditions. **Short clay** or **lean clay** is clay which is not fully plastic and tends to break when stretched.

See: **earthenware. stoneware, bisque, plasticity, kaolin.**

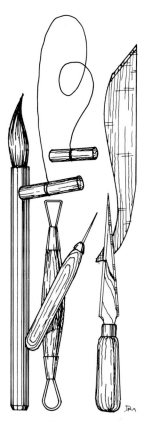

Tools used in clay work

Coiling

coiling

Pronounced: KOYL-ING (*oy as in boy*)

Origin

From the French *cuellier* meaning *to gather* or *collect*. It came to mean *to collect in rings or rounds* (i.e. as in coiling rope). Much of primitive pottery was made by the coil method.

Meaning

Coiling is a method of moulding clay by hand, by putting cylindrical, sausage-like rolls of clay ("*snakes*") on top of each other and then, using a pinching technique, joining the rolls together and smoothing over the joints to combine them into a shape required. Coiling is usually done from the base upwards.

Associations

See: **luting, slabbing, wedging, kneading.**

Collage

Pronounced: KOL-AHZ (*o as in pot, ahz as age in massage*)

Origin

From the French *coller* meaning *to stick* or *glue*. The technique was used by Georges Braque (1882-1963) and then by Pablo Picasso (1881-1973) in 1912 during their Cubist stage. It became part of the technique of artists in almost all the major art movements of the 20th century. Futurism, Dadaism, Surrealism, Constructivism, and Pop Art all used it.

Meaning

Collage is the sticking of bits of newspaper, letters, postage stamps, cloth, wood, photographs etc. into a pattern or onto paintings. **Assemblage** is three-dimensional and usually uses more than one kind of material; **collage** is two-dimensional and usually uses one kind of material. The technique is also used in papercraft. It refers, too, to the use of different types of needlework when combined in crewel embroidery work.

Associations

See: **decollage, decoupage, papier collé, assemblage, photocollage, Dadaism, Surrealism**.

See the Surrealist collages of: Max Ernst (German 1891-1976), Hans Arp (French 1887-1966), Joan Miro (Spanish 1893-), John Heartfield (German 1891-1968), Conrad Marca-Relli (American 1913-), Salvador Dali (Spanish 1904-1986) and the paper work of Kurt Schwitters (German 1887-1948).

Colour

Pronounced: KULA (*u as in dug, a as in ago*)

Origin

From the Latin *colare* meaning *to colour*. In 1672, Isaac Newton reported to the Royal Society in England that daylight (white light) when it passed through a **prism** splits into seven colours, **the spectrum**: red, orange, yellow, green, blue, indigo, and violet. Objects, he said, achieve their colour by absorbing or subtracting certain parts of the spectrum and reflecting or transmitting the parts left.

The names of many colours are derived from specific parts of our environment. Derived from plants are apricot, lemon, grass-green, hazel, rose-red. Derived from minerals and metals are alabaster, amethyst, copper, turquoise-blue. Derived from man-made products are chocolate, wine-red, bottle-green. Derived from fauna are beaver, canary-yellow, mouse-grey, fox, butterfly-blue.

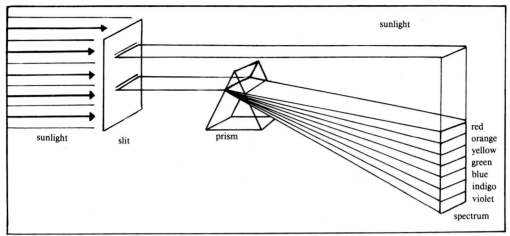

Derived from geographic names are Berlin-blue,
Copenhagen-blue, Naples-yellow, Spanish-green. Derived
from natural phenomena are aurora, spring-green, sky-
blue, fire-red.

Meaning

Light is the only source of colour and without it no
colour can exist. All things are reflectors, absorbers or
transmitters of one or more of the colours which make up
white light. For there to be colour, three elements are
needed: light (the source of colour), the object (and its
response to colour) and the eye, the perceiver of colour.
Every colour has three characteristics:

1 **Hue** is the quality which distinguishes one colour from
another. That is, for example, the yellowness or blueness
of something. There are said to be 150 differences of hue.

2 **Tone** (called also **brightness** by some artists) is the
lightness or darkness of a colour. All colours have a place
on a black-grey-white **tonal scale**. Yellow is close to white,
violet is close to black, etc. **High-key** colours fit into the
top of the range of a tonal scale; **Low-key** colours fit into
the bottom of the tonal scale. Some tones are: **white**-
ivory, alabaster, milk, chalky, hoar, pearly, blanched,
creamy, waxen, zinc white; **black**- sable, ebony, raven,
crow, jet, ink, pitch; **grey**- ashen, silver, steel, leaden,
livid, slate; **brown**- auburn, chestnut, cinamon, rust, khaki,
bistre, russet, hazel, chocolate, tawny, brunette, snuff,
fawn, puce, bay, tan, bronze, beige, zinc, sepia, umber,
caramel, mushroom; **red**- flesh-coloured, lake, pink,
cherry, cardinal, scarlet, carmine, crimson, damask, ruby,
claret, salmon, plum, blood, rose, magenta, carnelian,
vermilion, cinnabar, indian red; **green**- emerald, olive,
beryl, aquamarine, bottle, jade, sage, viridian; **yellow**-
crocus, gold, lemon, mars, amber, primrose, flaxen,
cobalt-yellow, buff, ochre, chrome, safffron, sandy,

37

Red results from the subtraction of green and blue wave lengths from white light.

Blue results from the subtraction of green and red wave lengths from white light.

Green results from the subtraction of blue and red wave lengths from white light.

Yellow results from the subtraction of blue only ,leaving red and green.

chrysoprase, gamboge, straw, sulphur, cadmium, strontium yellow; **purple**- violet, lavender, lilac, mauve, livid, crimson, maroon, heliotrope, mulberry; **blue**- indigo, turquoise, cobalt, navy, azure, manganese blue, aquamarine, sapphire, amethyst, cerulean, ultra-marine; **orange**- flame, apricot, ochre, cadmium orange, mars orange.

3 **Saturation** (called also **chroma** or **intensity**) is the purity, brilliance or richness of a colour and its strength or weakness (i.e.*high* or *low* saturation). The Latin word *satur* from which saturation comes, means *full*. It refers to the blueness of a blue or the greenness of a green. For example, orange has high intensity; brown has low intensity. One measure of intensity is how little white, black or grey is in the colour.

The sum of hue, tone and intensity is sometimes referred to as the colour **value**. Each colour has its **complementary colour** (see **Colour Wheel**). Coloured lights are termed **transmitted colour** and the colour in painting is called **reflected colour**. A red wall will absorb all colours except red which it reflects.

Primary colours (blue, red, yellow **in pigments** and red, green and violet **in lights**) are colours which cannot be made by mixing other colours. They can be used in different combinations to produce other colours. Two primary colours when mixed (e.g. red and yellow in equal proportions to produce orange) produce a **secondary colour**. The mixing of a primary colour with a secondary colour or two or three secondary colours produces a **tertiary colour**. Red with violet, for example, produces red-violet; orange, with violet and green produces citrine, olive and russet and all their tones.

Paint colours are mixed by an **additive** or **subtractive** process. Additive colour mixing has a starting point of black to which colours are added to produce the hue required. Subtractive colour mixing has a starting point of white (containing all the colours of the spectrum) to which colours are mixed to subtract the colour required.

In the paint industry, the primary colours are called yellow, cyan (blue-green) and magenta (blue red). **Colour blindness** is sensitivity to only two distinct colours rather than the three needed to match all colours in the spectrum. **Neutral colours** are black, grey and white, which give the impression of lightness or darkness. **Shade** indicates that a colour is changed by the addition of black to it. **Tint** is when a colour has been slightly changed by the addition of white to it.

Colours are said to have a **temperature**. **Hot** or **warm** colours are red, red-orange, red-violet, yellow, yellow-orange. **Cold** or **cool** colours are blue, violet, yellow-green, green, blue-green, blue. Cool colours suggest sensations of coolness and seem to *recede* in a painting and suggest depth; warm colours suggest sensations of heat and seem to *advance* towards the spectator and attract. Experiments have shown that there is a difference of 5-7 degrees in a person's feeling of heat or cold between a room painted in blue-green and one painted in red-orange. The term **local colours** is used for the natural colour of an object. For example, a road surface may be naturally grey but seen in sunlight through green foliage, it may appear violet. Some artists prefer to use the natural local colour; others, such as the **Impressionists**, emphasised the play of light on objects and preferred to show the colours which were *reflected* into their vision. Colours also have surface characteristics, such as being **opaque** or **transparent** and **gloss** or **matt**.

Associations

Coloration is the arrangement of colours. A **colorimeter** is an instrument for measuring the intensity of colours. A **colorist** is an artist who skilfully expresses forms more by the subtle use of colour than by the use of line. **Tache** (from the French for *stain*) means areas of flat, undifferentiated colour. **Criad colour** (pronounced *kree-ar* with *a* as in *far*) is from the French word meaning *shrieking*. It is a colour which is brilliant, loud and *shrieks* at you. (See **Fauvism**). **Chromatic** is from the Greek *Khroma* meaning *colour* and means *full of bright colours*. **Monochromatic** means a painting in various fine gradations of tones or tints in one colour, or the use of black and white only. **Achromatic** means tones without any hues-being mixtures of black and white to produce grey. **Earth colours** are pigments, such as brown, yellow, green, red, ochres, ambers etc. which are found naturally in earth and clay.

Much of twentieth century painting has been concerned with the study of, and experimentation with, colour.

See the paintings of Seurat, Van Gogh, Cezanne, Gaugin, Klee, Matisse, Albers, Rothko, Itten, Noland and Stella.

Colour Wheel

Pronounced: KULA(*u as in bonus, a as in ago*),
WEEL(*ee as in see*)

Origin

Colour wheels have been devised to attempt to give
precise terms for colours. One of the best known and
much used, after the language of colour was standardised
in the 1930's, was that produced by an American portrait
painter, Albert Munsell, in 1915. He devised his system in
the form of a tree which classified colours according to
the qualities of hue, value, and chroma. In this system
each colour can be specified by letters and numbers.

Meaning

A colour wheel is a wheel (or a circle or chart) which
shows the primary colours and mixtures of colours
organsied in order of hues and intensity. The colour wheel
shows the main gradations of colours.

Complementary colours (note the spelling. It should not be
confused with complimentary) are colours which are
opposite to each other and the greatest distance apart
from each other on a colour wheel. Each **primary colour**
(red, blue, yellow) has a **complementary colour** produced
by a combination of the other two primary colours. For
examples the complement of red is green (i.e.yellow and
blue), of yellow is violet, of blue is orange. **Analogous
colours** are colours next to each other on the colour
wheel. When complementary colours are placed side by
side, they intensify each other. For example, red
strengthens green. It is *Impressionist* theory that each
primary colour shows its complementary colour in the
shadow it casts. Thus, a yellow flower will cast a shadow
which is violet. Not all artists agree with this theory.

The colour system most often used is the **Munsell Colour
System** which has 1200 samples of colour, but other
systems are used, such as those by Ostwald, Michel-
Eugene Chevreul, Harold Kuppers, Frans Gerritsen, and
Johannes Itten.

Composition

Pronounced: KOM PA-ZISH-UN (*o as in bomb, a as a
in ago, i as in ink, u as in fun*)

Origin

From the Latin *com* meaning *with* and *ponere* meaning *to
put*. That is *to put together*.

Meaning

A composition is the combination of elements (colour,
shape, size, texture, tone, mass, direction and line) in a

work of art, which, by using the **principles** of balance, rhythm, dominance, contrast, harmony, and unity are harmonized into a unified whole. Each element in a work is important but the whole is more important than the parts. Sometimes the word refers to one work of art, such as a painting or a sculpture.

Associations

To compose is to arrange things in a specific manner for a particular purpose.

See: **elements, harmony, form, configuration.**

Computer Graphics/Art/Design

Pronounced: KOM-PEW-TUR (*o as in lot, ew as in few, ur as in fur*), GRAF-IKS (*a as in bat, i as in ink*), ART (*a as in far*), DE-ZIN (*e as in delay, i as in line*)

Origin

The word computer originates from the Latin *computare* meaning *to calculate* or *count*. The Latin *computus* was a Medievel set of mathematical tables used for calculating astronomical events and moveable dates in the calendar, such as Easter. In Old French the word *comput* was used for the calculation of the date for Easter.
Charles Babbage (1791-1871), an English mathematician, is usually given credit for inventing the computer, as he invented an *electronic calculating and problem-solving machine* in 1834. However, the first machine that stored information for later use was invented by Joseph-Marie Jacquard (1752-1834), a French silk weaver, who used a system in 1804 of punched cards to reproduce woven patterns automatically. The first fully electronic computer was ENIAC (electronic Numeral Intergrator and Calculator) produced at the University of Pennsylvania in 1945. It used more than 18,000 thermionic valves, weighed 30 tons and occupied 1,500 square feet of floor space. Dr. M.V.Wilkes designed the first all-electric computer in England, which had 18,000 valves, in 1949. *Graphics* is from the Greek *graphe* meaning *writing*. The **binary system** was developed by a German, Gottfried Leibnitz (1646-1716). The term **Computer Graphics** was first used by the Boeing Aircraft Company in the USA in 1900. The first exhibition of Computer Graphics was held in New York, in 1965. The first CAD (Computer Aided Design) systems appeared in an experimental form in the mid 1960's, and the first commercial drafting and design systems were produced in the late 1960's, mainly to meet the needs of the electronic industry in the designing of printed circuit boards.

Meaning

A computer is an electronic device which can store, retrieve and process data in accordance with a series of stored instructions (*commands*) called a **programme (or program)**. It can make extremely rapid calculations, using either numbers expressed as digits in a given number scale-usually **binary numbers** 0 or 1 (using a **digital computer**) or with numbers represented by measurable quantities of a given magnitude (using an **analogue computer**).

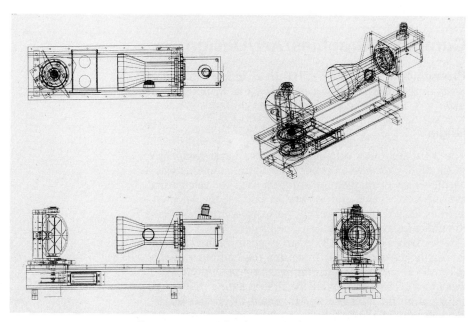

Computer graphics is a technique where programmed data in the form of basic shapes (called **entities** or **primitives**, such as points, lines, vertices, arcs, polygons or circles) are combined to produce **models** (pictorial or geometric). Designs, diagrams, charts and models can be produced. A **light-pen** attached to the computer terminal allows one to draw (or edit) direct onto a computer display screen. The images on the screen can be rotated, enlarged, modified etc.. The same computer equipment can be used for **computer-aided designs** (CAD) and **computer-aided art** (CAA). These are processes where a computer is used in the creation or modification of a design or an art work.

Computers can also be programmed to lighten or darken segments of an original image or a photograph to enhance its clarity or intensity. This is sometimes called **computer enhancement**. Multiple copies of computer graphics/art/ design work can be readily produced and there is some controversy whether this is advantageous or disadvantageous to art or design.

Associations

A **dot matrix printer** is used with a computer to produce graphic data as well as text. Any device attached to a computer (such as printers, plotters or digitisers) is called a **peripheral**. **MicroCAD** is a term for CAD systems which have recently been developed for microcomputers.

See: **pixelated images, typography, Industrial Design, Graphic Design, Design, loom, weave.**

Concept Art (or Conceptual Art)

Pronounced: KON-SEPT (*o as in on, e as in slept*)

Origin

A concept is derived from the verb *to conceive* which comes from the Latin *con* meaning *with* and *capere* meaning *to take*. That is *to take a thought with another to form an idea*. The term **Conceptual Art** has been credited to Sol de Witt, a Conceptual and Minimalist artist of the 1960's. The work of the movement was a reaction against the formalism of late **Modernism** and also a gesture opposing the commercialism of art at the time. The artists objected strongly to *art as a commodity*.

Meaning

Art always has an idea and usually a physical object as a product of the idea. What an artist presents materially in two or three dimensional forms is a reflection or interpretation of what occurred in his or her mind. The idea is the concept. Conceptual Art developed in the late 1960's and believed that an idea (or activity) and the interpretation of the idea was more important than a finished product. What the artist had in his or her mind (the concept and the process) is considered far more important than what results from creative making (the product). Some concept artists communicate their ideas through words, a happening, or body movement, as well as the conventional art forms. Examples of happenings are an act of self-burying where photographs of stages of the burial were recorded; professional grave-diggers digging a large hole in Central Park, New York and then filling the hole, and an example of Concept Art in an exhibition (in the Museum of Modern Art, New York) is Joseph Kosuth's work which shows a chair, a photograph of a chair and a dictionary definition of a chair.

Associations

See the works of Joseph Kosuth, Sol de Witt, Bruce Nauman, Keith Arnatt. Many terms have been used for Concept(ual) Art, including **Idea Art, Non-Object Art, Analytic Art, Impossible Art.**

Concrete Art

Pronounced: KON-KREET (*o as in rock, ee as in bee*), ART (*a as in far*)

Origin

The word concrete originated from the Latin *concretus* meaning *grown together*. That is for things or ideas which come together into a mass and then become firm and solid. The word concrete (as opposed to abstract) was first used in art in the nineteenth century. Max Bill, a Swiss artist, was the principal person in formulating the principles of concrete art in 1936 and he organised the first exhibition of concrete art in Basle, Switzerland, in 1944.

Meaning

Concrete Art (or **Concretism** as it is sometimes called) was first used as a descriptive term by Theo Van Doesburg, a Dutch painter and architect, to refers to art which depicts the real world and actual things (or, as was said, "*real material, real space*"). It avoided symbolism, abstract concepts, imaginative and expressive interpretations, illusion and lyrical and dramatic qualities. One of its main aims was "*to represent abstract thought in a sensuous and tangible form*". It developed throughout Europe from 1930 to 1960. As it developed, it became increasingly concerned with geometrical abstraction, relying on mathematical principles of proportion and the exact relationships of parts in the whole. **Constructivism** is similar in some respects to Concrete Art but it tends to use illusion more. Conrete Art influenced **Hard Edge Painting**.

Associations

See: **geometric, Hard-Edged Painting, Op Art, proportion.**
See the works of: Theo Van Doesburg (Holland 1883-1931), Jean Arp (Switzerland 1887-1966), Arne Jones (Sweden 1914-), Olle Baertling (Sweden 1911-), Aranasio Soldati (Italy 1896-1953), Bruno Manari (Italy 1907-), Wassily Kandinsky (Russia 1866-1944), Piet Mondrian (Holland 1872-1944).

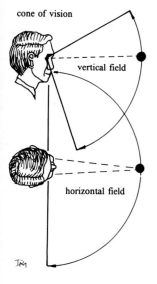

cone of vision

vertical field

horizontal field

Cone of Vision

Pronounced: KON (*o as in alone*) VI-SHUN (*i as in fit, shun to rhyme with station*).

Origin

From the Greek *konos* meaning *a pine cone, spinning top and a geometric figure.*

Meaning

A cone is a solid figure or body with a circular base and a summit (or vertex) which is a point. Every point on the surface of the figure is in a straight line from the base to the vertex. A cone of vision is a person's field of vision where everything can be seen with clarity when the person's eyes are looking in one direction. A clear field of vision extends for about 40° outside the object looked at. Beyond this, objects appear blurred.

Associations

See: **perception, landscape, panorama, viewpoint.**

Configuration

Pronounced: KON-FIG-A-RA-SHUN (*o as in rock, i as in big, a as a in ago, rashun to rhyme with station*)

Origin

From the Latin *con* meaning *with* and *figurare* meaning *to fashion*. That is the arrangement of things together.

Meaning

Configuration is the form or arrangement of elements in a painting or design. The meaning is closely related to that of **composition**.

Associations

See: **elements, composition, form, shape, format.**

Constructivism

Pronounced: KON-STRUKT-I-VISM (*o as in on, u as in luck, i's as in brick, sm as in prism*).

Origin

The word construct derives from the Latin *con* meaning *with* and *structuis* meaning *built*. The term **constructivism** was first used by two Russian brothers who were sculptors about 1920: Antoine Pevsner and Naum Pevsner (who was usually called Naum Gabo). They developed ideas generated by Vladimir Tatlin. The term constructivism comes from the artists wish to '*construct*' works deliberately and methodically rather than through impulse or spontaneous reaction. As Naum Gabo said in 1940, "*We call ourselves constructive because our ideal in life generally is construction not destruction*".

Meaning

There are quite wide interpretations of the term Constructivism, as it has found expression over the years. In Constructivism, artists aimed to make art a scientific investigation, involving composition, line, colour, materials etc.. They believed that sculpture should be more involved with movement in space rather than static values, consequently much of their work is **kinetic**. The artists wished their art to be linked to social, economical and architectural aspects of society. They influenced the **Bauhaus** movement. They objected to their work being called *abstract* and as Naum Gabo said "*We are demanding from the artist and from his work not an accidental and wanton fantasy, but a carefully considered creation executed with the full control of his emotions*". The artists used the latest materials available, such as glass, wire, sheetmetals, and plastic and they made use of highly-developed engineering techniques. In painting, Constructivism, as a non-representational, non expressive form of art, has mainly used geometrical forms.

Associations

See: **kinetic, movement, Concrete Art, Bauhaus, geometric, sculpture**.

See the works of the sculptors: Vladimir Tatlin (1855-1953), Naum Gabo (1890-1977), Kasmir Malevich (1878-1935), Lynbor Papova (1889-1924), Antoine Pevsner (1886-1902), Phillip King (1934 -) and Anthony Caro (1924 -) and the Dutch artists Theo Van Doesburg (1883-1931) and Piet Mondrian (1872-1944).

El Lissitzky, Russia 1890-1941, **The New Man** from **Victory over the sun** 1923
lithograph 31.1 x 31.6 cm, Collection: Australian National Gallery, Canberra. Reproduced by permission of the Australian National Gallery, Canberra.

Contrapposto

Pronounced: KONTRA-POST-O (*1st and 2nd o's as in got, final o as in go, a as in ago*)

Origin

From the Italian word meaning *opposed, constrasted* or *reversed*. The contrapposto position first appeared in statues of the Classical Greek period, and the term was first used by Italian sculptors of the **Renaissance**.

Meaning

Contrapposto refers to a means of showing the body so that parts of it are in different directions but they are nevertheless balanced. For example, the upper part of the body (torso) is turned in one direction; the lower parts (legs and hips) are twisted in the opposite direction, so that the weight of the body is placed on one leg. It was first used by Classical Greek sculptors to give flexibility and interest to their sculptures of the human form.

Associations

See: **Classical, sculpture, asymmetry.**

See Andrea del Verrochio's (Italian 1435-1488) statue of *David* and the sculptures of Buonarroti Michelangelo (Italian 1475-1564).

the contrapposto position

Contour

Pronounced: KON-TOOR (*o as in on, oor as in poor*)

Origin

From the Italian *contorno* meaning *a drawn outline*. Contour drawing was popularised by Kimon Nicolaides in his book "*The Natural Way to Draw*"(1941).

Meaning

A contour is the internal or external edge of a form in a drawing. That is the lines separating an area or shape from its surrounding background. Contour drawing attempts to produce a three dimensional quality and produce a tactile impression as well as a visual stimulus.

Associations

See: **line, drawing, texture, configuration, shape, ground.**

Copperplate

Pronounced: KOPA-PLAT (*o as in got, a as in ago, final a as in date*)

Origin and Meaning

Polished copper plates have been used in etching, engraving and printing since the 16th century. The writing on these plates had to be very neat and careful as a spoiled (scratched) plate could make the work expensive to produce. Consequently, writing which was exact and carefully executed came to be known as copperplate. The word came into general use about the beginning of the seventeenth century. Copperplate printing, which is produced on a polished plate which is slightly etched, is characterised by its sharpness of image. It is used for visiting and invitation cards.

Associations
See: **engraving, etching, print, calligraphy, cursive.**

Couch

Pronounced: KOOCH (*oo as in moon*)

Origin
From the Old French *coucher* meaning *to lay down*.

Meaning
In the production of paper, a couching cloth is a board covered with felt or flannel on which sheets of paper pulp are placed to be pressed, so that moisture is removed from the pulp and the fibres in the new paper mat together and the paper is easier to remove in a piece. **To Couch** is to transfer sheets of paper-pulp from moulds to a couching cloth.

Associations
See: **paper, deckle.**

Craft

Pronounced: KRAFT (*a as in fast*)

Origin
From Old English *craeft* meaning *strength*. It came to mean the *strength* one had in a particular manual activity. Somebody who had much strength was different from the average person. The old word *Skill* meant *distinction* or *difference*. So, a person who had *craft* also was one with *skill*.

Meaning
Craft means to make with skill or an occupation which requires skill. It also means a member of a skilled trade. It refers, too, to a very wide range of specialised activities which require not only manipulative ability and often precision and dexterity but also creative flair and imagination. Some of the crafts are: appliqué, basketry, batik, tie dyeing, beadwork, block printing, crewel work, crochet, decoupage, embroidery, enamelling, fabric printing, knitting, lacemaking, leather work, macramé, needlepoint, paper craft, papier maché, patchwork, puppetry, rugmaking, shell carving, silkscreening, spinning,

48

stenciling, tatting, tincraft, toy making, weaving and woodwork.

Associations
Among the people who promoted the development of crafts (sometimes called **handicrafts**) are Charles Robert Ashbee (1863-1942), William Morris (1834-1896) and John Ruskin (1819-1910).

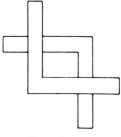

Crop

Pronounced: KROP (*o as in got*)

Origin
The origin of crop with a meaning of *to cut, prune or trim* is vague but it dates back to the seventeenth century. Its use in printing occurs in the early nineteenth century.

Meaning
To crop is to cut off or **mask** out an unwanted area of an illustration or photograph, usually to marks in a margin called **crop marks**. It also means to select a part of a picture or photograph for reproduction.

Associations
A **cropping mask** is a piece of material, usually cardboard, in the shape of the letter L. The overlapping of two cropping L's marks out a part of a work for further use.
See: **masking, blocking**.

an L cropping mask

Cross Hatching

Pronounced: KROS (*o as in loss*), HAT-CHING (*a as in bat, i as in ring*)

Origin
From the French *hacher* meaning either *to chop into small pieces* or *to engrave* or *to draw*. It is related to the French *hachure* meaning *to shade* (usually on a map) to show heights by means of crossed lines. The art was invented by Michael Wohlgemuth of Germany in 1486.

Meaning
Cross hatching is a technique in drawing, etching, engraving, painting and weaving, where parallel lines (straight or curved) are drawn close together (**hatching**) and then other parallel lines criss-cross them at right angles or at an oblique angle (**cross hatching**). The lines produce an effect of shadow, shading or **gradations** of light. Tones can be produced by varying the thickness of the lines. Hatching is used in textiles to describe shading, or shaded effects, obtained by the use of alternative threads, or groups of threads of different colours or tones.

Associations
See: **gradation, technique, drawing, etch, engraving, weave, transfer type**.

Cubism

Pronounced: KU-BIZM (*u as in due, i as in bit, zm as sm in prism*)

Origin

From the French *cubisme*. It is thought the term originated when the French critic, Louis Vauxcelle, in 1908 while attending an exhibition described the angular forms in the paintings of Georges Braque as "*cubes*".

Meaning

Cubism was an art movement which started about 1902, based to a considerable extent on the sculptures of Black Africa and the ideas of the **Post-Impressionist** painter Paul Cezanne, who said that painters *should look for the cone, the sphere and the cube in nature*. The leaders of the movement were Pablo Picasso and Georges Braque. Cubism attempts to give a structural sense of three-dimensional forms on a flat two-dimensional surface without creating an illusionistic effect. Its main features are:

it presents several views of a form presented together from different viewpoints in one composition, frequently making use of cubes and other geometrical forms;

it attempts to present a total form rather than one view of it and often one form is superimposed on another;

it tends to give little attention to perspective and often produces the effect of distortion;

it tends to repeat forms;

it relegates colour to a secondary position, but uses tonal values to great effect;

it tends to reduce subjects to their simplest geometric forms;

it experiments in the presentation of still life and the human form.

Cubism went through three distinct phases, although there is an overlap of the phases to a certain extent.

Phase 1. (1906-1909) saw the introduction and development of Cubism based on Cezanne's ideas.

Phase 2. (1910-1912) produced **Analytic Cubism** which had a low interest in colour and emphasised the form and structure of objects using geometric shapes. The artists superimposed one viewpoint on another and made time an entity in their paintings.

Phase3. (1912-1914) produced **Synthetic Cubism** where the artist synthesised numerous materials (paper, cloth etc.) into a painting, using collage (papier collé) techniques. Tactile qualities and decoration were features of the works. For example, in "*Still Life with Chair*" (1912), Picasso stuck a piece of oil cloth patterned with wickerwork chair caning among the painted objects.

The first Cubist painting using collage (papier collé) was "*Le Portugais*" by Braque, 1911. In 1918, a movement called the **Purists** reacted against the use of decoration in Synthetic Cubism and emphasised simple, basic, geometric (especially cuboid) forms. The leaders of the movement were Amédée Ozenfant and Charles Jeaneret (the latter usually called Le Corbusier).

Association

Orphism was a form of Cubism based on colour rather than form. The term *orphic* or *Orphism*, meaning *mysterious*, was coined in about 1912 to describe the kind of Cubism produced by Robert Delaunay (1885-1941).

See: **geometric, still-life, form, collage**.

See the paintings of: Pablo Picasso (Spanish, 1881-1973), Georges Braque (French, 1882-1963), Ferdinand Léger (French, 1881-1955), Robert Delaunay (French, 1885-1941), Albert Gleizes (French, 1881-1953), Alexander Archidenko (Russian, 1887-1964), Raymond Duchamp-Villon (French, 1876-1918),and the sculptures of Jacques Lipchitz (Lithuanian/French 1891-1973) and Alexander Archipenko (Russian 1887-1964).

Cursive

Pronounced: KURS-IV (*u as in fur, i as in bit*)

Origin

From the Latin *cursiva* meaning *running*. Note the words *current*-a flowing or running stream, also *curricula* meaning the *courses of study which are run by an academic subject area* in a school or college.

Meaning

The cursive style in **calligraphy** is a running, free-flowing manner of writing where letters are joined together rather than being separate. Some typefaces in typography are in cursive form, for example *copper-plate scroll*, or *chancery italic*.

Associations

See: **curvilinear, calligraphy, typography, copper-plate**.

There is nothing more certain than death, and nothing more uncertain than the time of dying. So, live life to the full.

51

Curvilinear

Pronounced: KURV-I-LIN-EE-A (*u as a in fur, i's as in big, ee as in bee, a as in ago*)

Origin
Curve is from the Latin *curvis* meaning *crooked, not straight* and linear is from *linearis* meaning *a line.*

Meaning
Curvilinear is the technique of emphasising curved lines as opposed to **rectilinear** which emphasises straight lines.

Associations
See: **drawing, arabesque, Art Nouveau, biomorphic, calligraphy, cursive.**

a curvilinear design

Cybernetic Art

Pronounced: SI-BUR-NET-IK (*i as in silence, u as in fur, e as in let, i as in ink*)

Origin
From the Greek *kubernetes* meaning *steersman*-the one who controls the ship and says which direction it should take. The word was coined by an American mathematician, Norbert Wiener, in 1948.

Meaning
Cybernetics is the science of systems of control and communication in animals and machines. Cybernatic Art is a development of **Kinetic Art**. It is usually expressed through mechanical sculptures or something similar, which are "*steered*" (moved) by some stimulus surrounding them, such as noises, air movement or the movement of spectators.

Associations
See: **kinetic, movement.**

Some modern artists who have produced cybernetic art are: Nicholas Schoffer, Enrique Castro-Cid, Charles Mattox, June Paik - all Americans.

Dadaism

Pronounced: DA-DA-IZM (*a's as in far, izm as in prism*)

Origin
Dada is a child's word in French for hobbyhorse - which is a horse's head on a stick, a rocking horse or a horse on a merry-go-round. The word was used as being deliberately meaningless. The Dadaist movement was started in 1916 by a French writer called Tristan Tzara and the artist Hans Arp. It is said that Tzara named the movement by opening a French dictionary and by sticking

a pin at random on a page and hitting the word *dada*. The movement's motto was "*Everything the artist spits is art*".

Meaning

Dadaism is a movement in Art following the First World War (1914-1918) at which time there was much political, social and psychological unrest, which led many people to have an anti-art, anti-everything attitude. Artists expressed their outrage against the way the world was going by doing absurd things. For example, the French-American artist Marcel Duchamp put a moustache and beard on a reproduction of the *Mona Lisa* and an obscene caption under it. One "happening" was a lecture by 38 lecturers-all of whom spoke at the same time. Another was an exhibition in the annexe to a café lavatory, where spectators were requested to destroy the exhibition with a chopper- which they did. The Dadaists main characteristic was to juxtapose unexpected images to surprise and shock. The movement is important in the history of art in that some of its ideas influenced **Surrealism** and also **Pop Art** and **Junk Art**.

Associations

See: **juxtaposition, sculpture, Pop Art, Surrealism, objet trouvé**.

See the works of George Grosz (German 1893-1959), Marcel Duchamp (French 1887-1968), Max Ernst (German 1891-1976), Francis Picabia (French 1879-1953) and Kurt Schwitters (German 1887-1948).

Decalcomania

Pronounced: DEK-AL-KOM-AN-EE A (*e as in neck, 1st a as in cat, o as in go, 2nd a as in late, ee as in see, 3rd a as in ago*)

Origin

From the French *decalquer* meaning *to transfer a tracing*. The French word is *decalcomanie* from *decalquer* and *manie* meaning *a craze* or *mania*. The process is said to have been devised by the artist Oscar Dominguez about 1936 and later applied to paintings by the German artist Max Ernst.

Meaning

Decalcomania is a process whereby a blot of ink or a dab of paint is put on a piece of white paper then either the paper is folded or another piece of paper is pressed onto the first. When the folded paper is opened, or one piece of paper is peeled from another, a random image is obtained. These processes can be repeated to produce images which have not been preconceived in subject or in form. It refers also to a process where a print is transferred to glass, china, ivory, alabaster, paper or stained glass work, and is sometimes referred to as **tonking**. The abbreviation **decal** is commonly used.

Associations

Blot drawing is similar to decalcomania. It was named by Alexander Cozens (1717-1786) and referred to a process where blots of ink or colour are allowed to fall at random on paper. Sometimes the paper is folded to produce a design.

See the works of Oscar Dominguez (Spanish 1906-1958) and Max Ernst (German 1891-1976).

Deckle

Pronounced: DEK-AL(*e as in let, a as in ago*)

Origin

From the Greek *deckel* which is the diminutive of *decke* meaning *a cover*.

Meaning

A deckle is an apparatus used in paper-making. It is a four-sided, bottomless, removeable, frame-like unit which fits snugly on top of a mould and keeps the paper pulp from flowing over the edges of the mould during dipping. The hand-mould method of making paper produces a rough, feathery edge to the paper, termed **deckle-edge**. At one time the deckle edge was cut off and the sheets trimmed squarely. Nowadays, the deckle edge is characteristic of hand-made paper and is left on.

a deckle

Associations

A **deckle** is also used in the manufacture of fibreboard.
See: **couch**.

Decollage

Pronounced: DE-KOL-AZH (*e as in let, o as in got, a as in far, zh as s in vision*)

Origin

From the French *decoller* meaning *to unstick* or *unglue*. Decollage is unsticking or ungluing. The word was first used by the French artists and photographers Raymond Hains and Jacques de la Villegle who met in 1949 and had an exhibition of collages (*affiches*) in 1957.

Meaning

Decollage is a technique of making collages from fragments of torn-down posters. The Surrealist artist Leo Malet first used decollage in 1934 when posters were partially torn down to reveal layers of imagery. Mimmo Rotella, an Italian painter, wrote in 1954: "*Tearing posters down from the walls is the only recourse, the only protest against a society that has lost its taste for change and shocking transformation*".

Associations

See: **collage**.

See the work of Mimmo Rotella (Italian 1918-), Raymond Hains (French 1926 -), Jacques de la Villegle (French 1926 -). These artists were sometimes called **affichistes** from the French word *affiche* meaning *a poster*.

Decoupage

Pronounced: DA-KOO-PAZH (*a as in late, oo as in soon, final a as in far, zh as s in vision*)

Origin

From the French *decouper* meaning *to cut up or cut out paper*, as in cutting paper shapes with scissors. It was very popular in Italy in the late seventeenth century and in France and England in the eighteenth century. Its popularity continued into the 19th century and it became a very fashionable pastime.

Meaning

decoupage

Decoupage is the art of cutting out shapes or motifs from any printed matter (e.g. calendars, gift cards, wrapping paper, magazines) or photographs and then gluing the shapes onto some material (including candles, ceramics and glass) to make a collage. The cut-out shapes are usually finished and sealed with layers of lacquers and varnishes. They are used in pictures or for the decoration of furniture, toys, boxes, screens and ornamental objects. Bits of other material (e.g. string, glass, plastic) are sometimes added for decoration to the contents.

Associations

The German equivalent of decoupage is *bilderbage*. A **decoupeur** is a person who uses the technique of decoupage. In England the art was called **japanning**, as it attempted to imitate the expensive, imported Japanese lacquer ware.

See: **collage, motif, trompe l'oeil, lacquer.**

Decorative Art

Pronounced: DEK-A-RA-TIV (*e as in let, 1st a as in ago, 2nd a as in cat, i as in lip*)

Origin

From the Latin *decorare* meaning *to make beautiful*. The French word *decorer* means *to beautify*. The word *art* comes from the Latin *ars*, which originally meant *skill*.

Meaning

Decorative Art applies to any of the products of the Applied Arts (e.g. textiles, metalwork, ceramics, glasswork etc.) which are used as decoration, for example in buildings . Decorative Art is distinguished from Fine Art in that its end is to ornament an object, whereas Fine Art exists as an end in itself. The distinction between Fine Art and Decorative Art is nowadays a matter of personal definition, as frequently they overlap.

Associations

Decor is the furnishings and decorations of a room or a stage.

See: **Art Deco, Art Nouveau, arabesque.**

Deflocculation

Pronounced: DEE-FLOK-U-LA-SHUN (*ee as in see, o as in got, u as in due, a as in late, u as in fun*)

Origin

From the Latin *flocculus* meaning *a floccule;* that is *a small portion of matter which is tufted like wool.* Deflocculation is action which prevents matter from massing in tufts. *De* is Latin for *away from, removal or reversal.*

Meaning

The term is used in ceramics. Potters need fine clay slip where the clay is suspended (mixed) evenly in water and does not sink to the bottom of the slip-container by force of gravity. To obtain this clay slip, and to prevent the clay from sticking in lumps or tufts (floccules), chemicals are added to the water and clay mixture. These chemicals (sodium carbonate or sodium silicate, soda ash) are electrolytes (a substance that can be dissolved in water to produce a solution able to conduct electric current) which act electrically on the clay. The electrolytes in this process are called **defloculants** because they ensure deflocculation. With defloculants, a slip can be produced which contains a large proportion of clay and a small proportion of water. For example, 450 grams of plastic clay can be made into slip with less than 56 millilitres (about a tenth of a pint) of water when a suitable deflocculant is added. Without the deflocculant, it would need 280 millilitres of water to obtain the same type of slip. The type and amount of deflocculant depends upon the type of clay used. Vinegar has a deflocculating effect on clay.

Associations

See: **slip, engobe.**

Design

Pronounced: DE-ZIN (*e as in delay, i as in sign*)

Origin

From the Latin *designare* meaning *to mark out*.

Meaning

The word design has the following meanings:

- the intentional choice and arrangement of elements (e.g. line, shape, space, colour, texture, balance, etc.) in a composition of a painting, drawing, print, photograph, graphic presentation or sculpture;

- the choice and use of materials to produce objects or create environments which meet human needs in functional and aesthetic ways (e.g. in ceramics, furniture, glasswork, interior decoration, jewellery and silversmithing, textiles and industrial design);

- a project or scheme in which objectives and the means to attain the objectives are stated ("*marked out*");

- a preliminary outline (e.g. sketch or model) showing the main features of a project.

In brief, a designed product must work, be reliable, be good value for money and look good.

The design of a product usually involves the following problem-solving processes:

- A concept is formed;

- A design brief is formulated in which the problem, the constraints imposed and the objectives to be reached are made clear;

- Research is undertaken to obtain sufficient knowledge and understanding to consider several solutions to the problem;

- Analyis of the data to sift significant from insignificant information;

- Synthesis of data and and the consideration of several choices of action;

- Experimentation with possible solutions, using models, sketches, mock-ups etc.;

- Final design to meet the requirements as set out in a design brief.

In Europe the word design tends to mean **industrial design**.

Associations

A **designer** is a person who through education and experience has the knowledge and understanding, techniques and skills successfully to complete design tasks for an agreed fee.

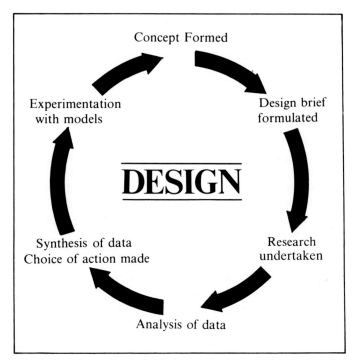

Concept Formed

Experimentation with models

Design brief formulated

DESIGN

Synthesis of data
Choice of action made

Research undertaken

Analysis of data

See the work of the following outstanding and influential, modern designers: **Industrial Design**: Peter Behrens (West Germany), Charles Eames (U.S.A.); **Graphic Design**: Milton Glazer (U S A), Paul Rand (U.S.A.); **Interior Design**: Le Corbusier (France), Raymond McGrath (Australia); **Glassware Design**: René Lalique (France); **Silversmithing Design**: Robert Welch (England), George Jensen (Denmark); **Furniture Design**: Alvar Aalto (Finland), Charles Rennie Mackintosh (Scotland); **Illustrative Design**: J.C.Leyendecker (U.S.A.), Heinz Edelman (West Germany).

See: **Bauhaus, Industrial Design, Graphic Design, layout, brief, specification.**

Die

Pronounced: DI(*i as in fine*)

Origin

From the Latin *datus* meaning *given* or *cast*, which changed in French to *de* and then in English to *die*, meaning *something cast in metal*.

Meaning

Die has a number of meanings, namely: a hollow mould used in casting metals; two segments of a hollow screw for cutting external threads of a screw or a bolt, either manually or by a machine; an attachment on a pugmill through which clay is forced to provide a specific shape of

a die

the clay; an engraved intaglio stamp which is used to make coins, medals or embossed paper; a metal form which determines the shape of plastics impressed on it or forced through it.

Associations
See: **stamp, pugmill, emboss, intaglio, casting**.

Diorama

Pronounced: DI-O-RAM-A (*i as in bite, o as in home, a as in cat, and final a as in ago*)

Origin
From the Greek *dia* meaning *through* and *horama* meaning *a sight* or *view*. The diorama was invented by Louis Jacques Mande Daguerre and Charles Bouton in 1822 and was first exhibited in Regent's Park, London.

Meaning
A diorama is a large scenic painting in a building where, by means of lighting effects and transparent areas, an illusion can be produced, so that spectators imagine they are present in a real-life scene. It is used, for example, to create realistic wildlife scenes in museums. It also means a scene painted and illuminated in such a way that, when viewed through a peep-hole in a box, a three-dimensional effect is produced of the scene.

Dipping

Pronounced: DIP-ING (*i as in lip*)

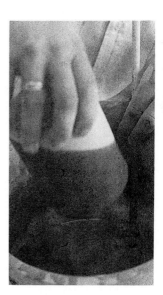

Origin
From the Old English *dyppan* which means *to dip deep*.

Meaning
Dipping is the process where potteryware is let down into a glaze solution. The dipped ware is then dried and **glost-fired**. Dip-decorated ware is pottery which is decorated by dipping it in coloured slip.

Associations
See: **slip, fire, glaze**.

Distortion

Pronounced: DIS-TOR-SHUN (*i as in miss, o as in port, u as in fun*).

Origin
From the Latin *dis* meaning *in two ways* and *tort* meaning *twist*; that is *twisted in two ways*.

Meaning
Distortion is a very personal and subjective interpretation by an artist of natural forms, or the visual changes made

by an artist to the size, shape, texture, position, character and colour of objects or people. Artists use distortion to emphasise or exaggerate particular features so that they stand out and are immediately noticed. For example, Paul Klee painted the sun black in some of his paintings and changed other local (natural) colours accordingly, so that the sun gained prominence in the paintings. Pablo Picasso distorted his human figures in his painting "*Guernica*" to draw attention to the message he wished to give. El Greco elongated the faces of most of the people in his paintings. These are controlled distortions, but distortions are not always controlled. It can occur in craft work sometimes when using metal or plastic and when over-heating or too rapid cooling can result in unplanned, distorted shapes. In metal work **strength** refers to the ability of a material to resist distortion.

Associations

See the works of the following artists who use distortion for planned purposes: Henry Moore (1898-1986), Paul Nash (1889-1946), Paul Klee (1879-1940), Salvador Dali (1904-1987). There are also distortions in Ancient Egyptian and Medieval paintings and sculptures.

See: **warp, asymmetry, proportion.**

Dominance

Pronounced: DOM-IN-ANS (*o as in pot, i as in pin, a as in ago*)

Origin

From the Latin *dominari* meaning *to rule, govern or control* or *to have a commanding influence on.*

Meaning

Dominance is the emphasis given by an artist to particular features in a composition, in order to stress their importance. Usually in any composition certain elements (e.g. size, shape, colour, texture, space, position, line direction) can be dominant and others subordinate (less important). Distortion always produces dominance as it tends to attract attention.

Associations

See: **accent, highlight, focal point, distortion.**

Draft

Pronounced: DRAFT (*a as in cast*)

Origin

Originally, the word was *draught* but the spelling has been simplified over the years, although the word draught is still in use. The word is from the Middle English *draht* meaning *to draw, to pull* or *extract from.*

Meaning

A draft is a plan, sketch or preliminary drawing of a work which will be substantially developed and elaborated on and then produced. It also means the skill of producing a draft.

Associations

A **draughtsman** is a person who makes drawings, plans or sketches, often using a **drafting machine**. A draft in design is similar in many respects to a **study** in painting. The following artists have excellent drafting abilities: Francisco Goya (1746-1828) (See his series of etchings "*The Disaster of War*"), James Whistler (1834-1890) (See his "*Le Depart pour Cythere*"), Edgar Degas (1834-1917) (See his many paintings of ballet dancers).

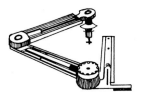

a drafting machine

Drawing

Pronounced: DRAW-ING (*aw as in saw*)

Origin

From the Old English *dragan* meaning *to draw, pull, carry or bear.* Drawing as we know it in art and design came to mean *what information is carried or borne in visual form.*

Meaning

Drawing communicates ideas and feelings by giving us information in a visual form. It is very close to writing, especially in Chinese writing. It is often used as the preliminary stage to a painting. Picasso made seventy or eighty drawings in preparation for his famous painting "*Guernica*" and it is an interesting fact that Picasso was trained intensively in classical drawing skills, which formed a foundation for his innovative work. Drawing or drafting (also spelled *draughting*) is the basis for most forms of artistic expression. It is, however, an art in its own right. Drawing is linear and is made more expressive by shading; painting, in contrast, is mainly the placing of masses of colour. Basically, to draw is to trace a line or figure by moving a pencil, pen or etching instrument across a surface in order to produce a picture or representation of an object. Drawing can also be produced by shading only.

In ceramics, drawing refers to the unpacking of potteryware from a kiln.

Associations

A **life drawing** is a drawing of a person (often a nude) using a living model. **Rendering** is a term, used mainly in design, for drawing or reproduction. It refers also to a detailed drawing, or water-colour painting, submitted to a client for inspection before the designer undertakes the finished work. **Rendition** is an alternative term for rendering. **Sciagraphy** is the art of shading in drawing. **Delineavit** preceded by a person's name was often put on the bottom of a drawing in former times. It meant (so and so) *drew it*.

See: **silhouette, contour, line, linear, cross-hatching, scumbling**.

Dry Mounting

Pronounced: DRI (*i as in kite*), MOWNT (*ow as in cow*)

Origin
From the Latin *montare* meaning originally *to ascend, lift, or raise*. A mount is the margin surrounding a picture or photograph, or the card on which a drawing is mounted.

Meaning
Dry mounting is a method used for mounting (setting in place) photographs on cardboard. Processed dry-mounting tissue is placed between the photograph and the cardboard. The tissue is touched in a few places by a hot tacking-iron and then placed in a press where heat is applied under pressure over the whole area. The shellac on the tissue melts adhering the photograph (or drawing) firmly to the mounting board, without producing wrinkles in the photograph.

a tacking iron

Associations
See: **layout, register, technique**.

Dry Point

Pronounced: DRI (*i as in kite*), POYNT (*oy as in boy*)

Origin
The technique of dry point was probably first used in the late 15th century.

Meaning
Dry point is an **intaglio** engraving technique where a design is drawn directly onto a copper plate with a needle **point**, or diamond-pointed tool (rather than gouged with a burin) which is held like a pen. No acid is used in this engraving technique, so the process is *dry*. A print is then produced from the plate which has been covered with etching ink. The point of the needle produces burred, soft lines which are characteristic of dry-point engraving. Great care has to be taken in this technique, as the slightest scratch is shown on the plate.

Associations
Roulette is a form of drypoint in which a roulette, a little wheel with spikes on it, is used as a drawing tool.

Mezzotint uses a rocker-shaped tool made of little spikes, which is used to produce solid-black texture, which can be scraped away to produce light and dark areas. **Scraping** and **burnishing** are methods of making tonal changes on a metal plate. Two of the greatest engravers of all times were the German Albrecht Dürer (1471-1528) and the Dutchman Rembrandt Van Rijn (1606-1669). See their work and also the work of James A. Whistler (American 1834-1903) and Pablo Picasso (Spanish 1881-1973).

See: **intaglio, copperplate, engraving, impression, edition.**

Mary Cassatt, America 1895-1926, **Simone, wearing a large bonnet, seated in an armchair** *drypoint 29.7 x 24 cm, Art Gallery of South Australia, Adelaide, South Australian Government Grant 1972*

63

Dunt

Pronounced: DUNT (*u as in bonus*)

Origin
From the Middle English *dunt* which is a variation of *dint* meaning *a dull sounding blow or stroke to shake something or somebody.*

Meaning
A dunt is a crack or number of cracks (sometimes invisible) which appear in clayware which has cooled too rapidly following firing in a kiln. Dunts are caused by stresses produced in the ware when there are differences between the amount of contraction between the body of a pot and the glaze on it. This is usually caused by not allowing sufficient time to elapse for the silica in the clay body to go through the various chemical changes which are essential to produce first-rate ware. The dunting can occur during cooling or even hours or days after the ware has been taken out of the kiln, as the chemical processes are still going on.

Associations
See: **earthenware, thermal shock, blowing, kneading, crazing, pyrometry**.

Dye

Pronounced: DI (*i as in bite*)

Origin
Dye is from Old English *deagian* of unknown origin. Dyeing has been practised since the earliest people existed on earth. The wall paintings in caves at Altamira in Spain and those at Lascaux in France show that people thousands of years ago had knowledge of, and skills in the use of, natural dyes long before spinning and weaving were common. Dyed fabrics have been found at Thebes in Egyptian tombs dating back to 3500 B.C.. Dyeing is mentioned in the Bible (Exodus SXX 23). Phoenicia (now Israel and Lebanon) was famous for its dyes. The first book on dyeing was published in English in 1548. Only natural products were used in the making of dyes until the 19th century. Sir William Henry Perkin (1838-1907) was the inventor of the first synthetic, man-made dye. In 1856, while trying to extract quinine from aniline, he discovered a purple dye (called mauveine) which he found would dye silk. This discovery led to the extraction of other dyes from coal derivatives. There are now over three million commercial dyes, of which the **procion** (or reactive) dyes form the bulk in the dyeing trade.

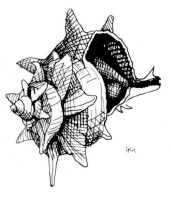

the Murex Brandaris snail from which Tyrian purple dye was obtained

Meaning
A dye is a solution used to impregnate a fabric, yarn, or fibre and give it a deep, ingrained stain or colour. To dye

is the action of dyeing where the stain or colour becomes a fixed part of a texture and not just a surface colour. Traditionally,dyes fall into two classes: **vat dyes** and **mordant dyes**. **Vat dyes** must first be converted by **reduction** (to remove oxygen from them) into a liquid form. Chemicals are used for this process. The material is then immersed in the dye and then exposed to the air. The dye absorbs oxygen and during this oxidation process the dye is fixed in the fibres of the material. In the **mordant dye** process, a **mordant** (which opens the material's fibres for the dye to penetrate the material) is required to fix the dye in the fabric. The principal mordants are alum, iron, chrome, copper, and tin. A mordant is either added to the dye in the dye-bath into which the material is immersed or the material can be treated with a mordant before it is steeped in a dye solution.

Indigo, a blue dye obtained from the indigo plant was one of the first dyes used by humans. The Portugese word for *indigo* is *anil*, from which the word **analine** is derived. Some natural dyes obtained from flowers, fruit or herbs are: brown from alder bark, walnut shells, and birch bark; blue from cornflowers, larkspur petals; orange from dahlias and sassafras; burnt orange from coreopsis and onions; yellow from dock roots, fig leaves, saffron and nettles; red from dogwood bark. Natural dyes are also obtained from insects, shellfish and minerals. Some well-known natural dyes are henna (red), madder (red), cochineal (scarlet) and indigo (blue). **Analine** is an oily liquid obtained from coal from which a dark blue dye (mauve) is made.

Associations

See: **bleeding, mordant, batik, weaving, tie-dye, fabric, jigging, oxidation, reduction, weld.**

Earthenware

Pronounced: URTH-AN WAR (*u as in fur, a as in ago, final a as in care*)

Origin

Earth is from Old English *eorthe* meaning *the land* or *soil*, and ware is from Old English *waru* meaning *object of care or concern* and later *articles of merchandise for sale.*

Meaning

Earthenware is pottery whch has a porous body which can be water-proofed by glazing. It is non-vitreous, opaque and usually terra cotta coloured. It is distinguished from stoneware by its greater porosity. When fired, if pottery

Distel Durch, Holland, *Vase* earthenware, Jugendstijl decoration, *Art Gallery of South Australia, Adelaide, South Australia*

has a porosity of more than 5% it is earthenware; if less, it is stoneware. It is glazed and fired at 1020°c - 1080°c.

Associations
See: **bisque, stoneware, greenware, pottery, stoneware, vitreous, opacity, porosity, glaze, oxidation, fire, raku, slip.**

Easel

Pronounced: EE-ZAL (*ee as in see, a as in ago*)

Origin
From the Dutch *ezel*. The easel was first used during the Renaissance and became very popular in Holland in the 17th century when it was used for painting small portraits and landscapes.

Meaning
An easel is a framework to hold a painting while it is being painted. There are different kinds to suit different needs. A studio easel can be adjusted so that the canvas it is supporting can be raised or lowered or tilted. It refers also to a device to hold two-dimensional material which is to be photographed.

Associations
See: **Renaissance, canvas, portrait, landscape.**

Ecorché

Pronounced: E-KOR-SHAY (*e as in let, o as in bore, ay rhymes with day*)

Origin
From the French *ecorcher* meaning *to flay or strip the skin off an animal.*

Meaning
Ecorché describes a picture or a sculpture of a human or an animal whose skin has been stripped off to reveal muscles and sinews. Such drawings are sometimes used by artists to study the anatomy and physiology of human or animal forms.

Associations
See "*Study of a Horse*" by George Stubbs (English 1724-1806), "*De Humani Corporis Fabrica*" by Andreas Vesalius (Italian 1514-1564) and works by Leonardo Da Vinci (Italian 1452-1519).

Edition

Pronounced: E-DISH-UN (*e as in naked, i as in fish, u as in bonus*)

Origin
From the Latin *editum* meaning *given out* or *put forward.*

Meaning

In printmaking, edition refers to a complete set of identical impressions taken from a plate or stone. The number of the impression and the total number of impressions taken is shown at the bottom of the print where the artist's signature is usually written. For example, 10/15 means that the impression is the tenth out of a total of fifteen impressions. In sculpture, edition refers to a number of castings taken from one mould.

Associations

See: **impression, printmaking, cast.**

Elements

Pronounced: EL-I-MENTS (*e as in bell, i as in bit, e as in met*)

Origin

From the Latin *elmentum* meaning *a first principle* or *main constituent of something*, such as air, fire, water and earth.

Meaning

The elements of an artistic composition are those basic visual qualities, such as line, colour, mass, shape, space and texture, which when combined produce visual images. The term also refers to any substance which cannot be split up into simple substances.

Associations

See: **composition, line, colour, shape, mass, texture, space, harmony, layout, form, configuration.**

Elevation

Pronounced: ELI-VA-SHUN (*eli as tele in television, a as in late, u as in fun*)

Origin

From the Latin *elevatum* meaning *lifted or raised up.*

Meaning

An elevation is the vertical face of a building or a drawing of a face of a building when looking towards the centre of the building. It is part of an **iosometric** drawing.

Associations

See: **callipers, geometric, line, projection, mechanical drawing, perspective, plane, proportion, rectilinear, sketch, symmetry, viewpoint.**

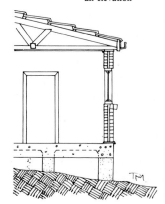

an elevation

Emboss

Pronounced: EM-BOS (*e as in lemon, o as on got*)

Origin

Boss is from Old French *boce* meaning *a swelling* or *bump*. Emboss means literally *to put bumps on something*.

Meaning

To emboss is any process (e.g. punching, hammering, moulding or using a die) which makes a design stand out in **relief** on metal, leather, paper, pottery, plastics, textiles or other material. Paper or other material can be embossed by placing the paper between a relief die and a hollow die. The relief die is struck into the hollow die to make a raised letter or design on the paper or material. Embossing on paper or card without ink is called **blind embossing**; with ink, it is called **die-stamping**.

William Maundy, Great Britain 17th century, *Sweetmeat dish* sterling silver, *Art Gallery of South Australia, Adelaide, South Australia*

Associations

See: **relief, repoussé, die, impression, symbol, chase, print**.

sprigging is the process of decorating pottery by pressing **bas-relief** figures onto ware. **Bossing** is the process of shaping malleable metals to conform to irregular surfaces. A **swage** is a tool used to shape metals.

Embroidery

a detail from the *Bayeux Tapestry*, showing the death of King Harold

Pronounced: EM-BROY-DARY (*em as in lemon, oy as in boy, a as in ago, y as in duty*)

Origin

From the French *embroder* meaning *to ornament with needlework* .Embroidery is the product of this action. The most famous embroidery in the world is the Bayeux Tapestry in France, which, although called a tapestry, is an embroidery. It was made in Medieval times and depicts graphically in seventy nine scenes the conquest of England by William the Conqueror of Normandy at the battle of Hastings in 1066. The embroidery is 70.34 metres long but only 50 centimetres wide. It was produced with two kinds of woollen threads in eight colours on a base of coarse linen. Embroidery produced on machines was first introduced during the Industrial Revolution in England.

Meaning

Embroidery is a term which describes all forms of decorating textiles with needlework, using threads of cotton, wool, silk and other materials. Stitches in needlework are usually hidden, but in embroidery docorative stitchery is revealed as part of the art of embroidery. The technique uses many kinds of stitches and many kinds of needles (e.g. crewel, tapestry, chenille, bodkins and bead). In the past, many kinds of hard materials were used for needles but nowadays they are mainly of steel. Frames (of various shapes, e.g. square,

an embroidered chair

tarbour, hoop) are used on which a design or picture is traced (called a **cartoon**) on a taut fabric ground, made from linen, velvet, leather, cambric, muslin, silk, nylon, chiffon, or some other material.

Associations

Brocade now means a textile very similar to embroidery which has a raised pattern woven into it. **Crewel work** is a type of embroidery with clear, strong designs, which uses colourful worsted, two-ply yarns on a background of linen cloth. It was used for hangings and upholstery in North America and England from the early 17th century and the work became very fashionable about 1860. **Zari** is a form of embroidery where gold and silver threads of metal are used to decorate leather goods and clothing.

Enamel

Pronounced: I-NAM-AL (*i as in ink, 1st a as in apple, 2nd a as in ago*)

Origin

From the Anglo-French *en* meaning *in* and *amel* or *email* meaning *to smelt or melt*.

The origin of the process is not known. The earliest known enamels in the form of jewellery are from Greece and were made in the 13th century B.C.. It was developed by Greek artisans in the sixth century and was then used extensively throughout the world. In 1799, Dr. Hinkling invented an enamelling process for saucepans.

Meaning

Enamel consists of a colourless, transparent compound called flux made of silica, potash or minium. The more silica there is in the compound, the harder it is. It is a very hard (vitreous) glass in powder form. It is coloured by metallic oxides, and the more oxide in the enamel the deeper the colour. Different oxides produce different colours: copper produces green, tin produces white and gold produces red. An object to be enamelled is cleaned with an abrasive (e.g. steel wool) and then covered with gum tragacanth, which ensures the enamel adheres to the object. The enamel is then fused onto the object by heating it from below with an air-acetelyne torch or by firing it in a kiln or a small, high-temperature furnace called a **muffle furnace**. Usually enamels, which can be transparent, translucent or opaque, are glossy and brilliantly coloured. Enamel is used to decorate pottery, metal and glass and for making the preservative linings of objects. It is used extensively in jewellery work. Enamel also refers to a paint with a high oil or varnish content, which dries to a brilliant gloss.

an enamelling kiln

Associations

If two colours of enamel are to be placed next to each other without a barrier, they may fuse during firing. To prevent this, a barrier of metal (called a **cloison**) is soldered between the enamels. This technique is called **cloisonné**. Another technique is to cut designs into a metal ground and then fill the incisions in the metal with enamels. This technique is called **champlevé**.

See: **flux, vitreous, opacity, Decorative Art, stained-glass, firing, pickle**.

Enamelling became popular during the Art Nouveau period in the early part of this century in Europe, particularly in France, where the work of René Lalique (1860-1945) was outstanding. One of the most famous **enamelists** in the world was Peter Carl Fabergé (1846-1920) who was born in Russia. He worked in precious metals and is best known for his superbly-crafted Easter eggs. See also the work of Alexander Fisher (1864-1963), a British enameller.

Encaustic

Pronounced: EN-KAU-STIK (*e as in pen, au as in daughter, i as in stick*)

Origin

From the Greek *enkaustikos* meaning *burnt in*. The technique was used by the Egyptians for mummy portraits, by the Ancient Greeks and Romans for mural paintings and by Cistercian monks to produce paving tiles, and later extensively in Victorian England. No Greek encaustic paintings have survived.

Meaning

In encaustic painting, pigments mixed with hot wax are applied with heated tools to a rigid base of plywood or masonite. The waxed pigments are burnt onto the surface to produce the painting. Encaustic bricks or tiles have a designed inlay of material of a different colour from the tile. The tile is glazed and then fired in a kiln.

Associations

See: **cerography, pigment, glaze, firing.**

See: *The Flag* by Jasper Johns (U.S.A. 1930 -). Probably the most famous examples of ancient encaustic paintings are the Fayum mummy portraits from Egypt, which can be seen in the British Museum, London.

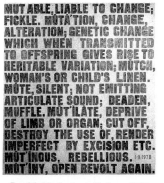

Bea Maddock, Australia born 1934, *Mutable* encaustic, collage on canvas 183 x 167 cm, *Art Gallery of South Australia, Adelaide, South Australia*

Engobe

Pronounced: EN-GOB (*e as in pen, o as in robe*)

Origin

From the French for *slip*. *Engober* in French means *to decorate or coat pottery with slip*.

Meaning

Engobe is a clay similar to slip which is applied by brush, dip or spray to a raw or bisque clay object to colour it, or to give it a smoother finish. To adjust for shrinkage in the object, the engobe usually contains flux and silica. Engobe can be in a jelly or stiff form. It is not quite a slip and not quite a glaze but a mixture of the two.

Associations

See: **slip, dipping, bisque, flux, shrinkage.**

Engraving

Pronounced: EN-GRAV-ING (*e as in pen, a as in brave*)

Origin

From the French *engraver* meaning *to carve* or *to cut*. Also, it is from the Old English *grafan* meaning *to dig*. Think of a grave for burial or a groove in a record.

The earliest known engraving is of "*Christ Crowned with Thorns*", dated about 1446. The Italian artist Parmigianino developed the technique from 1520 onwards. The earliest known copper engraving in England was made in 1461. The art of hatching and cross-hatching was invented by Michael Wohlgemuth of Germany in 1486.

Meaning

Engraving is a technique in printing using a tool called a **graver** or **burin**. An artist cuts a composition, design or lettering into metal, wood or stone. The deeper the cuts the more ink is eventually left on the material used and the darker will be the print. Engraving is most successful on copper and zinc because they are relatively soft metals and easy to work, but they wear away fairly quickly, so they are sometimes faced with steel in order to lengthen their lives. Very fine hatching and cross-hatching can be made on plates to produce shading effects. Engraving is also made on leatherhard clay, on glass and on gems.

Associations

xylography is the art of wood engraving; **chalcography** is the art of engraving on copper or brass. The three types of engraving are **intaglio, relief** or **cameo** and **surface** or **planar**. A **riffler** is a special file used in engraving. It is slightly curved and has narrow points at each end. It is especially useful for getting into difficult corners, for enlarging holes and for the filing of inside surfaces.

See: **burin, graver, wood block, copperplate, impression , edition, cerography, laser, scoring**.

See the engravings of William Hogarth (English 1697-1764) and Albrecht Dürer (German 1471-1528)

Opposite

Albrecht Dürer, Germany 1471-1528, **St Jerome in his study**
line engraving 24.4 x 19.3 cm, Art Gallery of South Australia, Adelaide, Morgan Thomas Bequest Fund 1962

a riffler

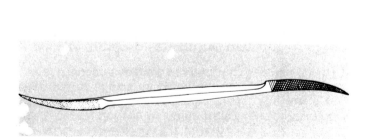

Ergonomics

Pronounced: URGO-NOM-IKS (*u as in fur, 1st o as in go, 2nd o as in got, i as in ink*)

Origin

From the Greek *ergon* meaning *work* and *oikonomos* meaning *one who manages* (e.g. a household). Literally, it is how work is arranged and managed.

Meaning

Ergonomics is the study of the relationship between individuals and their work or working environment. It is particularly concerned with the problems which people experience in their work from physical factors (e.g. the construction of benches or tables at which people must stand or sit to work), mental factors (e.g. the monotony of conveyor-belt work) and psychological factors (e.g. noise, colour of surroundings, and light). A work bench, for instance, can be said to be ergonomically sound if its form is appropriate for the activity and is such that it allows someone to work at it for relatively long periods without the person experiencing physical strain.

Software ergonomics deals with the ease with which a software computer package can be used by a computer operator.

The study of ergonomics is essential for designers who produce products which people will use.

Associations

Biotechnology is the application of technology to living things, including humans. **Bio-engineering** is similar. **Anthropometrics** is the science of the measurement of the human body.

See: **Design, Industrial Design**.

See the work of Henry Dreyfuss (American 1903-1972).

Etching

Pronounced: ET-CHING (*e as in pet, i as in ink*)

Origin

From the Dutch *etzen* or the German *atzen* meaning *to eat* or *to bite*. The first *dated* etching is by the Swiss artist Urs Graf (1485-1527), entitled *Girl Bathing Her Feet*, 1513. The German painter and engraver Albrecht Dürer (1471-1528) was a matchless artist in the use of the technique. European metalworkers began to use etching extensively for the decoration of armour and weapons in the 15th century.

Meaning

To etch is to produce a design on a metal plate by the use of a corrosive acid (e.g. nitric acid). A composition or

74

design is scratched onto a plate which has been treated with an acid-resistant substance, such as a **hardground** or a **softground** (usually using wax), or a **whiteground** (using soap). Where the resist substance is scratched, the metal plate is exposed. When the metal plate is dipped in acid, the acid "bites" into the exposed lines. The plate is cleaned and then inked and ink penetrates the etched lines. Ink is then removed from the unetched parts of the plate and prints can then be made. Traditionally, copper has been used for etching plates but zinc is cheaper and is often used. Experiments are constantly being made to find new materials for plates, such as masonite, steel and lucite. Etch also refers to an acid-gum solution which fixes a waxy or greasy drawing in place on a stone. In schools, where metal plates will probably not be readily available, a simple **drypoint** technique called **celluloid etching** is sometimes used. Here, compositions or designs are etched (scratched) onto rigid celluloid, perspex or some similar plastic material. Printing inks are applied and prints can be made as in the normal etching process.

Antonio Canaletto, Italy 1697-1768, **The Tower of Malghera** *etching 29.2 x 41.8 cm, Art Gallery of South Australia, Adelaide, Morgan Thomas Bequest Fund 1964*

Associations

An **etcher** is a person skilled in etching. A **dabber** is a pad used for inking an etching plate. An etching process can also be used in enamelling, jewellery work, glasswork and stained-glass work.

See: **hardground, resist, aquatint, Design, impression, edition, drypoint**.

See the works of Rembrandt whose etchings match his superb paintings, and the works of Giovanni Paolo Panini (1691-1765), Francisco Goya (1746-1828), Edouard Manet (1823-1883), J.A.M.Whistler (1834-1903) and Lucien Pissarro (1863-1944).

Expressionism

Pronounced: EX-PRESH-ON-ISM (*e as in let, presh as in fresh, o as in onion, ism as in prism*)

Origin

The term was first popularised by the German art critic Herworth Walden. The pioneers of the movement were the French artist Georges Rouault (1871-1958) and the Dutch artist Van Gogh (1853-1890). The Expressionistic tendency goes back to the work of Hieronymous Bosch (1475-1516) and Matthias Grunewald (1475-1528). The Expressionist movement, which incorporates *Symbolism* and *Art Nouveau* influences, lasted from 1885 until the early 1900's.

Meaning

Expressionism is a movement in Art where the artists' work emphasised feeling rather than reasoned thought. The artists attempted to communicate their emotional reactions to the confusing world around them rather than attempt to represent how things "*actually looked*". Expressionist form tends to exaggerate or distort natural objects in order to make clear an emotion or mood of the artist. Today Expressionism describes any art where the conventions of proportion or realism are disregarded in favour of personal expression. This usually results in some distortion of shapes and very personal use of colour.

Associations

Arthur Boyd, Australia born 1920, *The Sisters* 1954, earthenware 95.5 cm high *Art Gallery of South Australia, Adelaide, South Australia*

See: **subjective, distortion, painterly, facture, Romanticism, Art Nouveau, Symbolism**.

See the work of painters: Eduard Munch (Norwegian 1863-1944), James Ensor (Belgian 1860-1949), Henri de Toulouse-Lautrec (French 1864-1901), Georges Rouault (French 1871-1958), Oskar Kokoschka (Austrian 1886-1980), Chaim Soutine (Russian 1894-1943), Max Beckmann (German 1884-1950), Emil Nolde (German 1867-1956) and the work of sculptors: Ivan Mestrović

(Jugoslavian 1883-1962), Alberto Giacometti (Italian 1901-1966) and Elizabeth Frink (English 1930 -).

Fabric

Pronounced: FAB-RIK (*a as in fat, i as in ink*)

Origin

From the Latin *fabrica* meaning *a workshop* and *faber* meaning *a worker in hard materials*. Eventually, the word came to mean anything made by skill and labour, and then cloth which was made by hand through weaving.

The earliest-known textiles (wool) came from a neolithic burial site in Catal Hüyük in Anatolia, which is now Western Asia and Asiatic Turkey. They date from about 6,000 B.C. The production of fabrics goes back to Ancient times and probably the longest history of fabric decoration is that of Egypt, dating back to at least seven thousand years ago.

Meaning

Fabric is cloth material (textile) made by weaving raw materials, such as wool, cotton, flax, silk, hemp or jute. Fibre which is spun on a spinning wheel is called **yarn**. Fabric refers also to anything which is made or constructed by art and labour, for example the frame and structure of a building. To fabricate means to construct or manufacture (which originally meant *to make by hand*).

Associations

See: **batik, weave, appliqué, size, accent, loom, warp, porosity, sculpture (soft sculpture), wood-cut**.

Facet

Pronounced: FAS-ET (*a as in mass, e as in let*)

Origin

From the French *facette* meaning *a little face.*

Meaning

A facet is one of a number of flat surfaces (faces) on a gem stone or a crystal. Precious.stones (e.g. diamonds) are cut so that they have facets, which reflect and refract (i.e. break the direction of) light to make the stones sparkle.

Associations

See: **kaleidoscope, mosaic, prism, spectrum, highlight, Op Art**.

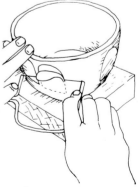

a facet on a pot

Facsimile

Pronounced: FAK-SIM-I-LY (*a as in back, i's as in bit, y as in duty*)

Origin
From the Latin *facere* meaning *to make* and *simile* meaning *like*. That is an exact copy of something, such as a piece of writing, a picture or a coin.

Meaning
A facsimile is a reproduction of a drawing, print, artefact or manuscript. Originally, it meant a precise copy in all respects, including the materials used. Nowadays, it usually refers to copies of original documents or graphics by the use of electronic reproduction machines, one of which is called a facsimile machine, which is often abbreviate to a **fax**.

Associations
reprography means all kinds of processes for the reproduction of facsimiles.

See: **squaring, life-drawing, still-life, pantograph,replica, Realism, template, stencil.**

Facture

Pronounced: FAK-TUR (*a as in fact, u as in sure*)

Origin
From the Italian *fattura* or the French *facture* meaning *handling*. That is how something is handled or made; its workmanship.

Meaning
Facture is the way an artist puts paint on a canvas to produce a picture. That is the artist's individual style, particularly in brushwork. Elements of a painting, such as composition, subject matter, colour, etc. can be related to a particular period or school of painting but facture, the way an artist handles his or her materials (not only paint but also other mediums) is personal to him or her and is difficult to imitate exactly. Facture is as individual as a person's signature or fingerprint. Facture is also termed **handling**.

Associations
See: **Expressionism, palette, painterly, subjective, style,.**

Fantasy

Pronounced: FAN-TA-SY (*1st a as in bat, 2nd a as in ago, y as in duty*)

Origin
From the Greek *phantasia* meaning *something made visible*. Later it came to mean *imagining in a fanciful way*.

Meaning

Fantasy is an expression ("*a making visible*") of a person's deep thoughts and feelings, often in a strange and unusual or fantastic manner, and sometimes revealing dreams or the unconscious. Surrealist and Cubist paintings and sculptures often reveal fantasy.

Associations

See: **Surrealism, Abstract Art, Cubism, Expressionism, Romanticism, Symbolism, illusion, cartoon.**

Sidney Nolan , Australia 1917, *The Temptation of St Anthony* synthetic polymer paint on composition board 122.0 x 96.5 cm *Art Gallery of South Australia, Adelaide, South Australia*

Fat

Pronounced: FAT (*a as in cat*)

Origin

From an Old English word *faet* which as well as meaning *plump and fleshy* also meant *thick and substantial.*

Meaning

Fat is a term to describe paint where the pigment contains a high proportion of oil to produce a rich paste (e.g. **impasto**). A saying in painting used to be: "*Start lean and finish fat*", meaning have thin layers of paint first and thicker layers next. In ceramics, it describes clay which has much plasticity. A fat clay, such as ball-clay or bentonite, which has high plasticity and is easily moulded, is sometimes added to short clay to make it more workable.

Associations

Lean colour is paint where the pigment has been thinned with turpentine so that the paint dries quickly.
See: **pigment, impasto, plasticity**.

Fauvism

Pronounced: FAW-VIZM (*aw as in paw, i as in bit, zm as sm in spasm*)

Origin

From the French *les fauves* meaning *wild beasts*. Fauvism (literally *wild-beast-ism*) was first used by a French art critic, Louis Vauxcelles, at an exhibition in 1902. Seeing a very conservative sculpture among paintings which had violent colours, he said the sculpture stood out like a Donatello (a Classical painter) among *fauves*- wild beasts. The first Fauve exhibition was in Paris in 1905.

André Derain, France 1880 - 1954, *Passage du Midi* oil on canvas 73.0 x 93.6 cm *Art Gallery of South Australia, Adelaide, South Australia*

Meaning

The term Fauvism applies to painters who used pure, violent, brilliant, bold and startling hues with stark contrasts and clashes and no play of light and shade.

Often the expressive brushwork was rough, with thick outlines. Perspective was of little concern to them and their works were essentially two-dimensional with flat planes of colour and forms, sometimes distorted, which were reduced to simple essentials, so that a rather primitive, child-like effect is often produced.

Associations
See: **colour, painterly, malerisch, plane, Primitive Art**.

An example of a Fauvist painting is that by Henri Matisse (the leader of the Fauvist movement) produced in 1905, called "*The Green Stripe: Portrait of Mme. Matisse*". The green stripe is down Madame Matisse's nose. See also his "*Still Life with a Goldfish*" and works by the French painters Georges Braque (1882-1963), André Derain (1880-1954), Maurice de Vlaminck (1876-1958), Raoul Dufy (1877-1953), and Georges Rouault (1871-1958).

Feldspar

Pronounced: FELD-SPAR (*e as in well, a as in car*)

Origin
From the German *feld* meaning *field* and *spath* (later *spar*) meaning a word for *a dull, easily-dug mineral stone*. That is a mineral dug with ease straight from a field.

Meaning
Feldspars are a group of white or flesh-red minerals found in crystalline rocks, containing aluminium silicates with potassium, sodium, calcium or barium. It is used as a flux in glazes. It is an essential ingredient of most true porcelains and it is used in the production of vitreous enamels. Other silicates (that is a combination of silica and an oxide) like feldspar, are clays and orthoclases. When it is decomposed, feldspar becomes **kaolin**.

Associations
Orthoclases are feldspars in crystals with two splits at right angles.
See: **flux, glaze, porcelain, enamel, vitreous**.

Figurative Art

Pronounced: FIG-A-RA-TIV (*i as in big, a's as in ago, i as in give*)

Origin
From the Latin *figurativus* meaning *like an emblem* or *metaphor*. That is not literal or realistic. In Art, it came to mean *like a human figure*. That is realistic and actual.

Meaning
Figurative art comprises works which pictorially represent a clearly-recognisable, objective depiction of nature,

human beings and the world , rather than works which are a subjective, abstract or symbolic interpretation of them. Ocassionally, an artist's expression results in a distorted, but nevertheless valid, interpretation of reality, as he or she sees it (as there are many interpretations of *reality*).

Associations

See: **Realism Naturalism, Formalism, genre, icon, landscape, Classical, objectivity, Pre-Raphaelite. Representational Art** (as opposed to **Abstract Art**) is sometimes used for the term figurative art. Figurative art is shown, for example, in the work of Rembrandt (1606-1669), Goya (1746-1828) and Degas (1834-1917), and non-figurative art is shown in the work of, for example, Mondrian (1872-1944), Klee (1879-1940) and Salvador Dali (1904-1986).

Filigree

Pronounced: FILI-GREE (*i's as in sit, ee as in see*)

Origin

From the Latin *filum* meaning *a thread* and *granum* meaning *a grain*. Filigree is an abbreviation of *filigreen* or *filigraine*. Originally, it meant delicate work made in threads and beads or grains. The process was used in Ancient Greece and Rome. It was a popular form of ornamentation for jewellery and vessels among the Anglo-Saxons in the 7th and 8th centuries. Venetian metalworkers in the 13th and 14th centuries produced filigree which was enriched by enamelled cloison work.

filigree work

Meaning

Filigree is the very fine and delicate use of elaborate openwork patterns (with lace-like effect) using metals which are sometimes precious. Such work is usually produced from fine, flattened, twisted wires which are made into patterns and then soldered. The work is either attached to a solid backing or left as unsupported open work. It is used extensively in jewellery-making and in decorative metal work for gates, fences and varandahs. **False filigree** is produced by the **lost wax** casting process, where delicate forms are modelled in wax.

William Fountain, Great Britain, *Dessert dish cover* 1803, sterling silver, *Art Gallery of South Australia, Adelaide, South Australia*

Fine Arts

Pronounced: FIN (*i as in line*), ART (*a as in far*)

Origin

Fine is from the Latin *finis* meaning *end*. It came to mean *the end or finished thing* and then *beautiful and excellent*. Art is from the Latin *ars* meaning *skill*. It was used to mean skill (applied to many crafts and professions) with no emphasis on any specialisation until the 17th century. The use of art and artist to apply **only** to drawing, painting, sculpture and engraving, etc. did not become established until the 19th century. The French for Fine Arts is *Beaux Arts* meaning *beautiful Arts*. The use of the term Fine Arts can be traced to the Renaissance when artists, such as Leonardo Da Vinci, argued that painters practised an intellectual activity not just a manual skill. The term Fine Arts became established in about the middle of the 18th century.

Meaning

The plural Fine Arts, rather than the singular Fine Art, is usually, although not always, used. The term includes drawing, painting, sculpture, printmaking , photography, electronic media, film-making, music and poetry. It refers to art which requires refined and subtle skills but which does not necessarily fulfil a practical function, in distinction to crafts, the applied arts and decorative arts and design which usually do.

Associations

See: **aesthetics, Decorative Art, movement, plastic arts, sculpture.**

Firing

Pronounced: FI-RING (*1st i as in line, 2nd i as in ink*)

Origin

From the Old English word *fyr* meaning *to burn, fuel* and *bake*. It probably came from the Latin *Pyr* and Greek *pur* meaning orginally *wood for burning dead bodies.*

Meaning

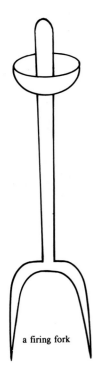

a firing fork

Firing is a process in ceramics of converting clay into a hard substance. It is the hardening, glazing or fusing process for ceramic, glass or enamel objects by intense heat in a kiln. The temperature in a kiln can be controlled with precision, and is varied according to the type of ware being fired- usually about 1000°c for earthenware and 1450°c for true porcelain. Some ware requires several firings before the process is finished. Clay breaks up in water but is changed by firing into a stone-like substance which is not affected by water and is often impervious to it. This is called the **ceramic change**. When firing occurs, (at a mimimum of 573°c) organic matter is burned away, with a change in the colour of the clay. The second firing brings about a fusion of glass onto the surface of the ware. The addition of oxide to the glaze produces a variety of colour, depending on the fluxes chosen to fuse the glass.

Associations

See: **pyrometer, pyrometric cone, pottery, ceramics, kiln, bisque, flux, frit, oxidation, saggers, thermal shock, periodic table, glaze, glass, enamel, porcelain**.

Flux

Pronounced: FLUX (*u as in dug*)

Origin

From the Latin *fluxus* meaning *flowing*.

Meaning

In ceramics, flux is a substance which is added to glaze materials to allow the basic components of a glaze to fuse at a lower temperature than they would without the flux. It causes other substances to become fluid. One can use a flux to ensure a glaze matures (that is melts) at the required temperature. The most common fluxes are calcium, potassium, sodium, lead and boron. When a metal is heated (by annealing, soldering or welding), an oxide of the metal forms on its surface (sometimes referred to as *firescale*). It is rather like rust. The oxide prevents metals from fusing in a heating process. Fluxes (which are often a borax mixture in paste or liquid form) which clean the oxide from the metals, so that they can be joined together by solder, are called **corrosive fluxes** (e.g. hydrochloric acid, zinc chloride and ammonium chloride, which is also called sal ammoniac). Some fluxes, however, do not remove oxides before soldering but only stop them from forming during the soldering operation. These are **non-corrosive fluxes** (e.g. resin).

Associations

entetic is a word to describe a substance which when mixed with another substance will melt and fuse at a lower melting point than will the separate substances. **Borax** is the most common flux for most ferrous and non-ferrous metals. It does not, however, dissolve oxides of aluminium and lead.

See: **glaze, frit, oxidation, solder, feldspar**.

Focal Point

Pronounced: FO-KAL (*o as in go, a as in ago*)

Origin

From the Latin *focus* meaning *the hearth* or *fireplace*; that is the main point of entry or comfort in a house, and the point to which people are drawn.

Meaning

The focal point of a work of art is that area to which the eyes are drawn most strongly. An artist may draw a spectator's attention to a particular part of a work (the focal point) by the use of contrasting shapes, vivid colours, changes in size, spotlighting, changing of values, by the addition of detail or by distortion.

Associations
See: **highlight, perspective, dominance, distortion, accent**.

Folio

Pronounced: FO-LIO (*o as in so, io as in radio*)

Origin
From the Latin *folio* meaning *in leaf-form* (compare with *foliage* which means leaves on a tree). That is a folded sheet of paper with two leaves.

Meaning

a portfolio

Folio means a page number of a publication and a leaf in a book or manuscript. It means also a sheet of paper folded to make two leaves and four pages and a book or volume of the largest size. It refers also to a large, flat container holding samples of an artist's or designer's work. This is also called a **portfolio**, meaning a folio which can be carried (from the French *porter* meaning *to carry*).

Associations
recto refers to the righthand page of a folded sheet of paper; **verso** refers to the lefthand or even page.

Foreshortening

Pronounced: FOR-SHORT-EN-ING (*o's as in port, e as in token*)

Origin
Fore is an abbreviation of *before* or *afore* meaning *in front of*. *Shortening* originates from Old English meaning *to make smaller*. That is something immediately in front of you that appears to get smaller.

Meaning

foreshortening

Foreshortening describes an object that is at an angle to the plane which appears to become narrower and less clear as it recedes. It is a perspective effect in painting and drawing whereby objects or persons appear to be smaller than they really are. The spectator readjusts the objects or persons into their correct proportions. In foreshortening, the picture does not give a usual or characteristic view of the objects or persons. Geometrically, every projection involves foreshortening to some extent. A common example of foreshortening is where a figure in a picture stands with arms outstretched towards the viewer. The hands appear very large, the arms very short.

Associations

See: **proportion, focal point, perspective, plane, projection, illusion, distortion.**

Form

Pronounced: FORM (*o as in worn*)

Origin

From the Latin *forma* meaning *shape* or *configuration.*

Meaning

Form is the shape, design and size of visual elements and their organisation and relationships in a work of art, in order to create unity in a composition. It is how the content of a work is revealed visually. Three-dimensional form is attained by (a) the method of addition, such as modelling, collage or assemblage, which is called **construction**; (b) the method of subtraction, such as carving, milling or lathe work, which is called **destruction**; (c) the method of manipulation, such as origami, the shaping of rubber, plastic, clay, or cardboard and changing the shape of metals, which is called **manipulation**.

Associations

morphology is the study of the forms of plants, animals, etc.

See: **shape, format, organic form, biomorphic, structure, composition, elements, configuration.**

Formalism

Pronounced: FORM-A-LIZM (*o as in port, a as in ago, izm as in prism*)

Origin

Form is from the Latin *formalis* meaning *having a set form or manner* and *ism* is from the Greek *ismos* meaning *act* or *the action of.*

Meaning

Formalism is the critical writing about a work of art, where the formal elements of the work (e.g. composition) are excessively considered, rather than the content of the work. It means also a strict keeping to prescribed forms and an emphasis on the conventional aspects of things and the prevailing system, rather than on innovative and off-beat ideas. Formalism in Art at the beginning of the 20th century (which lasted as **an attitude** for more than sixty years) refers to a concern shown by artists increasingly to reject illusion in favour of an accentuation on the art-object expressed through form, colour and scale. Cubism and geometric abstraction (emphasising basic line forms and flat colour planes) were part of Formalism.

Associations

See: **composition, elements, form, Classical, Impressionism, Neo-Impressionism, Cubism, geometric, Hard Edge Painting.**
See the work of Georges Seurat, Paul Cezanne, Henri Matisse, Pablo Picasso, Georges Braque, Piet Mondrian, Hans Hoffman, Jean Helion, Cesar Domela, Frank Stella, Kenneth Noland, David Smith.

Format

Pronounced: FOR-MAT (*o as in port, a as in cat*)

Origin

From the French *format* meaning *the form and size of something*, for example a book.

Meaning

Format refers to the size and general shape and composition of a work of art or design. For example, the appearance of a publication through its layout, typography, binding, size and shape makes up its format

Associations

See: **composition, configuration, form, layout, typography.**

Fresco

Pronounced: FRES-KO (*e as in let, o as in go*)

Origin

From the Italian word *fresco* meaning *fresh* or *cool*, because lime-proof pigments were painted on freshly-laid lime plaster in the making of murals.

Meaning

Frescos are wall paintings where water-soluble pigments are put on a ground consisting of fresh plaster, lime and sand. As the plaster dries, the pigments are bound. This is called *fresca buon* meaning *true fresco*. Another method, called *fresco secco*, meaning *dry fresco*, is when pigments are ground in glue or a polymer emulsion or cassein and then applied to a dry plaster wall which has been dampened with lime water. True Fresco was used in Italy from the 13th to 16th centuries.

Associations

See: **ground, pigments, mural.**
See: The Giotto's Scrogegni Chapel in Padua and the ceiling of the Sistine Chapel in the Vatican in Rome painted by Michelangelo; the frescos of Fra Angelico in

the Convent of San Marco and the reproductions of
Leonardo Da Vinci's *The Last Supper*, orginally in the
Convent at Milan.

Frieze

Pronounced: FREEZ (*ee as in see*)

Origin

From the Italian *fregio* meaning *a border* or *fringe
ornament.*

a frieze in geometric form

Meaning

Nowadays, a frieze usually means any painting or relief
sculpture which is used to decorate a wall in the form of
a long, horizontal band. It refers, too, to the space
between a picture rail on a wall and the ceiling of a room.

Frit

Pronounced: FRIT (*i as in bit*)

Origin

From the Italian *fritta* meaning *roasted.*

Meaning

A frit is a carefully-proportioned mixture of materials
(silica, flux, texturing and colouring ingredients) which are
fused in a high-temperature furnace to form a glass. This
glass mass is pulverised to a fine powder which is sold in
packages for glazing purposes. The frit is dispersed in
water and then the liquid is applied to potteryware.
During firing in a kiln, the solution melts to form a finish
of glaze on the ware. Fritting can prevent health problems
in a ceramics studio. Lead, for example, is very poisonous
as a glaze by itself but it loses its toxicity when fritted
with silica.

Associations

See: **glaze, feldspar, flux, glass, pottery, kiln.**

Frottage

Pronounced: FROT-IDGE (*o as in got, idge as in
bridge*)

Origin

From the French *frottage* meaning *rubbing.* It is said to
have originated when Max Ernst was in a tavern in
Brittany in 1925 and during a period of rain he passed
the time by admiring the grain in a scrubbed wood floor
of the tavern. He was inspired to take samples of the
wood grain by placing sheets of paper over the floor and
rubbing them with a soft pencil.

Meaning

Frottage is the technique of producing a visual representation of a texture by laying pieces of paper or canvas over an object (of wood, stone, fabric etc.) and then rubbing the paper or other material with a pencil, crayon, charcoal or paint. This technique was used by some painters, who called the technique **grattage** when using paint. The technique is often used to copy images from tombstones, brasses or bas-relief objects. The technique allows chance to become an important factor in the images an artist produces. Max Ernst used the technique of cutting up frottages and then arranging them in a collage, sometimes with added drawings. The term refers, too, to any reproduction of a texture, such as that produced by dabbing a water colour with a sponge.

Associations

See: **texture, Surrealism, relief.**
Frottage is also referred to as **rubbing**.
See *The Great Forest* and *Vox Angelica* by the German Surrealist painter Max Ernst (1891-1976).

A rubbing of a brass made in 1393 in Wanlip, Leicestershire, England of Sir Thomas Walsch

Funk Art

Pronounced: FUNK (*u as in bonus*)

Origin

The word *funk* originated in jazz in blues music where *funky* means a heavy , uncomplicated beat and a rich, sensual and emotional sound. Funk art originated in the 1960's in San Francisco. The first exhibition of Funk Art was at the University of California in 1967. Funk Art was also called *Sick Art* and *Grotesque Art*.

Meaning

Words associated with the Funk Art movement and which best describe its variety are: anti-intellectual, anti-formal, eccentric, vulgar, erotic, vicious, visceral, exhibitionist, bizarre, shoddy, macabre, aggressive, kitsch, and humorous. The style tended to borrow objects and ideas from whatever was available and popular at the time and all sorts of materials (plastic, fibreglass, vinyl polychromed metal, etc.) were used in the works created. Funk pottery is invariably satirical or joke pottery.

Associations

See **Dadaism** and the works of Jeremy Anderson, Susie Bitney, William Wiley , David Gilhooly, and Edward Keinholz.

Furniture

Pronounced: FUR-NI-CHA (*u as in burn, i as in ink, a as in ago*)

Origin

From the French word *fourniture* from *fournir* meaning *to equip* or *to supply*.

Meaning

In ceramics, furniture refers to pieces of refractory (resistant to heat) objects used to support potteryware while it is being fired in a kiln. In printing, it refers to the wood supports which surround a relief printing block or pieces of type to hold them in position to give a perfectly level surface on which paper may be laid for printing purposes.

Associations

See: **pottery, relief, kiln, bat, refractory, saggers.**

kiln furniture

stilt

thimble

Futurism

Pronounced: FUCHA-RISM (*u as in due, a as in ago, ism as in prism*)

Origin

Futurism was a movement from 1909 to 1915. The term was first used by Filippo Marinetti, an Italian poet and dramatist, in an article in *Le Figaro*, a Paris newspaper. The movement's artistic leader was Umberto Boccioni, who died in 1916.

Meaning

Futurism was a movement which started in Italy. It was a reaction against what some writers and artists considered the static art of the day, which they said did not represent the dynamic and energetic modern world. The movement hated history and aimed to destroy the *"cult of the past"*. It praised originality and scorned imitation and emphasised speed, power, energy, machines and technical development. It was indebted to the ideas and forms of Cubism. The movement flourished in Italy for ten years and then lost its significance following the outbreak of war in Europe in 1914.

Associations

See the works of: Giacoma Balla (1871-1958), Umberto Boccioni (1882-1916), Luigi Rossola (1885-1947), Gino Severini (1883-1966).

Gauge

Pronounced: GAJ (*a as in late*)

Origin

Probably from an Old French word *jange* which became *gauger* meaning *the action or result of measuring.*

The micrometer gauge (*micro* being a prefix meaning *one millionth of*) was invented by an Englishman, William Gascoyne, in 1640. This was improved in 1848 by a Frenchman, Jean-Laurent Palmer, who produced the first micrometer which could measure to 0.05 millimetre.

a gauge wheel

Meaning

The word gauge has a number of meanings. In woodwork, it is a tool used to measure or control the depth and angle of a hole drilled into wood. In metalwork, it is a term for the grading of sheetmetal less than 3.125 mm. thick. The higher the grade number, the thinner the metal. Gauge 18 is for metal 1.3 mm.; gauge 22 is 0.7 mm. metal. It is used also to measure the spaces between metal parts (*feeler gauges* and *sheet and wire gauges*), to determine the type of thread and the pitch of various screw threads (*screw pitch or thread pitch gauge*), to measure the angle for screws of cutting tools (*screw cutting gauge*), to measure radii (*radius gauge*) to measure the internal diameters of objects (*telesscopic bore gauge* or *small hole gauge*). A *snap gauge* is a gauge preset to measure correct sizes in production work.

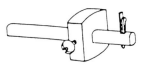

a marking gauge

In crochet, it refers to the number of horizontal stitches and the number of vertical stitches in a square inch of crochet. In stained glass work, it is the grading of wire or metal where the higher the gauge number the thinner the metal.

Associations

A **gauge wheel** is used for measuring the thickness of sheetmetal or the diameter of a wire. **Micrometers** are precision instruments which can measure directly to 0.01 mm. There are three kinds: **outside micrometers** to measure external dimensions, **inside micrometers**, which measure between internal surfaces and **depth micrometers**, which measure the depth of holes and grooves and the distances between the shoulders of objects.

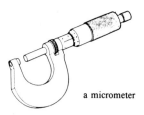

a micrometer

See: **stained glass.**

Genre

Pronounced: ZHON-RA (*the sound of zhon is close to that of John, zh as s in vision, o as in long, a as in ago*)

Origin
From the French word *genre* meaning *kind or variety, sort or style*. Genre painting began in the 16th century and became very popular in the 17th century, especially in Holland.

Meaning
Genre refers to a type of painting, such as portrait, landscape, seascape, still-life, abstract, etc.. Some paintings have mixed genres, such as history and portrait (e.g. the works of Reynolds or Turner) or abstract and history (e.g. Picasso's "*Guernica*"). It also refers to the subject matter in a painting which depicts everyday, unidealised life (including entertainment, recreation and business activities), especially that of a particular group of people, such as peasants. These genre paintings often aim to tell a story or make a moral point.

Associations
See: **portrait, landscape, still-life, Realism**.
See the painting called "*Supper*" by the Dutch painter Jan Steen (1625-1679), and "*A Woman Reading*" by the Dutch painter Jan Vermeer (1632-1675). See also the works of Dutch painters Pieter de Hooch (1629-1683), Nicolas Maes (1634-1693), and Jean Baptist Greuze (1725-1805), the Spanish painter Manuel Velazquez (1599-1660), the English painter William Hogarth (1697-1764) and the French painter Jean Baptiste Sinéon Chardin (1699-1779).

Geometric

Pronounced: JEE-O-MET-RIK (*ee as in see, o as in go, e as in let, i as in brick*)

Origin
From the word *geometry* meaning *the science of the size of things in space* (e.g. lines, surfaces and solids). It is from the Greek *geo* meaning *earth* and *metria* meaning *measurer*.

Meaning
Geometric means created by the precise mathematical laws of geometry. Usually geometric art uses simple shapes such as circles, rectangles and triangles, although more complex shapes are sometimes used. The use of geometric shapes forms an important part of non-representational art, especially Abstract Art.

Associations
See: **Abstract Art, Hard-Edge Painting, rectilinear, Concrete Art, Constructivism, Art Deco, Art Nouveau,**

a geometric design

shape, space, perspective, plane, projection, mechanical drawing, scale, drawing, symmetry.

See the works of: Frank Stella (U.S.A.1936), Victor Vasarely (Hungary 1908 -), Fritz Glarner (Switzerland 1899-1972), Richard Mortensen (Denmark 1910 -), Otto Freundlich (Germany 1878-1943), Piet Mondrian (Holland 1878-1944).

Gesso

Pronounced: JES-O (*e as in yes, o as in go*)

Origin

From the Latin *gypsum* meaning *chalk (calcium sulphate)*. It has been used in Europe since about the fifth century. In the past gesso was mixed with shredded cotton to form a thick paste which could be moulded into various shapes. Ornamental picture frames were often made from gesso. The purest form of gypsum is alabaster which comes from the Egyptian town of Alabastron.

Meaning

Originally gesso was made from chalk or gypsum mixed with gelatin or glue. It forms a brilliant white ground for **tempora** painting (and also **oil painting** if the surface is sized) on solid surfaces. It is sometimes called **plaster of paris**. It used to be too brittle for use on a canvas. Synthetic gesso is now produced which can be used on a canvas and other fabrics as well as on solid surfaces. The term gesso nowadays, however, refers to polymer primers and not to the true gesso.

Associations

See: **size, ground**.

making gesso

Gilding

Pronounced: GILD-ING (*i as in ink*)

Origin

From the Old English *gyldan* meaning *gold*. When gold was first used is not known for certain, but gold utensils found in Iraq show that things made with great craftsmanship were being made in gold more than 5000 years ago. The process of gilding has been used for thousands of years in China, Japan, Egyypt and Ancient Greece and Rome.

Meaning

Gilding is the technique of applying real gold in either very thin leaf or dust form to objects (e.g. to porcelain). Gold, unlike bronze or paint, does not lose its sheen, even when left outdoors and is subject to changing atmospheric variations. It can be bought in books consisting of gold leaves about nine inches square or in gold dust. Gold is the most malleable and ductile of all metals When it is beaten into thin sheets, it is called **foil** and in the very thinnest sheets it is called **leaf**. The leaf or foil is applied to objects using an adhesive called a **mordant**, which *bites* into the leaf to provide a surface which makes the gold adhere. Gold leaf is usually **tooled** to provide textual variations instead of the plain,flat texture of the gold leaf.

Associations

The term **gild**, or **gilt** as it is sometimes called, also refers to silver as in **silver-gilt**. **A gilder's tip** is a brush which when brushed through an artist's hair produces enough static electricity for delicate leaves of gold to be picked up by the artist to be placed carefully on an object which is being decorated. Gold is measured in **carats**, a carat being a twenty fourth part. Twenty four carat gold is pure gold; 18 carat is 18 parts gold and 6 parts of other metal. **Noble metals** refer to gold,silver and platinum, which do not change despite atmospheric changes.

Netherlandish, late 17th century,
Ceremonial Goblet
*Glass, 31.5 cms x 10.2 cms, Felton Bequest
1968, National Gallery of Victoria,
Australia.*

Glass

Pronounced: GLAS (*a as in craft*)

Origin

From the Old English *glaes*. The word appears in English writings in the ninth century. Glass production was practised in Egypt and countries of the Middle East as early as 3000 B.C.. Wealthy Romans during the time of the Ancient Roman empire had glass in the windows of their houses. Byzantine glass (called *smalti*) is considered the finest glass for making **mosaics**. The glass **blowpipe** was invented in Phoenecia (now Israel and Lebanon) in the first century B.C.. The Venetians were the first to produce almost colourless glass (called *cristallo* because it resembled rock crystal) in the 15th century.

Meaning

Glass is a unique material as it fits into neither solid nor liquid categories. The main ingredient of glass is **silica** in the form of limestone and soda ash, so glass is a mixture of sodium and calcium silicates. Note that the words silica, flint, and quartz are often used separately in different books but mean the same thing.
Glass is transparent or translucent and colourless. Liquid glass can be shaped by blowing, drawing, floating, casting, rolling, and binding (also called sagging or slumping). Silica melts at a temperature of 1700°c. but when combined with a **flux**, such as broken glass (called **cullet**), it will melt in a kiln at 650°c. A slow cooling, or

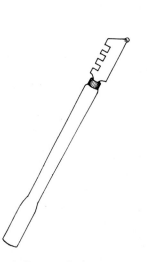

photograph by Jos Jensen

A glass cutter for plate glass

annealing process is necessary in the production of glass.
Glass is strong, hard and brittle when cold, is resistant to
attack from most chemicals (see: **hydrofluoric acid**), will
not burn nor leak, repels staining, is easy to clean, is a
good electrical insulator and can stand much compression
but not much tension. There are two main divisions of
glass, namely transparent glass and opalescent glass, both
of which can be coloured or streaky. Recently, fibre-glass
(or glass-fibre) has been woven into cloth and it is used
for making many products, including car and boat
bodywork. Fibre-glass was first used to reinforce some
contact-pressure resins in 1944. It is also used
substantially in sculpture.

In 1952, an Englishman, Alistair Pilkington invented the
float process of making flat, plate glass, which was
manufactured in 1959. By floating molten glass over a
surface of dead-flat molten tin, large plates of perfectly
flat glass can be produced.

Associations

See: **stained-glass, annealing, hydrofluoric acid, frit, firing,
flux**.

See the work of René Lalique (French 1860-1945), Emile
Gallé (French 1846-1904), Simon Gate (Swedish 1883-

1943), Henry Holiday (British 1839-1927), Louis Comfort Tiffany (American 1848-1933), Maurice Marinot (French 1882-1960), Keith Murray (New Zealand 1892-1981), and Tapio Wirkkala (Finland 1915 -).

Glaze

Pronounced: GLAZ (*a as in late*)

Origin

Glaze is a Middle English form of *glass*. In 1283, Lucca della Robbia invented tin-glazing of pottery. Dr. John Dwight was the first English potter to experiment on a systematic, scientific basis in the use of glazes. He produced the first salt-glazed stoneware in 1671.

Meaning

A ceramic glaze is a glass-hard (silica) coating which is fused onto potteryware which is leatherhard or has been **bisqued** fired. The glaze not only decorates the ware and gives it a smooth, brilliant surface but it also water-proofs it. Ware may be glazed by being dipped, brushed or sprayed with glaze or by having glaze solution poured over it. The main component of glaze is silica (in the form of silver sand, ground flint or quartz) but it also must have a **flux** (such as lead, soda, pottasium, borax or calcium), a colouring agent (a metallic oxide) and (unless a clear glaze is required) an opacifier which is a chemical (e.g. titanium alumina or zirconium) which makes a glaze opaque.Alumina also acts as a stiffener. The chemistry of glazes is complex, as is the chemical reaction between a glaze and a clay body at different temperatures in a kiln during firing.

Glaze also refers to the placing of layers of transparent film of paint onto the ground or colour masses of an oil painting in order to achieve a depth and brilliance of colour. Generally, a darker colour is placed over a lighter one. A glaze must be thoroughly dry before another layer of glaze is added. The famous Italian painter Titian (1485-1576) is said to have applied thirty or more layers of glaze to some of his paintings to get the richness of colour characteristic of his work. Both he and Rembrandt used much glaze in their paintings.

Associations

See: **ground, feldspar, firing, flux, frit, dipping, annealing, slip, engobe**.

A **frit** is a pre-packed mixture of materials which can be used as a glaze. Frits can be bought from a shop selling ceramic materials. **Sregazzi** (Italian for *rubbing*) is a technique in oil painting of applying a dark glaze on flesh colours and then rubbing the glaze with a fingertip to produce shadows on the flesh.

applying glaze

spraying

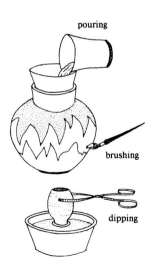

pouring

brushing

dipping

Glyptic

Pronounced: GLIP-TIK (*i's as in tin*)

Origin

From the Greek *gluptikos* meaning *carved*.

Meaning

Glyptic means related to carving (either **relief** or **intaglio**) on stone and usually on precious or semi-precious stones.

Associations

See: **sculpture, bust, form, relief, intaglio, manipulation**.

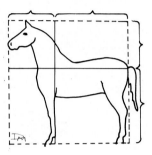

Golden Section

Pronounced: GOL-DAN (*o as in go, a as in ago*), SEK-SHUN (*e as in let, u as in bonus*)

Origin

The term *Golden Section* (also called *Golden Ratio, Golden Mean*, and *Golden Number*) was first used in the nineteenth century but the concept goes back to Ancient Greek times and was used by the famous Greek mathematician Euclid in about the year 300 B.C.. It was applied first to architecture in the first century B.C. by Vitruvius in his treatise "*De Architectura*".

Meaning

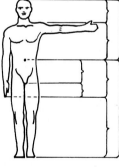

Golden section is the name given to a geometric proportion or ratio where a line is divided so that the smaller part is to the larger part as the larger part is to the whole. This works out at a ratio of about 5 to 8 (1: 1.618). It is expressed algebraically as a: b = b : (a+b). It has been used extensively in art, especially painting-for example, in the relationship of the area of space above the horizon line to the space below the line. It is said to express the secrets of **visual harmony** and is regularly found in nature, for example, the widths of curves upon a shell's spiral, the number of leaves on a plant's stem, the proportions of the human body, or the structure of a crystal.

Le Corbusier, a French designer and architect, devised what he called his **modulor** system of architectural proportion based on the Golden Section.

0.618   1.0

A   B   C

Golden section

Associations

See: **proportion, harmony, Classical**.

See the work of Piet Mondrian. The proportions of much of his Abstract Painting are based on the **golden mean**.

Gouache

Pronounced: GWASH (*a as in wash*)

Origin

Gouache is the French for *wash* or the Italian *guazzo* meaning originally *pool, puddle or water splashed about.*

Meaning

Gouache is an opaque water-colour paint made by colours ground in water and thickened (as a binder) with gum-arabic, honey or glycerine. When it is dry, the gouache produces a soft sheen. Pure water should be used when making gouache as hard water can spoil the effects of a painting. A layer of gouache prevents the whiteness of paper showing through. It is often used to highlight or to emphasise **local colour**. It is particularly useful in design in the presentation of **artwork** (called *mechanicals* in the U.S.A.) for reproductions.

Associations

See: **water colour, opacity, aquarelle**.

Other words used for gouache are **poster paint** and **body colour**. **Aquarelle** is transparent **water-colour**; gouache is opaque water-colour.

See: "*The Poetess*" by Joan Miro (1893), the water-colours of François Boucher (1703-1770) and the work of Paul Sandby (1725-1809).

Dante Gabriel Rossetti, Great Britain 1828 - 1882, *The Loving Cup* gouache on panel 52.6 x 35.9 cm *Art Gallery of South Australia, Adelaide, South Australia*

Gradation

Pronounced: GRA-DA-SHUN (*a's as in late, u as in bun*)

Origin

From the Latin *gradus* meaning *a step*. A grade is one "**step**" as you advance and one level of something (e.g. artistic ability, or tone in colour) on a total graded scale. The Latin *ation* means *forming* or *showing*, so gradation is *how grades are shown*.

Meaning

Gradation describes steps, stages or degrees of gradual, progressive change in an orderly fashion. Gradation in art and design can be shown by regular changes in colour, shape, size, space, direction, position, tone, texture, and gravity or a combination of some of these. Speed of change is decided by the number of steps (grades) in a gradation process. To **gradate** is to arrange things in gradation.

Associations

See: **half-tone, animation, sfumato, transfer type, chiaroscuro**.

artist's stump

stumping is when an artist uses a **stump**, which is a cylinder of tightly-rolled paper with a sharp point at the end, like a pencil. It is used to smooth over pastels, chalk or soft pencil to obtain gradations of tone and colour, almost with a **sfumato** effect.

Graffito

Pronounced: GRAF-EET-O (*a as in ant, ee as in see, o as in go*)

Origin

From the Italian for *a scratched drawing*. The technique was used extensively in Italy in the 16th century.

Meaning

Graffito (plural *graffiti* and also called **Sgraffito**) is a technique of scratching through superimposed layers of coloured plasters (or some other material) or through pastel, crayons or oil pastels to reveal different layers in a different colour and to produce a composition in this manner. It is similar to **scumbling** as a technique but a scratching implement is used instead of dry-brush work, as in scumbling. The technique is also used in ceramics, china, glass and enamel work. Nowadays, it means also writing or drawings painted, sprayed or penned on a building. Some **graffiti** of this kind are concise, witty, humorous or moving; others are childish, obscene and vulgar.

Associations

Famous graffiti are those on the walls at Pompei and in Aboriginal cave drawings.

The pointed tool used in (s)graffito work is called a **sgrafio**.

sgraffito work

Graphic Design

Pronounced: GRAF-IK (*a as in hat, i as in bit*) DI-ZIN (*1st i as in lift, 2nd i as in line*)

Origin

From the Greek *graphikos* meaning *drawing* or *writing*. The term came into the English language by way of the German *graphik*. In the past, graphic design has been referred to as **commercial art** and **advertising design**. Graphic design is now the accepted term.

Meaning

Graphic design is concerned with the communication of information and ideas by visual means. Nowadays, it encompasses posters, book illustrations, product packaging, fabric production, printmaking, advertisements, postage stamps, all kinds of signs (signage), film-making, cartoon animation, and television presentations. A graphic designer is able to conceptualise visually and then reveal the concept in a two-dimensional form, which frequently gives the illusion of a three-dimensional form. The designer must be able to manipulate effectively form, shape, colour, texture, scale, movement, images and symbols and be skilful in drawing, layout, lettering, typography, photography, diagram drawing and the technique of using film.

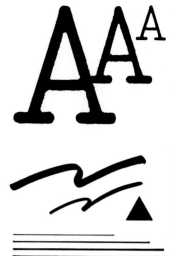

Associations

See: **Design, specification, print, register, rendering, stencil, template, transfer type, typography, calligraphy, copperplate, draft, folio, form, gradation, grid, half-tone, juxtaposition, line, literals, pattern, motif, logo, poster.**

Graphically means *vividly descriptive.*

See the works of: Milton Glazer (U.S.A.), Paul Rand (U.S.A.), and the graphic design-group practices of Michael Peters (U.K.), Fletcher, Forbes and Gill (U.K.) and Total Design (Holland).

Greenware

Pronounced: GREEN-WAR (*ee as in see, a as in fare*)

Origin

Green has many meanings, one of which for centuries has been *not thoroughly dried or seasoned.* It was used in ceramics in the early 19th century to mean *ware not fired.*

Meaning

Greenware is a ceramic object which has been shaped and finished and is in the process of drying by natural means before it is fired.

Associations

See: **clay, feldspar, bisque, ceramics, leatherhard, pinchpot, pottery, earthenware.**

Grid

Pronounced: GRID (*i as in bit*)

Origin

From *gridiron* or *griddle* which are early English words for a cooking utensil, consisting of inersecting metal bars with spaces between them. It was used for boiling or grilling food over an open fire.

Grids (as a network of vertical and horizontal lines) were used by Renaissance artists for scaling their sketches and cartoons which would be used in murals. Grids were also used extensively by early typographers in the 15th century to design letters and to layout printed pages.

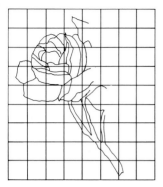

a grid

Meaning

A grid is a system of parallel lines which cross each other at even intervals to create equal rectangles or squares (as on graph paper). Often a grid is on transparent material so that an image under the grid can be seen. It can be used for arranging printed matter or images in a regular pattern, to check whether lines are parallel, to identify positions on a picture or photograph, to measure distances and to enlarge or reduce the size of a drawing. A grid with lines spaced 1.5 centimetres apart will increase the size of the original by a half. A five centimetre grid will double the size of the original drawing. In graphic design, columns of type, captions, headings, illustrations and photographs can be aligned accurately using a grid.

Associations

The term **graticule** is an alternative word for grid.

See: **squaring, Graphic Design, pointing**.

Grisaille

Pronounced: GRIZ-AL (*i as in ink, a as in late, l is only slightly pronounced*)

Origin

From the French *gris* meaning *grey* and *grisailler* meaning *to paint something gray* or *to go gray*. The Ancient Greeks did not use the technique of **chiaroscuro** and used shades of gray to obtain shading effects.

Meaning

Grisaille is a technique in **monochrome** painting in which only neutral grays are used. It may be used for a finished painting or as an underpainting. It applies also to paintings in black and white which are finished by the application of transparent glazes, or to pencil sketches on grey-tinted paper. It means, also, a pigment used in stained-glass work, which consists of burnt umber, red lead and quartz. It refers, too, to a style in enamelling where no coloured enamels are used but where an opaque or semi-opaque layer of white or gray is applied over a dark ground and then the top layer is engraved to reveal the darker layer to create a composition.

Associations

See: **chiaroscuro, monochrome (see** *glass***), opacity, stained glass**.

Grisaille is the French word for glass used in stained-glass work where crushed glass is added to pigments and resin. Compositions are created from this material.

See the work of Jean-Auguste Dominique Ingres (1780-1867).

grisaille glass in Salisbury Cathedral, England

Grog

Pronounced: GROG (*o as in log*)

Origin

Probably from the French *gros grain* meaning *coarse grain*. Probably the word was applied to ceramics as the *grog* comprised pieces of coarse, rough **bisque** clay which was then ground.

Meaning

Grog is **bisque** clay (i.e. clay already fired) which is finely ground. Adding bisque to ordinary clay gives the mixture increased **plasticity** and decreases the shrinking and warping of the clay. It is more **refractory** than the clay to which it is added. Grog can be purchased in different mesh sizes (i.e. the size of a hole in a sieve). It is used for large sculptures, tiles and **raku**.

Associations

See: **bisque, plasticity, raku, refractory**.

Ground

Pronounced: GROWND (*ow as in cow*)

Origin

From the Old English *grund* meaning *foundation* or *groundwall* or *earth*.

Meaning

A ground is a smooth, even (usually white) surface on a canvas which is specially prepared as the base for a painting. The ground can be oil paint, gesso, emulsion or acrylic. The ground heightens colours put on it, prevents a chemical reaction between the paint and the canvas and stops absorption of paint into the canvas. More generally, the ground can be a foundation material on which a painting or drawing is made, e.g. canvas, paper, or plaster. It refers also to the background to a painting (that is the area behind any figures) where the main features of the composition are in the foreground. In etching, it refers to an acid-resistant, waxy layer (usually consisting of beeswax, bitumen and rosin) on the metal plate on which a drawing is made with a sharp instrument. This substance, which can be bought in the form of dark brown cakes or balls, is often referred to as **hard ground**. In ceramics, it is the condition of the surface of potteryware when it is ready to accept decorative glaze.

Associations

See: **gesso, size, primer, etch, oil paint, composition**.

Half Tones

Pronounced: HAF-TON (*a as in far, o as in bone*)

Origin

The first photographs were made by a Frenchman, J.N.Niepce, in 1822 and his invention was developed by an Englishman William Henry Fox Talbot, who published the first illustrated book with photographs, called *The Pencil of Nature* in 1844. Talbot discovered the principle of half-tones. The first person to reproduce photographs in printers ink was a Swedish engraver Carl Gustaf Wilhelm Carleman in 1871, who used line half-tones (rather than dot half-tones which came later). The photo-mechanical process was invented by Frederick E. Ives of the U.S.A. in 1880. The first half-tone photograph in a newspaper appeared in the *Daily Graphic* in New York. The process allowed photographs to be reprinted at the same time as text, instead of as a separate operation, which meant that photographs could be used extensively in all printing operations, especially in newspapers.

50% square dot screen

50% elliptical dot screen

Meaning

A printing press (e.g. letterpress or litho-press) can lay down ink on paper only of one density. It cannot make the ink in one area of a page darker than another area. Therefore, in order to produce the range of tones present in a photograph for a printing process, a new technique had to be devised. As the new process did not produce continuous tones (i.e. the gradual merging from black to white) but had areas of tone and areas without tone, it was called **half-tone**. In half-tones, an image on a photograph is broken down into lines of separate dots, or elliptical dots, where the larger the dots the darker is the image. The areas of least density are the **highlights**; those with the greatest density produce shadows. To produce the dots on a photograph, a half-tone screen is used, which consisted in the past (and to some extent today) of a sheet of glass onto which fine, intersecting lines are etched, but which nowadays is more often a contact screen made on a film base. The screens vary in the number of lines they have on them, ranging usually from 20 to 80 lines to the *centimetre* (but they can exceed this). The greater the number of lines, the finer is the screening. Under normal viewing conditions the eye is not able to see the dots which make up the images which vary from light grey to almost black. Very fine screens (in excess of 150 lines) can be used only when top-quality art paper is being used for reproductions. The half-tone screen is placed behind the lens of a copy camera which makes negatives for printing plates. In engraving, half-tone effects can be produced by fine cross-hatching or by the use of dots as in photography.

Associations
See: **negative, gradation, tone (see colour), engraving, lithography, highlight.**

Hard-Edge Painting

Pronounced: HARD (*a as in card*), EDJ (*e as in net*)

Origin

Hard Edge Painting is a a term first used in 1959 by Jules Langsner, an American art critic, to describe the work of some painters who reacted against some of the Abstract Expressionist painters who had blurred, *brushy* edges to their forms.

Meaning

Hard Edge Painting is a technique in painting whereby the composition is given forms which are precisely defined and where straight lines usually separate areas of the composition. Usually flat colours of two or three hues are used which stretch from one edge of the canvas to the other. There is no perspective and foreground and background are not distinct. It is closely associated with **Post Painterly Abstraction** and **Minimal Art.**

Associations

See: **Abstract Art, Minimal Art and Concrete Art.**

See the works of the American artists - Frank Stella (1936 -), Al Held (1928 -), Ad Reinhardt (1913-1967), Ellsworth Kelly (1923 -), Alexander Liberman (1912 -), Kenneth Noland (1924 -) and Barnett Newman (1905-1970).

Highlight

Petrus Van Schendel, 1806-1870, Holland **The Poultry Vendor**
Oil on panel, 36.3 cms x 35.3 cms, National Gallery of Victoria, Australia.

Pronounced: HI-LIT (*i's as in bite*)

Origin

Highlight is a word which was introduced into the language this century. The word *high* is used in the sense of *full and intense*, as it was used with one of its meanings in the 18th century.

Meaning

A highlight is the clearest, brightest part of a picture, print or half-tone, because it receives the most direct light. Often it is a dot or a small area of white to represent the point of the highest reflection of light. **To highlight** something is to illuminate it or to give it prominence or dominance.

Associations

See: **accent, dominance, half-tone, facet**.

Holography

Pronounced: HOLA-GRAFY (*o as in pot, 1st a as in ago, 2nd a as in raft, y as in duty*)

Origin

Holography is from the Greek *holographos* which comes from *holos* meaning *whole* and *graphein* meaning *written*. Originally, it meant any document written wholly by an author and in his or her own hand. The technique used today was invented by Professor Dennis Gabor of London University in 1947 and developed by two scientists from Michigan University, Emmett Leith and Juris Upatnieks in 1963.

Meaning

Holography is a technique for producing what appears to be three-dimensional images on photo-sensitive material without the use of a camera lens, by using lasers and mirrors. An image produced is called a **hologram** (from the Greek *holos*, and *gramme* meaning *a letter in the alphabet or something drawn*). The holographic technique for producing holograms is as follows:

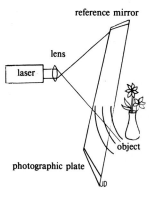

reference mirror

lens

laser

object

photographic plate

● In a vibration-free, totally dark environment (These conditions are essential.), a laser beam is sent through a beam-splitter, which divides the original beam into at least two beams. One beam is called the *object beam* and the other the *reference beam*.

● The object beam is passed through mirrors which diffuse it.

● The reference beam is reflected off mirrors and then passed across the object beams, so that two types of beams intermingle. This is called an **interference pattern**. The effect is rather like the overlapping of circles on the surface of water when two pebbles are dropped near to each other in a lake.

- The intermingled beams of light pass over and around the object being produced and then strike a plate or reflective surface covered with light-sensitive material, which is close to the object. A three-dimensional image **(the holograph)** is produced on the plate.

- The plate can be developed in the same manner as in the photographic process.

The hologram has a three-dimensional image which when viewed from different angles appears as it would appear from that angle in reality. It is possible to look around an object and see what is behind it. As a hologram has the ability to store several images rather that just one, it will be used in the future as an important storage system of data.

Associations

See the work of the American artists Robert Indiana, George Otman, Bruce Nauman.
See: **laser, illusion**.

Hydrofluoric Acid

Pronounced: HI-DRO-FLU-O-RIK (*i as in bite, 1st o as in go, u as in due, 2nd o as in pot, i as in ink*)

Origin

From the Greek *hydro* meaning *water* and *fluorine* a pale, yellow, highly reactive gas. Hydrofluoric acid means fluoric acid disperesd in water. In 1771, a German, Carl Wilhelm Scheele, was able to obtain free hydrofluoric acid gas. Attempts were made to produce free fluorine (e.g. by Sir Humphrey Davis, in 1818) but all were unsuccessful. It was achieved by Henri Moissan of France in 1886.

Meaning

Hydrofluoric acid is a very strong, colourless, fuming, corrosive liquid. It is the only acid which will attack silica and silica products, consequently when it is purchased it is supplied in non-vitreous containers. It is used for etching glass and sometimes for removing unwanted marks on glazed materials. When used pure it eats away glass and leaves it clear. To get an etched effect on the glass, it is mixed with an alkali, such as sodium or ammonia. A useful resist material to use with the acid is a self-adhesive vinyl, such as Fablon. Hydrofluoric acid is very dangerous and should be handled with great care.

Associations

See: **glass, vitreous, etch, glaze**.

Icon

Pronounced: I-KON (*i as in bite, o as in got*)

Origin

From the Greek *eikon* meaning *an image* or *portrait*. Icons date from the sixth century within the Greek Orthodox Church and changed very little up to the seventeenth century.

Meaning

An icon is a painting or carving of Christ or of angels or saints. Some are in the form of **mosaics** and many are painted on panels. They can be single or can be hung in groups. An icon in **computer graphics** is a symbol used to represent visually a choice of commands available to a user of the computer.

Associations

Iconology is the study of images. **Effigation** is the representation or presentation of a likeness.

See: **iconography, mosaic, Baroque, computer graphics.**

an icon of *Saint Basil Vasilios,* kind permission of the Greek Orthodox Archdiocese of Australia

Iconography

Pronounced: I-KON-O-GRAF-Y (*i as in find, 1st o as on gone, 2nd o as in go, a as in bat, y as in duty*)

Origin

From the Greek *eikon* meaning *an image* and *graphos* meaning *writing or drawing.*

Meaning

Iconography refers to the systematic study of the content of paintings rather than of their forms or styles. It means also a number of images or symbols (such as the images used in works of art which deal with western religions) and the meanings given to the images. For example, a dove often represents the Holy Spirit and lilies are symbolic of purity. Iconography refers, too, to a collection of pictures giving a total visual record of a subject-for example, a collection of portraits, or scenes from a particular locality. An example is Anthony Van Dyck's (1599-1641) series of portraits entitled "*Iconography*".

Associations

See: **icon, symbol, portrait.**

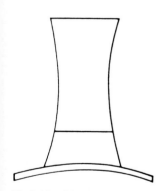

The height of the top of the hat and the brim are equal. The hat gives the illusion of being taller than it is wide.

Illusion

Pronounced: IL-U-ZHON (*i as in fill, u as in due, zh as s in vision, o as in flagon*)

Origin

From the Latin *ludere* meaning *to play* and *to attribute reality to what is unreal*, and then *illusio* meaning *deceit, mockery, deceiving the eye by false or unreal appearances.*

Meaning
Everything seen by the human eye has the potential for ambiguity (That is uncertainty, doubt, and more than one interpretation.). When visual ambiguity occurs, illusion can follow. Illusion in art and design is a technique where visual devices (e.g. perspective, foreshortening, light and dark shading, shape contrasts, figure and direction distortion) are used to suggest to a viewer that what she or he sees on a flat surface is three-dimensional and real The illusions of space and depth are created. By using such techniques as figure repetition, multiple images, fuzzy outlines, zig-zag lines, changes of curviture, the illusion of **movement** can be created.

Associations
See: **foreshortening, perspective, trompe l'oeil, chiaroscuro, Op Art, plasticity, perception, movement**.

The *Camera Degli Sposi* at Mantua in Italy, by Andrea Mantega (1431-1506) is one of the first works of **illusionism**.

The white sides can appear to be at either the top or the bottom

Impasto

Pronounced: IM-PAS-TO (*i as in bit, a as in fat, o as in go*)

Origin
From the Italian *impastore* meaning *to knead, make into paste* or *stick with paste.*

Meaning
Impasto is a technique in painting where paint (usually oil paint) is applied thickly, often with a palette knife, on a canvas. The rough texture produced, often with brush and palette knife marks showing, stands out in relief. It refers also to a technique in ceramics where pigment is applied to potteryware in such a way that it stands out in slight relief from the glazed surface of the ware. An example is the use of brilliant red (e.g. Armenian red) in the decoration of **Isnik** pottery.

Associations
Dry brush painting is a technique of applying thick oil paint to a canvas with very little paint on the brush, so that the pigment sticks to the canvas in clumps and streaks.

See: **relief, fat, malerisch, painterly, texture**.

See the works of Van Gogh, Cezanne, Rembrandt, Soutine, de Stael, and modern painters, such as Jackson Pollock.

Arthur Boyd, Australia born 1920, *Nebuchadnezzar caught in a forest* (detail), *Art Gallery of South Australia, Adelaide, South Australia*

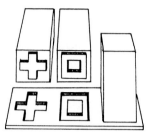

Impression

Pronounced: IM-PRESH-AN (*i as in dim, esh as in fresh, a as in ago*)

Origin
From the Latin *imprimere* meaning *to press upon, or force upon,* and later *impressio* meaning *emphasis* and *the act of stamping something.*

Meaning
An impression is the contact of paper with a printing surface or the print obtained from any relief printing process. It means also the number of copies printed at one printing operation. It refers, too, to the result of pressing a mark or symbol or design into soft material, such as wax or clay.

Associations
See: **chased, repoussé, symbol, print, die, edition, emboss.**

Impressionism

Pronounced: IM-PRESH-AN-ISM (*i as in dim, e as in fresh, a as in ago, ism as in prism*)

Origin
When the French painter Claude Monet (1840-1926) exhibited a little painting entitled *"Impression: Sunrise"* at an exhibition in Paris in 1874, he did not expect that the the word *impression* in the title would describe a new movement in painting. But it did, as the word *impression* attracted attention, was used by an art critic writing about the exhibition and gained such popularity that the term *Impressionism* was used extensively and has been used since.

Meaning
Impressionism refers to the work of group of French painters (the **Impressionists**) in the 19th century whose work was basically a reaction against **Romanticism**. Their work also owes much to **Realism** and the unidealised slice of "reality" that is found in many photographic images. The major emphasis in their work was the effects of light on objects. Claude Monet, one of the leaders of the movement, said, *"Light is the principal person in a picture"*. Form and content were not considered nearly as important as technique, which stressed nature's luminous qualities. To get the effects of natural light, the artists often painted in the open air (see **plein air**). In their paintings, shadows appear as colours rather than the conventional black and greys. The artists discovered that if they applied pure colours in separate brush strokes, side by side (called *broken colours*), spectators, if standing some distance from a canvas, would blend the colours

themselves and the resultant colours would be more brilliant than usual. For example, to obtain brown, they sometimes placed strokes of green, red and yellow side by side and obtained a brilliant, lumimous brown.

Associations

Luminosity is the effects of light on a painting.

See: **plein air**.

See the works of: Claude Monet (1840-1926), Camille Pissarro (1830-1903), Edouard Manet (1832-1883), Edgar Degas (1834-1917), Pierre Auguste Renoir (1841-1919) and Alfred Sisley (1839-1899).

Imprimatura

Pronounced: IM-PRIM-A-TURA (*i's as in dim, a's as in ago, u as in pure*)

Origin

From the Italian word *imprimatura* meaning *the primary coat of a painting*.

Meaning

Imprimatura is the application of a **wash** or **glaze** of thin colour to a canvas to act as a coloured ground before the composition of a painting is started. The imprimatura affects the colours which are superimposed.

Associations

Note that **imprimatur** (without a final a, as in *imprimatura*) is Latin for *let it be printed*, and it was originally a licence for a book to be printed. It now means that some action has the appproval of a group that has the authority to make a decision. **Imprimatura** is sometimes called **coloured ground**.

See: **wash, glaze, ground, priming**.

Industrial Design

Pronounced: IN-DUST-RI-AL (*i's as in pin, u as in dust, a as in cat*), DE-ZIN (*e as in delay, i as in sign*

Origin

Industrial designers have been employed in industry and commerce since the middle of the 19th century when the significance of producing machine-made articles which are both pleasing to look at and practical, efficient and effective was recognised. Schools of Design were founded in England in 1836. The development of the profession of Industrial Design is linked closely with the history of Industrialism. The term *Industrial Design* was first used by the Americans Raymond Loewy and Henry Dreyfuss in the early 1900's to describe their professional activities

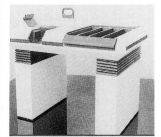

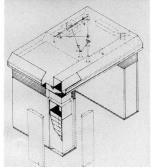

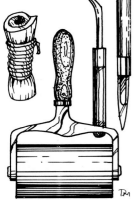

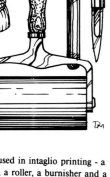

Tools used in intaglio printing - a dabber, a roller, a burnisher and a scraper

in consultancies which provided services to American manufacturers.

Meaning

An Industrial Designer is a member of a product development team which is professionally responsible for enhancing the daily lives of people by designing products and environments which meet human needs in functional and aesthetic ways.

Associations

See: **design, aesthetics, ergonomics, Bauhaus.**

See the works of: Peter Behrens (Germany 1868-1940), Walter Teague (American 1883-1960), Wilhelm Wagenfeld (German 1900 -), Norman Bel Geddes (American 1893-1958), Henry Dreyfuss (American 1904-1972), Charles Eames (U.S.A. 1907-1978), Marcello Nizzoli (Italy 1887-1969), Walter Gropius (Germany 1883-1969).

Intaglio

Pronounced: IN-TAL-YO (*i as in tin, a as in tar, yo as in yodel*)

Origin

From the Italian *intagliare* meaning *to engrave, etch* or *cut out*. In Italy an engraver is an *intagliatore*.

Meaning

Intaglio is the technique whereby a composition is hollowed out or scratched out from the material worked on. In **relief** work, the image required is above the material worked on; in intaglio work, the image is below the surface of the object. Intaglio includes the techniques of **etching, mezzotint, aquatint and drypoint.** An intaglio is also an incised carving in a gem. It is the opposite of a **cameo.** Probably the commonest example of intaglio work is in a ring which is used as a seal.

Associations

Another term for intaglio is **diaglyph** and its opposite, the relief form, is called an **anaglyph.**

See: **relief, etching, mezzotint, aquatint, cameo, drypoint.**

Italics

Pronounced: I-TAL-IKS (*i's as in pin, a as in cat*)

Origin

From the Greek *italikos* meaning *Italy.* The word refers to the handwriting of the people in Ancient Italy. The first version of italics as a writing style was introduced by Aldus Manutius of Venice in 1500.

Meaning

Italics is a type face which is sloped or slanted to the right. It is now used for titles of books, names of books or journals, for foreign words or to emphasise a word in a text and make it *stand out* (as here) and to draw special attention to its importance.

Associations

The verb used is **italicize** or **italicise**.

See: **accent, highlight, dominance**.

Jigger

Pronounced: JIGA (*i as in pin, g as in good, a as in ago*)

Origin

The word *jig* probably comes from the Old Norse word *giga* meaning a *fiddle* or the Old French *giguer* meaning *to hop or dance*. Both words imply moving in a lively but ordered manner. Before the 1st century Romans used jiggers to make multiple clay objects, as did the Chinese. It was then applied to a horizontal lathe used to make flat ware, such as plates and dishes.

a jigger

Meaning

In ceramics, a jigger is a machine for making flat ware on a large, commercial scale. It consists of a convex mould on which clay is placed. The mould revolves and a **profile (or die)** is lowered by means of a pivoted arm onto the clay, which is squeezed between the mould and the profile. The mould shapes the inside of the plate and the profile forms the outside and the footring. In fabric dyeing, a **jig** is a machine in which a fabric is transferred from one roller to another, having passed through a bath of dye.

Associations

See: **dye, die, fabric, profile, jolley, porcelain**.

Jolley

a jolley

Pronounced: JOLY (*o as in got, y as in duty*)

Origin

See *jigger*. The origin of jolley is not known but as with jigger it probably came from an English dialect.

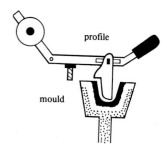

Meaning

A jolley is a machine which is used for forming hollow ware (e.g. cups and bowls) on a fairly large scale. It consists of a revolving concave mould into which clay is injected. As the mould revolves, an adjustable arm (a **profile**) shapes the interior of the ware. The mould forms the outside of the ware and the profile the inside. The process of the operation is the obverse of that for **jigging**.

Associations

See: **jigger, ceramics, profile, potteryware.**

Justification

Pronounced: JUST-I-FI-KA-SHUN (*u as in rust, i's as in pin, a as in late, u as in fun*)

Origin

From the Latin *justus* meaning *just and right* and *facere* meaning *to make.* That is to prove or show something to be just and right and worthy of being defended.

Meaning

Justification is a term used in printing which refers to the spacing of letters and words so that they are proportionally equal, and so that each line of words in a text is exactly the same length as all other lines. There is vertical alignment on the left and right hand sides of the text. Each line is adjusted equally, so each line has, as it were, been treated **justly**.

Associations

See: **alignment, proportion, typography.**

Juxtaposition

Pronounced: JUXT-A-PA-ZISHUN (*1st u as in run, 1st a as in apple, 2nd a as in ago, i as in pin, final u as in fun*)

Origin

From the Latin *juxta* meaning *near* and *positum* meaning *placed.* That is something placed near or next to another thing.

Meaning

Juxtaposition means the placing of objects (or mediums) together, side by side. In art, it usually refers to the placing together of objects which are not usually associated or placed near each other. Dadaism and Surrealism used juxtaposition, for example, to produce shock, surprise or the dominance of particular objects or qualities. Pointillism juxtaposes certain colours to gain special optical effects.

Associations

See: **Dadaism, Surrealism, fantasy, objet trouvé, contrast, dominance, pointillism.**

Kaleidoscope

Pronounced: KAL-I-DA-SKOP (*a's as in ago, i as in bite, o as in rope*)

Origin

From the Greek *kolos* meaning *beautiful* and *eidos* meaning *form* or *shape* and *skopo* meaning *to look at*. That is, literally, *looking at beautiful things*. The kaleidoscope was invented by an Englishman, Sir David Brewster, in 1817.

Meaning

A kaleidoscope is an optical instrument or toy consisting of a cylindrical tube which can rotate, with two mirrors set lengthwise inside and with fragments of loose, coloured glass between them. At one end of the cylinder is an eye-hole. When the cylinder is rotated, the moving coloured glass is reflected in the mirrors and constantly-changing, coloured, symmetrical patterns are produced. **Kaleidoscopic** now means a constantly-changing arrangement of bright and coloured lights. The term also refers to an all-over pieced quilt made up of Maltese cross blocks. When the blocks are sewn together there is an illusion of a Maltese cross.

Associations

See: **symmetry, cross, illusion, Op Art, facet, highlight.**

a kaleidoscope

Kaolin

Pronounced: KA-O-LIN (*a as in late, o as in flagon, i as in bit*)

Origin

From the Chinese *gaoling* meaning *high hill or high ridge* which describes the area in Ching-te-Chen in China where the white china clay was first found. It is found also in England, France and the United States.

Meaning

Kaolin is the purest clay, containing very little iron impurity. It is almost pure aluminium silicate. It is white and remains white after being fired. It has little plasticity, and kaolin with the most plasticity is from China. It is refractory and melts at over 1770°c. It is used in glazes and to provide bulk to other clays and is an essential ingredient for all types of porcelain.

Associations

Kaolin is referred to also as **china clay**, especially in the United Kingdom.

See: **clay, porcelain, plasticity, refractory, glaze.**

Key

Pronounced: KEE (*ee as in see*)

Origin

From the Old English *caeg* meaning *an iron instrument for moving bolts of a lock forward or backward to fasten or unfasten*. Key came to mean what opens up anything to reveal its importance. Key as a term in art was first used in the mid 19th century.

Meaning

Key refers to the average of the tonal values in a painting. A **high-key** painting has hues closer to black than white; a **low-key** painting has the opposite. It is also another term for a wedge which is placed at each corner of a stretcher to expand the corners and make the canvas taut. Also, it is an insert in the seam of a mould which is made in two or more pieces, which when removed enables the mould to be taken to pieces without damage. In metal work, it refers to a small, removeable, rectangular piece of metal which fits into slots in both a shaft and a hub to lock a gear or a pulley on a shaft.

Associations

See: **colour (values), wedge, stretcher, accent, dominance.**

Kiln

Pronounced: KILN (*i as in pin*)

Origin

From the Latin *Culina* meaning *where the baking takes place*. The word *culinary* means *related to cookery*. The word kiln came to mean the container in which clayware is baked or *cooked*. Kiln sites have been found during excavations in China which date back to 6000 years ago. High-temperature kilns to produce proto-porcelain existed in the Shang Dynasty in China from the 16th to 11th century B.C..

a gas kiln
by kind permission of Shimpo Industrial Co., Kyoto, Japan

Meaning

A kiln is a high-temperature oven or furnace heated by electricity, gas, oil or combustible material such as wood. It is used to fire ("*bake*") pottery, to fuse enamel objects and for glass staining. It must be heavily insulated and various methods are used, including double refractory walls, and refractory foam and filament fibres. There are many kinds of kilns, which are sometimes described by their shapes, e.g. beehive kiln, tunnel kiln, hovel kiln (like a bottle). A small studio kiln is usually fired by electricity or gas. It is often a simple box construction weighing, depending upon the materials used, about 50kg. (opening at the top or in front), which has inside a length of resistance wire and refractory brickwork for insulation. It is easy to operate as the normal fuel supply (electric power) is easy to control and there are no waste disposal problems. It is readily installed and, if fitted with silicon carbide elements, will stand the strain of reduction.

Associations

A **muffle** is an internal chamber in a small kiln, made from heat-proof (refractory) material, which protects ware from direct contact with flames and gases in the kiln.

See: **reduction, oxidation, refractory, firing, frit, pyrometry, furniture.**

Kinetic

Pronounced: KIN-E-TIK (*i's as in pin, e as in let*)

Origin

From the Greek *kinetikos* meaning *movement*. The word first entered the vocabulary of scientists in the mid 19th century. The first moving sculpture called "*Kinetic Sculpture: Standing Ware*" was created by the Russian sculptor Naum Gabo in 1920. Kinetic Art flourished in the 1950's.

Meaning

The word *kinetic* means *depending on movement* and Kinetic Art covers both real movement and the illusion of movement. The terms describes:

• The construction of objects which gain their effect by movement, often by having mechanically-controlled moving parts.

• Paintings which create optical illusions and visual uncertainty in order to produce in a viewer a sensation of movement. Such paintings are often referred to as **Op Art.**

• Paintings whose appearances change dramatically as a spectator changes his or her viewpoint of them.

Associations

See: **movement, mobiles, Op Art, laser, Cybernetic Art, Constructivsm.**

See the works of: Naum Gabo (Russian 1890-1977), Alexander Calder (American 1898-1976), Victor Vasarely (French 1908 -), El Lissitzky (Russian 1890-1941), Yaacov Agam (Israeli 1928 -), Jesus Raphael Soto (Venezuelan 1923 -),and Jean Tinguely (Swiss 1925 -), whose sculptures are often moved by motors or electric magnets and which occasionally self-destruct.

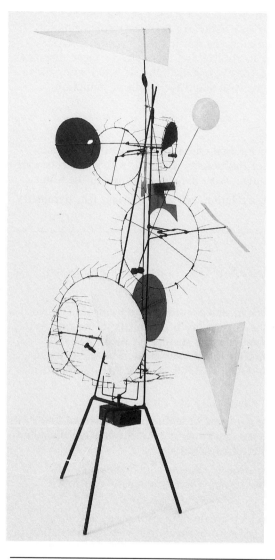

Jean Tinguely, Switzerland, France, United States, born 1925, **Meta Mechanique (Meta-Herbin)** 1954-55 *painted steel, electric motor 174.0 x 108.7 x 81.7 cm, collection: Australian National Gallery, Canberra. Reproduced by permission of the Australian National Gallery, Canberra.*

Kitsch

Pronounced: KITCH (*i as in bit, ch as in church*)

Origin

From the German *verkitchen* meaning *to make cheap, and to cheapen*. Originally, it was used in South Germany to refer to art which was false or unauthentic. That is it pretends to be art but it is not.

Meaning

Kitsch refers to poor quality artefacts or paintings, usually mass-produced, which are showy, inartistic or excessively sentimental. Most very cheap souvenirs bought in shops catering exclusively for tourists tend to be kitsch.

Associations

The French word **toc** is similar in meaning to **kitsch**.

See: **Dadaism**.

Kneading

Pronounced: NEED-ING (*ee as in see*)

Origin

From the Old English *cnedan* meaning originally *to tread* or *press* and then *to press into a mass with one's hands*.

Meaning

To knead clay is to roll, stretch, fold, squeeze and mix it with one's fingers and palms until all the air bubbles in it have been expelled and it has the consistency of dough or firm paste. There are different techniques of kneading. In Europe, the *ram's head* or *bull's head* technique is used; in the Orient the *spiral* or *shell* technique is more common. These words to describe the technique indicate the shape the clay takes while kneading. Once kneaded, the clay is ready for shaping. If insufficient kneading takes place, there may be **blowing** during firing.

Associations

See: **wedge, pugging, technique, dunt, thermal shock.**

kneading

Lacquer

Pronounced: LAK-A (*1st a as in cat, 2nd a as in ago*)

Origin

Lacquer has two different meanings and two origins. One is from the Hindustani word *lakh* meaning a resinous substance produced by the females of many species of insects, especially the *coccus lacca*. The insects feed on the sap of the Sumae tree in Siam and India. The resin hardens around them and their young. It protects them from predatory birds and other insects. This secretion forms into flakes and is collected at night. The word changed from the Portugese *lac* (from the name of the insect) to the French *lacre* (meaning *sealing wax*) and then to *lacquer*. The second meaning and origin is from the sap of the lac or lacquer tree which has grown in Eastern Asian countries for thousands of years and is a native of China. Lacquer ware was used in China in the 7th century B.C.. It was introduced into Japan in the 8th cenury and developed into one of the outstanding art forms in Japan in the 17th century. Lacquer work became very popular in Europe in the 18th century.

Japan, Edo period 1614 - 1867, *Tray* negro lacquer on wood, *Art Gallery of South Australia, Adelaide, South Australia*

Meaning

Lacquer is a very hard, durable, heat-resistant, coloured varnish. When built up in layers, it is hard enough to be carved. There are natural lacquers (gum-lacs) made from the secretion of a Sumae tree and from the Lac tree, and man-made lacquers produced from plastic resins and acrylics. Natural lacquers tend to turn yellow and become brittle after long exposure to sunlight. Synthetic lacquers (made up of cellulose and a solvent) are easy to apply in sprays, weather well, dry quickly and produce good glossy finishes. They are used extensively for automobiles and to prevent tarnishing and oxidation of polished metal surfaces.

Lacquer is also used on a large scale in ceramic decoration, as, unlike enamel, it does not require firing but still achieves great hardness.

Associations

Japanning refers to an 18th century word which describes artefacts of tin, wood or paper, which were painted black and then covered with lacquer to produce a high gloss sheen. The artefacts were relatively inexpensive imitations of expensive Japanese lacquer ware. **Shellac** refers to *lac* from a Sumae tree which is melted and formed into thin plates or shells (*shell-lac*). It is now a type of varnish.

See: **acrylic, ceramics, varnish**.

Laminate

Pronounced: LAM-IN-AT (*1st a as in lamb, i as in pin, 2nd a as in late*)

Origin

From the Latin *lamina* meaning *a thin scale, layer, sheet or flake* of metal, bone, rock, vegetable tissue etc. and from *ate* a suffix forming a verb. That is *to layer*.

Meaning

A laminate is the sandwiching of two or more layers of paper, cardboard, plastic, wood, plywood, foil, glass-fibre, etc. by means of an adhesive or thermosetting resin. The layering of materials increases not only the thickness but also the strength of the laminate. Materials which are laminated are usually stronger than solid materials of the same weight and dimensions (e.g. layers of glass and fibre-glass for security windows). A laminating machine is usually used for the process. Laminating is also used in book binding where a layer of plastic is placed on the the front and back of a book cover in order to protect it and to give it a glossy effect.

Associations

A **thermo-setting** process is where materials are subjected to heat and pressure.

Landscape

Pronounced: LAND-SKAP (*1st a as in hand, 2nd a as in late*)

below *South Australian Landscape* by I.G.Pedersen

Origin

From the Dutch word *landscap* from *land* and *scap* which is a suffix for *ship*, as in for example, hardship. *Landship* or *landscape* meant *concerning or related to the land.* Landscape as a **genre** of painting is relatively new, dating from the end of the 16th century during the Renaissance period. Prior to this time, few artists painted a landscape for its own sake but as a background to people or events. Landscape painting as a completely independent genre developed during Romanticism.

Meaning

A landscape is a picture representing either natural scenery or an idealised, pastoral scene. Landscape paintings can be large (Constable's "*six footers*") or small with just a few brush strokes (e.g. Carot's "*The Roman Campagna*"). Many landscape paintings are noted for their delicate nuances of colour and effects of light and shade. Most landscapes are of country-side scenery but there are also landscapes depicting disasters such as storms, avalanches and shipwrecks. Landscape painting flourished in the 17th century and was the most important aspect of **Romanticism** and a significant part of **Impressionism**. It continues to be very popular today. In printing, landscape refers to a page or illustration which is wider than it is deep, particularly when the book is turned sideways.

Associations

Picturesque originally referred to picture-like scenery (e.g. paintings of Nicholas Poussin and Claude Lorraine). Towards the end of the 18th century, it referred to scenes which showed the rougher beauty of humans and nature (e.g. ruins or peasants at work). In the 19th century, it referred to charming landscapes (e.g. paintings of the Barbizon School).

See: **plane, sfumato, ground, genre, figurative, cone of vision**.

See the works of: Turner, Constable, Monet, Cezanne, Ruisdale, Gainsborough, Claude, Poussin, Crome, Richard Wilson.

Laser

Pronounced: LAZA (*1st a as in late, 2nd a as in ago*)

Origin

Laser is an acronym of *Light Amplification by Stimulated Emission of Radiation.* In 1917, Albert Einstein, a famous German mathematician and scientist, proposed the mechanics of stimulated emission - the principle of the laser action. A number of American scientists contributed to the development of the laser in the 1940's and 1950's but T. H. Maiman, who worked for the Hughes Aircraft Company in California, made the first laser in 1960 and J.Townes of Columbia University is generally credited with being the first person to apply laser knowledge to the making of practical things.

Meaning

A laser produces a narrow beam of light of only one wave-length (that is one colour) which goes in only one direction. The light is very highly concentrated and generates intense heat (ten million times the intensity of sunlight). It cuts very easily the hardest of substances (e.g. it can burn holes in steel plate and set carbon on fire). Yet, it can be quite easily controlled. It can be used for low-cost, high-speed engraving. The number of uses to which it can be put increases continuously and it will be used much more in the future in art, especially sculpture, all kinds of metal and plastic work and in kinetic and optical art and design. There are several kinds of lasers, used for varying functions, but their basic principles are the same.

Associations

See: **holography, engraving, sculpture, kinetic.**

A ruby laser, which can produce for a few millionths of a second light ten million times more powerful than the light of the sun.

Layout

Pronounced: LA-OWT (*a as in late, ow as in cow*)

Origin

The word appears in Samuel Johnson's dictionary of 1775 meaning *to plan*. Its usual meaning today is a 20th century derivation. It was first used with its modern meaning in 1852 by an American journalist in the *San Diego Herald*, and it was also used by the author Rudyard Kipling in 1903.

Meaning

In graphics, layout refers to the arrangement and positioning of elements in the design, such as text, illustrations, photographs, typography (size and type, etc.) in conjunction with information related to spacing (including white space), size, colour and texture.

Associations

See: **Design, Graphic Design, Industrial Design, composition, elements, typography.**

Leatherhard

Pronounced: LETHA (*e as in let, th as in that, a as in ago*), HARD (*a as in far*)

Origin

From the Old English *lether* meaning *the tanned skin of an animal*, which is very tough and hard when dried and the Old English *heard*, meaning *hard*.

Meaning

Leatherhard is the condition of raw clay when most, but not all, of the moisture has left it and it is no longer plastic and when it is hard enough to be carved or burnished without crumbling. Leatherhard pottery can be decorated by fluting, faceting, incising, sprigging and by transfer slip.

Associations

See: **clay, glyptic, burnish, facet, sprigging**.

Line

Pronounced: LIN (*i as in fine*)

Origin

From the Latin *linum* meaning *flax*, from which *rope* was made. Rope was used to mark out a series of objects in horizontal order. The word then came to mean a long, narrow mark made horizontally on a surface. Drawings using lines have been made since pre-historic times. The oldest use of line to communicate visually is that in the drawings of animals scratched on cave walls 20,000 years ago.

Meaning

A line is the path of a visual moving point (e.g. from a pencil, pen, chalk, crayon or brush) as it draws across a surface. Its visual impact is usually created by its contrast with the surface on which it is drawn. Artists give much thought to their use of line, as different forms of line convey different ideas and feelings, as follows:

- **horizontal lines** suggest rest, repose (e.g. a fallen tree), but can also suggest movement and speed, particularly when there are a series of such lines (e.g. trailing lines from a comet or spaceship);

- **vertical lines** suggest alertness, life, dignity and nobility. The eyes are carried upwards (e.g. a church steeple, an *upright* man);

- **diagonal lines** suggest movement and action and jagged or zig-zag lines suggest movement, pain or tension;

- **curved lines** suggest delicacy, tranquility and, when free-flowing, gentleness, grace and sensuousness;

- **round lines** suggest smoothness, restfulness or completion.

Lines can also convey a sense of texture (by cross-hatching, stipple, etc.) and their weight (i.e. thick or thin

A line drawing, where a wide range of lines are used, based on Van Gogh's *Cottages Des Saintes Maries*

lines) can suggest ideas. For example, a heavy line can emphasise importance or in some cases movement as the eye is attracted towards the emphasised line.

In graphic art, line refers to a half-tone dot frequency. That is a forty line screen is one that produces forty dots per *centimetre*.

Associations

Linearity is the reliance of a painter or designer on lines for a drawing rather than colour or tone.

See: **drawing, contour, shape, graphic art, half-tone, configuration**.

Lino Block (or Cut)

Pronounced: LIN-O (*i as in fine, o as in go*), BLOK (*o as in rock*)

Origin

Lino is an abbreviation of linoleum, which is from the Latin *linum* meaning *flax* and *oleum* meaning oil. Originally, linoleum was a floor covering of canvas (made from flax) which was covered with solidified linseed oil (also from flax) to preserve it. Linoleum was invented in 1861 by an Englishman named Frederick Walton, who patented a process of oxidising linseed oil with added resin and cork dust which was placed on a cotton or flax backing. He built a linoleum factory in Staines, England and another was established in Kirkcaldy, in Fife, Scotland in 1877. Linoleum was very popular until the 1950's, when it was superseded by synthetic coverings. Aubrey Beardsley (1872-1898), an English artist, was the first great book illustrator to use lino-block reproduction.

cutting a lino block

Meaning

Linoleum is a floor covering made now from a mixture of boiled linseed oil, used as a binder, and finely-ground cork. The backing was originally burlap (a coarse canvas) but nowadays it is usually felt saturated with asphalt (or bitumen or pitch).

To make a lino block, linoleum is usually placed on a block of wood and then a design is drawn on the lino with particular attention being paid to producing contrasts of light and dark areas and an interesting variety of textural effects. Using a variety of lino-block cutting tools (including a **burin**), the design is gouged out of the lino to produce a relief composition. The block needs to be carved deeply for printing on fabric. The block is inked with a water-soluble ink or painted with textile colour, using a roller or a brush. Then the block is carefully pressed against the paper or fabric under pressure (from a washing-roller, a book-press or the back of a large spoon), so that a print can be made. Registration should be worked out before a repeat pattern is printed.

Associations

See: **canvas, relief, print, composition, registration, engraving, impression.**

Literals

Pronounced: LITA-RALS (*i as in bit, a's as in ago.*)

Origin

From the Latin *litera* meaning *a letter of the alphabet.*

Meaning

Literals is a term used in typography. It is an abbreviation of **literal error**. That is an error in the use of letters or words. Literals now refer to a misprint of a letter or word, a misspelling or the use of the wrong type-face. In the U.S.A., a literal is called a **typo** (typographical error).

Associations

See: **graphic design, typography.**

Lithography

Pronounced: LI-THOG-RA-FY (*i as in fine, o as in dog, a as in ago, y as in duty*)

Origin

From the Greek words *lithos* meaning *stone* and *graphe* meaning *writing*. Literally, it means *writing in stone.*

The process was invented by Alois Senefelder (1772-1834), a musician born in Prague of German parents) in 1796. It was introduced into England in 1801 by André d'Offenbach. The process was not perfected until later.

Meaning

Lithography is a printing process which is based on the chemical principle that oil or grease and water will not mix. A slab of smooth-grained, porous limestone, usually from Bavaria, is used. A composition is drawn on the stone using a black, greasy, water-soluble ink called **tusche** or a litho crayon. The stone absorbs the greasy material. Then gum arabic, containing a little nitric acid, is spread over the surface of the stone, which *fixes* the grease on the stone. Only the composition areas are receptive to the gum arabic. The grease continues to penetrate the stone while the gum-arabic dries. The surface drawing is then removed with turpentine and the stone is washed and moistened. Ink is then applied with a roller. The moisture prevents the ink from spreading all over the surface of the stone. Paper is then pressed against the stone (usually using a press) and impressions can be taken.

Lithography also refers to printing where an off-set printing press with three rollers or cylinders is used. A large rubber roller goes over an inked plate (usually made of aluminium, but it can be of zinc, combined metals such as chromium and copper, plastic or paper), which also has water on it, to pick up an impression which it

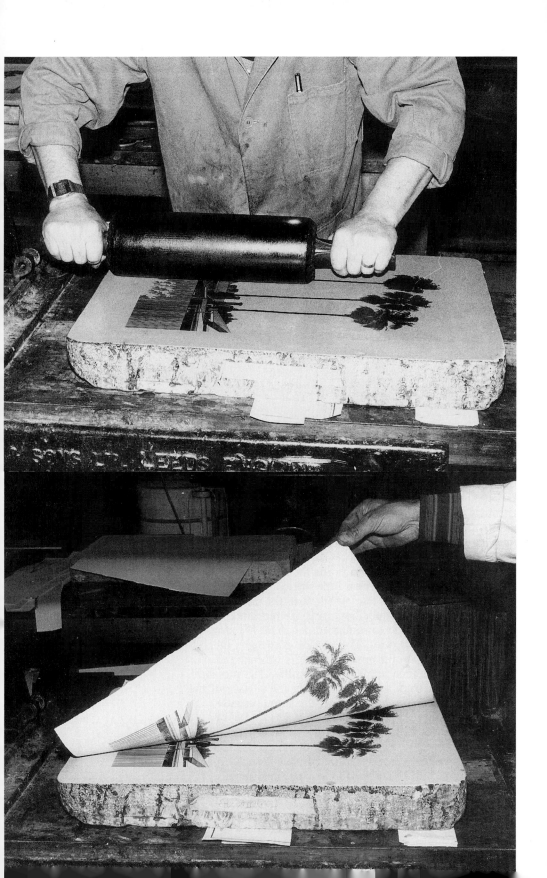

transfers, via another roller, onto paper. In this process, it is not necessary to draw a composition in reverse, as it is in the former process. The litho plates are now invariably produced by photo-mechnical means.

Associations

Bed refers to a flat, horizontal part of a printing press on which a printing plate, stone or block is held firmly during a printing process. The bed may be firmly fixed and pressure applied to it from above or it may move mechanically until it reaches a point where pressure can be applied to the plate or stone. A **levigator** is an instrument for grinding off an old image from a lithographic stone and also for grinding a stone's face level.

See: **planograph, resist, brayer, porosity, print, register, impression**.

See the works of: Aubrey Beardsley, Honoré Daumier, Theodore Gericault, Eugene Delacroix, Francisco Goya, Henri de Toulouse-Lautrec, Edgar Degas, and contemporary lithographers Robert Rauschenberg, Ken Tyler and David Hockney.

Logo

Pronounced: LO-GO (*o's as in go*)

Origin

Logo is an abbreviation of *logotype*, which is from the Greek *logos* meaning *word* and *tupos* meaning *an impression* from *tupo* meaning *to strike*.

Meaning

A logo is a distinctive, designed image, often using one or more letters, which represents or symbolises an organisation. A company's logo is used on letterheads, business cards, notepaper and in some advertisements. Almost every commercial, industrial and public company now has a logo, which is usually created by a graphic designer.

a logo of the wool industry

Associations

See: **symbol, Graphic Design, shape, emboss**.

Loom

Pronounced: LOOM (*oo as in room*)

Origin

From an Old English word *geloma* meaning *a tool*. Evidence found in Ancient Egyptian tombs at Badari shows that looms were used in 4400 B.C.. They were introduced into England in 1131. In 1730, Henry Kaye invented a flying shuttle which advanced the art of

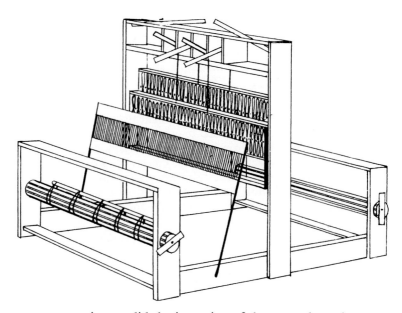

weaving, as did the invention of the power loom by Edmund Cartwright in 1785, and the Jacquard pattern-weaving loom (by Joseph Marie Jacquard of France, 1752-1854) in 1801, which was introduced into England in 1850.

Meaning

A loom is a frame or machine on which yarn is made into cloth. The simple basic **draw loom**, which was used in Ancient China and Middle East countries thousands of years ago, was devised so that warp threads could be *drawn up* (originally by strings and later by treadles) in a planned sequence, in order that weft threads could be inserted alternately above and below the warp threads. The lines of horizontal threads were then *beaten* against the already woven cloth to form part of it. In hand weaving, where a simple frame loom is used, a **heddle** (consisting of a metal device with alternate slits and eyes) is used to lift the warp to provide a gap (called a **shed**) through which a shuttle (around which yarn is wound) can pass. A number of looms are used in weaving, namely the card loom, frame loom, roller loom, shaft loom and rug frame. Modern high-speed, industrial looms work on similar principles to the original loom. Looms are now available which are operated by computers, which ensure that very accurate, complex designs can be produced on woven fabrics in a fraction of the time taken on hand-operated looms.

Associations

See: **technique, composition, dye, manipulation, motif, weave, tapestry**.

a heddle

Lute

Pronounced: LUT (*u as in due*)

Origin

From the Latin *lutum* meaning *mud* or *clay*. To lute is to use clay.

Meaning

In ceramics, luting is the joining of leatherhard parts of ware in order to stop a hole or to make a joint airtight, by using slip as an adhesive. The parts to be joined are scored and covered with a thick clay slip to ensure a secure grip between the parts being joined.

Associations

See: **clay, scoring, leatherhard, slip, manipulation, form, slab, sprigging.**

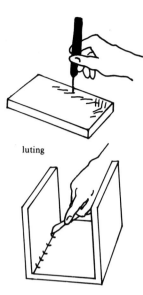

luting

Macramé

Pronounced: MA-KRA-MA (*1st a as in ago, 2nd a as in far, 3rd a as in late*)

Origin

From the Turkish *makrama* meaning a *bedspread* or the Arabic *migramah* meaning *a fringe*. Turkish bedspreads and towels usually have fringes or trimmings of knotted threads or cords. Knotting techniques go back to the earliest times, especially among sailors. The word came into use in English during the nineteenth century.

Meaning

Macramé is a technique in craft of knotting strands of material together to create a fabric design. Most materials that are flexible enough to be tied into a knot can be used but the material should have little elasticity, so that it does not pull out of shape. Cords which do not fray are best for this work.

Associations

See: **fabric, design, technique, medium.**

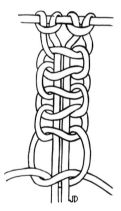

a macramé knot

Mahlstick

Pronounced: MAL-STIK (*a as in far, i as in pin*)

Origin

From the Dutch *maalstock* from *malen* meaning *to paint* and *stock* meaning *a stick*.

Meaning

A mahlstick is a light rod of bamboo, rubber, or aluminium about a metre long with a padded leather ball at one end. It is held in the hand not used for painting in order to steady the painting hand, especially when the

using a mahlstick

painter is involved in detailed work. It is also called a **rest stick**. Some mahlsticks are made in detachable sections, in order that they may be taken to pieces to be kept in a sketch-box.

Marbling

Pronounced: MA-BAL-ING (*1st a as in far, 2nd a as in ago*)

Origin

From the Greek *marmos* meaning *shining stone*, which became *marble* in French. Marble stone has a variety of veins of colour of different flowing shapes within it. The process probably originated in Persia and was introduced into Europe towards the end of the 16th century. Marbling was popular for the decoration of end papers and edges of books in the 18th and 19th centuries in Europe and in the U.S.A. in the 19th century.

Meaning

Marbling is a technique in decoration where liquid colours which will not mix (e.g. oil colours and water colours) are intermingled by the process of disturbing the surface of the liquids with a steel, wide-toothed comb, in order to produce a design. Paper or fabric is placed on the surface of the liquids and then carefully removed so that a swirling, flowing pattern is transferred to the material. It also refers to the decorating of ceramic ware with coloured slips which are put on a ground of wet slip. The ware is shaken so that the coloured slips run together to create what appears to be like the veined design in marble.

Associations

Marbleizing describes a finishing process used to make surfaces appear like marble.

See: **slip, water colour, oil paint.**

Marquetry

Pronounced: MA-KET-RY (*a as in far, e as in let, y as in duty*)

Origin

From the French *marqueter* meaning *to variegate*. That is to mark with irregular patterns of different colours to produce varied effects. The art was practised in Ancient Egypt, Greece and Rome. The wood carvers of Italy developed the technique of wood inlays (called *intarsia*) to a very high level in the 15th. and 16th centuries, often working from **cartoons** produced by eminent artists, such as Botticelli (1444-1512). The process became popular in

an intarsia donkey

Holland and Germany in the 17th century and became a distinctive feature of their furniture. Later it was highly regarded in France. It was first introduced into Britain during the middle of the 17th.century.

Meaning

Marquetry is a decorative woodwork process where shaped pieces of wood of the same thickness or wood **veneers**, of different colours and grains are glued to a wood ground (in much the same manner as a jigsaw), in order to create a design for furniture or wood utensils. Wood was the main material used but sometimes slivers of metal, tortoise-shell, mother-of-pearl, ivory or other textured materials were inlaid into the designs. The invention of a marquetry **donkey** (a type of jig saw) in 1780 allowed marqueteurs to cut up to ten pieces of veneer at a time, which increased production substantially. Floral and arabesque designs were popular in marquetry.

Associations

Inlays of wood are called **intarsia** in Italy. The inlay process is different from the marquetry process, in that intarsia fit inside a base on which they are placed but marquetry veneers are placed on top of the base. André-Charles Boulle (1642-1732, born in Paris of Swiss parents), a cabinet maker to Louis X1V of France, produced marquetry which was inlaid with ornamental patterns in

An intarsia panel in the Church of Santa Maria Novella in Florence

brass, pewter, copper, enamel, or tortoise-shell. This kind of work is known as **Boulle work**. One of the finest **marqeteurs** was the German cabinet maker David Roentgen (1743-1807).

Mass

Pronounced: MAS (*a as in cat*)

Origin
From the Latin *massa* meaning *a kneaded lump* (to make a barley cake). The idea of *lump* as a quantity or a number of materials developed from this early meaning.

Meaning
Mass refers to the physical bulk of a solid body of material. In an art composition, it refers to an area or a group of forms expressed in colour and is the main portion of a painting to which the eye is usually attracted. Mass is the positive element in a composition, whereas space is the negative element. Both are essential in any composition or design.

Associations
See: **composition, space, positive, negative, elements**.

Masterpiece

Pronounced: MAST-A-PEES (*1st a as in mast, 2nd a as in ago, ee as in see*)

Origin
Originally, a masterpiece was a test-piece of work given to an apprentice or a journeyman artist or craftsman which was submitted to the governors of a Medieval Guild for them to decide whether the work was of a sufficiently high standard for the applicant to be considered worthy of the rank of *master* in the Guild. A Guild limited the number of masters it approved; consequently, the standards required were exceptionally high.

Meaning
Masterpiece nowadays applies to any artistic work which is among the finest examples of a genre, or to a famous artist's or designer's best work.

Matt

Pronounced: MAT (*a as in cat*)

Origin
From the Persian *mat* meaning *dead* and from this anything which is not bright and alive is matt or dull.

Meaning
To matt is to give a pebbled or grained texture and a dull, unglossed finish to a surface, in contrast to a smooth,

polished, gloss surface. On a wood or metal surface, this is called **matting**. Water-based paints produce a matt finish; oil-based paints usually produce a gloss finish. Artists can produce a matt finish to their work by the inclusion of a matt medium or varnish can be used with a matt finish. In ceramics, a matt glaze is one with a dull surface, produced by adding barium or alumina to the clay.

Associations

See: **acrylic, glaze**.

Mechanical Drawing

Pronounced: MEK-AN-I-KAL (*e as in let, a's as in ant, i as in pin*), DRAW-ING (*aw as in saw*)

Origin

From the Greek *mekhane* meaning *a contrivance, a device* and the suffix *ic* meaning *in the form of*. Mechanical came to mean anything associated with machines or devices.

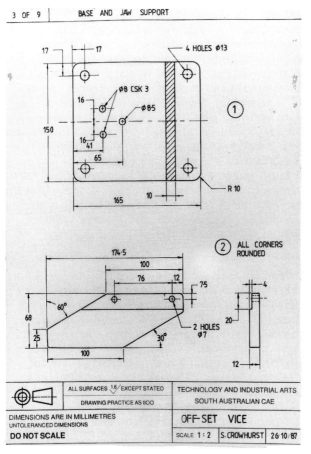

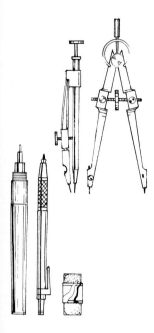

technical drawing tools

Meaning

Mechanical drawing is a precisely - controlled form of drawing to convey exact and detailed information in graphic form. From a mechanical drawing, it should be possible to construct what has been designed. Some of the tools used to produce mechanical drawings are: divider-spacer, compass, French curves, ellipsograph, lettering-guides, bow pen, parallel rules, protractor, templates and T-square. The term is used to describe all kinds of engineering and architectural drafting and work involving projections.

Associations

See: **cross hatching, projection, shape, perspective, format, drawing, line, draft, geometric, Golden Section, grid, Industrial Designer, rectilinear, plane**.

Medium

Pronounced: ME-DI-UM (*e as in me, i as in bit, u as in bonus*)

Origin

From the Latin for *middle* or *middle quality*, then *an intervening substance, instrument or means*. That is something which must be used to make something else work effectively (e.g. oil must be added to pigment to make oil paint) or to make something happen (e.g. a pencil is needed for drawing). The earliest medium for painting was wax, used by the Greeks and Romans up to the 8th.century. In the Middle Ages (5th.to 15th.centuries) *tempera* bound with egg white was used. Oil painting was first described by a German monk named Theophilus in 1100, but it was first used in the 15th.century by Dutch painters, such as Jan Van Eyck (1390-1440) and later by Leonardo da Vinci (1452-1519). Since the 20th.century an *acrylic* medium has also been used by some painters, made from *polymerised resin* .

Meaning

A medium is the liquid in which a pigment is suspended to make paint, for example gum arabic for water paint or size for distemper. Also, it refers to the material which an artist uses for her or his composition, e.g. clay, marble, paint, glass, etc. In drawing or painting, the range of mediums is very wide, such as: graphite or coloured pencils, conté (a French brand of grease-free crayon), crayons, wax crayons, charcoal, black pastel (oil or dry), indian ink, felt-tipped markers, water-based markers, pastel crayons, oil pastels, etc.. Artists also use combinations of mediums. The term also means a liquid used to render paint more fluid and workable or to alter its drying time and durability. The term can be used too for the technique used by an artist or designer, such as engraving, etching, modelling or painting.

Associations

Media can be the plural of medium, but the alternative plural **mediums** is probably less confusing in art, craft and design, as the word media now applies more often to television, newspapers and journals.

See: **vehicle, accelerator, technique, tempera, oil paint, acrylic.**

Metamorphosis

Pronounced: MET-A-MOR-FO-SIS (*e as in let, a as in ago, 1st o as in more, 2nd o as in go, i as in list*)

Origin

From the Greek *metamorphosis* meaning *a complete change of form, a transformation*

Meaning

Metamorphosis is when something completely changes its appearance, for example from a caterpillar to a butterfly, from a tadpole to a frog, and, in art, from a slab of marble into a sculptured form of a person. Each time an artist or a designer takes materials and creates a new form from these materials a metamorphosis takes place. Creation is a **metamorphic** process.

Associations

See:**morphology, manipulation, technique.**

Mezzotint

Pronounced: MEZO-TINT (*e as in met, o as in go, i as in tin*

Origin

From the Italian *mezzo* meaning *half* and *tinto* meaning *a dye* or *a colour*. Ludwig Von Siegen, a German army colonel from Hesse, is said to have invented the technique in 1642 and first used it for a portrait of a German countess. It became popular for printing in the 18th and 19th centuries.

Meaning

Mezzotint is a relief or intaglio technique in engraving in which the ground on a plate is formed by regular fine burred dots, using a tool called a **cradle** or a **rocker**. The dots are scraped to produce half-tone areas which vary in strength according to the depth of the scrapings. The ground is inked to form a black background to the composition. The design of the composition is then scraped carefully to deepen or smooth the burring on the plate. The composition parts do not attract ink and appear in a print as white. Half the composition is tinted; half is not. The process is the reverse of line engraving and etching. It is able to show subtle variations of light and shade.

Associations
See the work of: Joshua Reynolds (1723-1792), John Constable (1776-1837), and J.M.W.Turner (1775-18510.

See: **engraving, print, impression, edition, composition**.

Minimal Art

Pronounced: MINI-MAL (*i's as in pin, a as in ago*), ART (*a as in far*)

Origin
From the Latin *mimimus* meaning *smallest*. The Minimal Art movement began in the U.S.A., mainly in New York and Los Angeles, in the 1950's and lasted throughout the 1960's. A major exhibition of Minimal Art entitled *Primary Structures* was held in New York in 1966.

Meaning
Minimal Art is a form of sculpture and, to a lesser extent, painting, which avoids personal expression, emotion or illusion. Artists aimed to define what they believed essential by stripping away anything they considered unesssential and by reducing art to its most basic form. It used simple, repeated geometric shapes and often hard-edged, smooth, uninterrupted surfaces and neutral colours or bright plastic colours. Carl André's Minimal Art sculpture, called "*Equivalent V111*", consists of a rectangle of 120 fire bricks arranged in two layers. Some artists had their works produced by industry under their supervision.

Associations
See the works of the following artists from the U.S.A.: Ellsworth Kelly, Kenneth Noland, Carl André, Frank Stella, Donald Judd, David Smith, Barnett Newman, Robert Morris.

See: **facture, Hard Edge Painting, geometric**.

Mirror Image

Pronounced: MIRA (*i as in pin, a as in ago*), IMIJ (*i's as in pin*)

Origin
Mirror is from the Latin *mirare* meaning *to look at*, and the French *miroir* meaning *a looking-glass*. Image is from the Latin *imago*, which means *likeness* and later a *statue*

or a *conception*. It derives from the Latin *imitari* meaning *to imitate*.

Meaning

A mirror image is a reflection where an object or a person is completely reversed in shape and appearance. It can also mean **identical**. Mirror images are produced in printing processes, other than in off-set printing.

Associations

See: **replica, facsimile, printing, lithography**.

a mirror image

Mobile

Pronounced: MO-BIL (*o as in go, i as in file*)

Origin

From the Latin *mobilis* meaning *moving*. The word mobile was first used by the French artist Marcel Duchamp (1887-1968) to describe the moving sculptural forms of the American sculptor Alexander Calder, who held his first exhibition of mobiles in France in 1932.

Meaning

A mobile is a three-dimensional, kinetic sculptural form made originally in metal but now made from most man-made materials (including stained-glass) or from natural materials, such as shells. Multiple shapes are suspended in space in a delicately balanced arrangements on fine metal rods or wires, fishing lines or threads (and, occasionally on drink straws), so that by air currents or structural tension or the movement of spectators, they move and revolve. The forms reveal the imaginative use of mass and space. Mobiles have become a popular aspect of interior decoration.

Associations

A **Stabile** is a term coined by Alexander Calder to describe some of his sculptures. They are similar in form to mobiles but they do not move. They are fixed to a *stable* base rather than suspended. See the works of Alexander Calder (1898-1976).

See: **kinetic, Op Art, Constructivism, mass, space**.

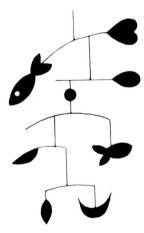

a mobile

Monoprint

Pronounced: MONO (*1st o as in log, 2nd o as in go*), PRINT (*i as in pin*)

Origin

From the Greek *monos* meaning *alone* or *single* and print from the Old French *preinte* meaning *something pressed*. The Italian artist Catiglione (1616-1670) is thought to have first used the technique in Rome in 1635.

Meaning

A monoprint is a simple printing technique where one print at a time is made and every print is different (as distinct from an **edition** of prints). There are several processes. One is where a composition or design is made using a brush and printing ink on sheet glass or a metal plate. Paper is pressed onto the plate and then peeled off carefully to produce a single impression. Poster paint or tempera can also be used. A second is where ink is rolled onto sheet glass, using a brayer, and a line-drawing is made on the ink with a small stick or a brush handle. The drawn lines appear as white lines on the print. A third method is as given above except that paper is stuck to the ink and the composition or design is made with a ball-point pen on the reverse side of the paper. The paper is then peeled from the glass to reveal the monoprint.

Associations

Monotype is an alternative term for monoprint. See the works of Giovanni Castiglione (1616-1670), William Blake (1757-1827), Edgar Degas (1834-1917). Paul Klee, Pablo Picasso, Henri Matisse, Max Ernst and Georges Rouault also used the technique.

See: **print, impression.**

Montage

Pronounced: MON-TAJ (*o as in on, a as in far, j as s in vision*)

Origin

From the French *monter* meaning *to mount* or *to fix objects into or onto something* (e.g. to set gems in gold or place pictures in a mount).

Meaning

A montage is a composition made up of overlapping images from pictures, prints or photographs. It refers also to a composition made up of parts of cinema or television films or prints. In **collage** the pictorial elements do not overlap or blend; in **montage** they do.

Associations

A **photomontage** is a montage using only photographs. It was a technique used frequently by Dadaist and Cubist artists. It was used by the German graphic artist John Heartfield, during the 1930 for propaganda purposes against Nazism.

See: **collage, Cubism, Dadaism, composition, assemblage, elements.**

Mordant

Pronounced: MOR-DANT (*o as in more, a as in ago*)

Origin

From the Latin *mordere* meaning *to bite*. A mordant bites
and holds fast to a material to become part of it.
Mordants were used in India and Egypt more than five
thousand years ago. It was originally thought that
mordants *bit* open the surfaces of fibres to open passages
through which dyes could get inside fibres.

Meaning

A mordant is an etching solution (e.g. nitric or
hydrochloric acid) which *eats away* those lines on a metal
surface which are not protected by a **resist** material. The
depth of the "*bite*" depends upon the strength of the
mordant and also how long the metal is exposed to it. In
photography, it is used in **dye-toning** and some **colour-
printing** processes. In **gilding**, it is an adhesive size which
holds gold leaf put on it. In the **dyeing** of fabrics, it is a
substance which causes fibres to swell and to absorb dye,
which lessens the chances of the dye being washed out.
The dye is said to be *fixed*. The main mordants, which
are metallic salts, are alum, chrome, copper, iron, and tin.
Salt and vinegar are sometimes used to assist mordants to
fix the dye in fabrics in batik.

Associations

Dutch mordant is a solution of hydrochloric acid and
potassium chlorate used for etching fine lines on copper.
The formula was discovered in Holland in the
17th.century.

See: **etching, gild, size, resist, dye, batik**.

Mosaic

Pronounced: MOZ-A-IK (*o as in got, a as in late, i as
in ink*)

Origin

From the Latin *mosaicus* meaning *related to the Muses*.
The Muses in Ancient Greece and Rome were the nine
godesses who were daughters of the chief god, Zeus. They
were the inspirers of poetry, music and drama. The
earliest mosaics depicted the Muses. Mosaics were one of
the earliest forms of decorative art. They were used
extensively by the Romans and the Greeks not only in
their public buildings but also in their homes. Their
origins date back to 5000 years ago. They were the most
dominant part of Byzantine art (in the 11th and 12th
centuries) and reached the highest artistic levels among
the Aztecs of Mexico. The art of mosaic patterning
declined from the 14th.century, being superseded by

Head of a Parthian woman,
kingdom of Edessa, Syria, late 2nd/
early third century A.D. *collection of
the Art Gallery of South Australia,
Adelaide, South Australia*

fresco and wall paintings. There was a brief revival of the art in the 19th.century. In the 1950's mosaics were used extensively on public buildings in Mexico City.

Meaning

A mosaic consists of regular or irregular pieces of glass, marble, stone, shells, tiles or other hard materials of different colours (called **tesserae** which is Latin for *four sided*) which are inlaid into an adhesive material (e.g. mastic grout, plaster or cement) to form a design. Wood is not used in mosaics. When fragments of material are used they are usually set with their broken parts facing upwards or tilted at an angle to reflect light, which often produces a sparkling effect. Mosaic is also used more generally to mean any design which is created by joining sections of material together on a flat base to which they stick.

Associations

smalti are glass tesserae and **tessella** are miniature tesserae. Both Titian and Raphael produced cartoons (using the original meaning of the term) for mosaics. See the works of Antonio Gaudi (1852-1926), Lazlo Barta (1902 -) and the American *mosaicist* Louis Comfort Tiffany (1848-1933). An excellent example of contemporary mosaic work is that of Eduardo Paolozzi who has produced mural mosaics at the entrance and on the platforms of the Tottenham Court Road underground station in London. See the book *Eduardo Paolozzi Underground*, edited by Richard Cork.

Motif

Pronounced: MO-TEEF (*o as in go, ee as in see*)

Origin

From the Latin *motivus* meaning *movement* or *to repeat a move*.

Meaning

A motif is a visual element, pattern, subject or theme in a work of art that is repeated a sufficient number of times in the same or slightly different form in a composition or design to give it dominance. It is similar to a melody or theme in a musical composition. In sculpture, it refers to the manner in which a sculptor arranges figures he or she has produced. It means also the subject for a landscape sketch.

Associations

See: **elements, composition, dominance, landscape**.

Mural

Pronounced: MU-RAL (*u as in pure, a as in ago*)

Origin

From the Latin *murus* meaning *a wall*.

Meaning

A mural is a painting made usually directly onto a wall or ceiling of a building, either indoors or outdoors.
Sometimes murals are painted on canvas or on panels and then stuck to a wall or a ceiling. A mural is given a matt surface in order that it can be seen from any angle without the glare of reflected light. It also refers to a large painting designed to be fixed to a wall. In the past fresco was the medium used for murals but nowadays oils, tempera and polymer paints are used. External murals are becoming increasingly popular, especially to brighten up some dreary modern environments.

Associations

See the work of Duncan Grant (British 1885-1978), Vanessa Bell (British 1879-1961), Arthur Mathews (American 1860-1945), Lucia Mathews (American 1870-1955).

See: **fresco, matt, tempera**.

Movement

Pronounced: MOOV-MENT (*oo as in moon, e as in token*)

Origin

From the Latin *movimentum* meaning *to be in motion, to make progress*.

Meaning

A movement in Art and Design refers to a group of people who are moved (motivated) to take the same action, who have the same aims and produce artistic works which identifies them as members of the group. For example, Op Art, Minimal Art and Pop Art are art movements. Movement in art and design also refers to the illusion of activity, speed or vitality created in a composition or design by the skilful use of visual techniques

Peter Paul Rubens, 1577-1640, Flanders, **Hercules and Antaeus**
Oil on panel, 64.6 cms x 49.5 cms, Felton Bequest 1947, National Gallery of Victoria, Australia.

Associations

Gestural refers to brush work which emphasises an artist's broad, vigorous movement.

See the works of Rubens (1577-1640), a master of rhythm and movement, and Sandro Botticelli (1445-1510), Eugene Delacroix (1798-1863), and Edgar Degas (1834-1917). See the works from the Futurist Movement, e.g. Giacomo Balla's "*Dog on a Leash*". See also "*La Cirque*" by Georges Seurat.

Negative

Pronounced: NEG-A-TIV (*e as in egg, a as in ago, i as in if*)

Origin

From the Latin *negare* meaning *to deny, say no, contradict* and *ivus* a suffix meaning *tending towards or having the nature of* (e.g. *descriptive* means *tending to describe*). It came to mean anything not positive or the reverse or opposite of something. The negative-positive process in photography was invented by an Englishman, William Henry Fox Talbot in 1839.

Meaning

A negative is a photographic film on which lights and shadows of images are the reverse of what they are in reality. The light tones are reproduced as dark and dense, the dark tones as light and thin. It is the opposite of a positive. **Negative space** refers to the areas in a composition or design between the outlines of shapes (objects or figures) and between shapes and the edges of the material being worked on. Shapes take up positive space. A composition or design results from the combination of negative as well as positive space. A negative is also a mould which is shaped in the reverse form from the original prototype shape used.

Associations

See: **gradation, half-tone, bromide, space.**

Neo-Classicism

Pronounced: NEE-O (*ee as in see, o as in go*), KLAS-I-SISM (*a as in pass, i's as in pin, sm as in prism*)

Origin

From the Greek *neos* meaning *new* and the Latin *classicus* from *classis* meaning *assembly or group* (usually of patricians not plebeians) and later *first class or rank* and *of the highest standard*.

Neo-Classicism was a movement which started in Rome about 1750 and spread rapidly throughout Europe, lasting about a decade. It was established as a reaction to the ornate Baroque and Rococo styles but also from a desire to reproduce the art and spirit of Ancient Greece and Rome. Findings from archaelogical excavations of the buried cities of Herculaneum (in 1706) and Pompeii (in 1748) in Italy stimulated and inspired the movement. The first spokesmen of the movement were Johann Joachim Winkelmann (1717-1768), a German art historian, and Anton Raffael Mengs (1728-1779), a noted German portraitist. The movement had an influence on painting, ceramics, sculpture and particularly on architecture.

Meaning

Neo-Classicism was a movement which consciously set out to imitate the art of Ancient Greece and Rome. The elaborate excesses of Rococo were rejected in favour of Classical restraint,and, as Winkelmann put it, a style of *"noble simplicity and calm grandeur"*. The style is characterised by deliberate imitation of Classical themes, ideas and forms (e.g. bas-relief), symmetry, sharp linear outline and a preference for flatness rather than plasticity. It de-emphasised colour and made little use of chiaroscuro. The clean lines and restrained colour of Nicholas Poussin (1594-1665), of the French Classical School, was much admired. It included the fine arts (including architecture) and the practical and decorative arts.

Associations

In France, Neo-Classicism was called the **Louis Seize Style**.

See the work of: Jacques-Louis David (French), Jean Auguste Dominique Ingres (French), Anton Raffael Mengs (German), John Flaxman (English), Gavin Hamilton (English), Angelica Kauffman (Swiss)- all painters; the sculptors Antoine Houdon (French), and Antonio Canova (Italian), the engraver Giovanni Battista Piranesi (Italian), the ceramist Josiah Wedgwood (English) and the English furniture designers Thomas Chippendale, Thomas Sheraton, and George Hepplewhite.

See: **Baroque, Rococo, symmetry, linearity, plasticity, chiaroscuro**.

Neo-Impressionism

Pronounced: NEE-O (*ee as in see, o as in go*) IM-PRESH-A-NISM (*i's as in pin, esh as in fresh, a as in ago, sm as in prism*)

Origin

From the Greek *neos* meaning *new* and the Latin *impressio* meaning *what is pressed into something*. It came to mean *what is pressed into and retained in the mind.*

The movement started in the early 1880's and lasted a decade. Its leader was Georges Seurat, a French painter. He (and Odilon Redon, who is better known as a **Symbolist**) held the first exhibition of the movement in 1884. The term *Neo-Impressionism* was first used by a French art critic, Félix Fénéon in a magazine article in 1886 and it was then used by other art critics and by artists.

Meaning

Although the word *Impressionism* is part of the term *Neo-Impressionism*, the Neo-Impressionists were distinct from the Impressionists and what the two movements had in common was relatively small. The Neo-Impressionists reacted against the Impressionists but they were also a clear development of them. The movement emphasised the relationship of art with science, particularly to the psychology and physiology of vision and to optical phenomena and to the analysis of colour and light. The artists developed the theory and practice of optical mixtures. The law of Simultaneous Contrast propounded in 1839 by Michel Eugene Chevreul (1786-1899), the director of the famous Gobelins tapestry works in France, said that a colour placed next to its complementary colour is made more powerful by the contrast. This law very much influenced the thinking and artistic practice of the Neo-Impressionist artists. The movement's work is characterised by strict, formal composition (often reduced to basic geometric structures), methodical fragmentation of brushwork, (**pointillism**- which the movement preferred to call **divisionism**) and an emphasis on light, luminosity and harmony. The artists were very exact and painstaking and it was common for painters to produce several **studies** before work began on a major composition.

Associations

See the works of Georges Seurat, Camille Pissarro, Paul Signac, Henri-Edmond Cross, Albert Dubois-Pillet and a later painter Robert Delauney (1885-1941).

See: **pointillism, Impressionism, study, colour, juxtapose, plein air**.

Objectivity

Pronounced: OB-JEK-TIV-ITY (*o as in rob, e as in let, i's as in ink, y as in duty*

Origin

From the Latin *objectum* meaning *something thrown in the way of someone* or *something placed before you so that you see what it is*. *Ivity* means *the extent of a quality or condition* (e.g. humid-ity or poros-ity). Objectivity came to mean the extent to which you consider what is actually in front of you.

Meaning

Objectivity refers to a person's attitude or approach to something, which is based on facts placed before the person for consideration. What is real, practical, actual and there to be seen is considered rather than sensations, emotional responses, ideals and personal likes or dislikes. The opposite of objectivity is **subjectivity**. For example, one can show objectivity in discussing obvious elements in an artistic composition or a design, such as line, mass, shape, texture, colour, content, etc.. Subjectivity occurs when one expresses a personal response to the work. Realism attempts to be as objective as possible. Dadaism, Surrealism and fantasy consciously reject objectivity. All artists and designers, in fact all people, are subjective; some more than others.

Associations

See: **Realism, perception, illusion, fantasy, Symbolism, Surrealism, figurative, aesthetics, genre, landscape, specification, still-life.**

Objet Trouvé

Pronounced: OB-ZHA (*o as in got, zh as s in vision, a as in late*), TROO-VA (*oo as in soon, a as in late*)

Origin

From the French *objet* meaning *object* and *trouvé* meaning *found*. That is something that is found rather than created. Marcel Duchamp, a French artist (1887-1968), is usually credited with the introduction of **found objects** and what he called *ready mades*. One of Duchamp's ready-mades consists of a bicycle wheel which is attached to a stool The difference between a ready-made and an an objet trouvé is that a ready-made is totally manufactured.

Meaning

An objet trouvé is an object, natural or man-made, which is found or selected and then presented by an artist as a work of art, either in its original state or in a modified form. Such presentations were practised by the Dadaists and the Surrealist artists. The artists intentions were to draw people's attention to aspects of an object which they may not have noticed or to shock and surprise people by the presentation of the objects or by the juxtaposition of seemingly incongruous objects. Nowadays, drift wood, stones and shells are often arranged and presented as works of art, as are man-made objects, especially in sculpture.

a Japanese pebble toy

Associations

See the works of Max Ernst (1891-1976), Kurt Schwitters (1887-1948), Marcel Duchamp (1887-1968), Edward Kenholz (1922 -), Paul Nash (1889-1946).

See: **assemblage, Pop Art, Dadaism, Surrealism, juxtaposition.**

Oil Paint

Pronounced: OIL (*oi as in coil*), PANT (*a as in late*)

Origin

Oil is from the Latin *oleum* which is from *olea* meaning *an olive*. It is not certain who first used oil paint on canvas to produce a painting. Some have said it was the Dutch painter Jan Van Eyck. Whether it was he or not, it is certain that he and his brother used oil paint in their work in the 15th. century (about 1400). It was first used in Venice in 1450 by the painter Veneziano. It became a popular medium for artists of all countries from then on.

Meaning

Oil paint is made from pigments (from natural earths or man-made oxides) mixed with linseed (made from flax), poppy, safflower or walnut oil to a paste consistency. Nowadays, thinners and siccatives (a drying agent) are sometimes added. It is applied to a slightly absorbent surface, such as a primed canvas. As it is slow drying, it allows a fairly long time to be spent on a work and colours to be blended over many hours, so that, unlike as in water colour painting, large-scale works can be done. It also allows corrections and changes to be made, as the paint can be readily scraped off. As the paint is thick, it does not run to make accidental mixings. Also, as new colours can be applied to existing colours, great depth and brilliance of colour can be achieved and deep richness of texture produced. It is able to show subtle gradations and variations of tone and light, and also depict minute detail.

Stanley Spencer, Great Britain 1891 - 1959, *Garden View, Cookham Dean* oil on canvas 91.4 x 61 0 cm
Art Gallery of South Australia, Adelaide, South Australia

Associations

Tonking is a method of removing surplus oil paint from a canvas by laying a sheet of absorbent paper (e.g. newspaper) over an area of a painting, then rubbing the paper gently with the palm of the hand before carefully peeling off the paper. Among the masters in the use of oil paint are: Jan Van Eyck (1390-1440), Titian (1485-1576), Rubens (1577-1640) Velazquez (1599-1660), and Rembrandt (1606-1669).

See: **glaze, scumble, fat, impasto, painterly, Renaissance, medium.**

Op Art

Pronounced: OP (*o as in top*), ART (*a as in far*)

Origin

Op Art is an abbreviation of *optical art*. Optical is from the Greek *optikos* meaning *eye*, and *optical* means *related to sight*. Several artists in the 1930's (e.g. Victor Vasarely) pioneered what was later to be called **Op Art**, but it was in the late 1950's and 1960 that the Op Art movement thrived. The term came into use about 1965 when a major exhibition called "*The Responsive Eye*" was held in New York. It was to some extent a reaction against the imprecise, informal art of Abstract Expressionism and Tachisme.

Meaning

Op Art was a movement where artists exploited the wide range of ways to produce visual stimuli which resulted in the effect on a spectator of flickering or vibrating movement. By the precise use of geometric abstract forms and subtle use of black and white or combinations of complementary colours, artists were able to create compositions which gave the illusion to a spectator of pulsating or disappearing and reappearing forms. They were able to create surfaces which appeared to warp, swell or vibrate. Technically, they were very accomplished. In the 1960's and 1970's, Op Art designs were popular in textile design and decorative art.

Associations

Moiré patterns are wave-like effects which are produced by juxtaposing identical patterns which are not quite in parallel.

See the works of Bridget Riley (1931 -), Victor Vasarely (1908 -), Peter Sedgeley (1930 -), Yaacov Agam(1928 -), Josef Albers (1888-1966).

See: **illusion, juxtaposition, movement, Tachisme, kinetic, pattern**.

Opaque

Pronounced: OPAK (*o as in rope, a as in late*)

Origin

From the Latin *opacus* meaning *shady, darkened and obscure*. The word became *opaque* in French, from which we derive the English word.

Meaning

Opaque refers to something which cannot be seen through. It reflects light rather than transmits it. It is something which is neither transparent (e.g. as in a clear-glass window) or translucent (e.g. as in a frosted-glass window). Some varnishes and glazes are opaque; some are transparent. Opaque materials are used frequently for **resist** or **blocking** purposes. An opaque paper prevents *see through* or *show through* of images or type. **Opacity** is the noun from opaque.

Associations

See: **resist, blocking, matt, medium, translucent.**

Origami

Pronounced: O-RI-GAM-I (*o as in go, i's as in ring, a as in arm*)

Origin

From the Japanese *ori* meaning *fold* and *kami* meaning *paper*. Origami is a Japanese traditional custom which dates back to the 12th century. Symbolic designs made from folded paper have been significant parts not only of Japanese festivals and ceremonies but also of their entertainment. Origami is now an art practised throughout the world.

Meaning

Origami is the traditional art of folding lightweight paper called **origami paper**. It is sculpture in paper. Traditionally, animals, figures and birds of many kinds are made according to laid-down instructions of paper folding. The paper must always be square and nothing can be cut away from the square or added to the shape produced. The Japanese practice of attaching to gifts a folded-paper token design, called a **noshi**, is a development of the ceremonial act. An origami crane is a symbol of peace.

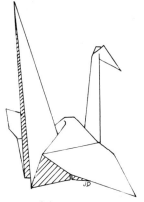

a sitting crane

Associations

See: **paper, sculpture, manipulation, mobile, shape, technique.**

Overlay

Pronounced: OVA-LA (*o as in go, 1st a as in ago, 2nd a as in late*)

Origin

Overlay is a 20th century word which originated with the development of colour printing.

Meaning

To produce multiple copies of art work in colour, a printing plate must be made for each colour to be used in the composition. An **overlay** of the work in each separate colour is made on transparent or translucent material, so that when the various overlays are put on top of each

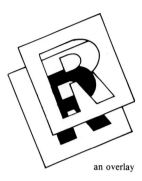

an overlay

other, the total composition in the colours used can be seen. The various parts of the art work in each colour must register precisely. To ensure precision of positioning of the various parts, register marks are placed exactly the same on each of the pieces of art work and each overlay, usually by placing three marks on the sides and bottom of the art work and the overlays. It can also mean the overlap of printing colours.

Associations
See: **Graphic Design, composition, register, print, technique.**

Oxidation

Pronounced: OXI-DA-SHUN (*o as in box, i as in pin, a as in late, u as in sun*)

Origin
From the Greek *oxus* meaning *sharp* or *keen* and *genes* a suffix meaning *that which produces*. Oxygen, therefore, is that which produces keenness, and later vitality or life. Oxygen ,a colourless, tasteless, scentless gas, is essential to human, animal and vegetable life. It is also necessary for things to burn. *Oxidation* (or *oxidising*) is a 19th century word, derived from oxygen, which means *to cause to combine with oxygen*. The term *oxide* was coined by a French scientist G.de Morveau.

Meaning
Oxidation is essential in the ceramic process where an oxide (used for colouring and glazes) has to combine with potteryware. During the firing process in a kiln, the ware usually requires enough oxygen to cause the burning of carbon gases to get rid of the carbon in a ware. Oxidation can be seen to be taking place in a kiln when the chamber shows a clear, bright flame and there is no smoke. Earthenware needs a full oxidising atmosphere in a kiln when it is being fired.

In vat dyeing, fabrics which are coloured by oxides need to oxidise as the final process in making the colour permanent.

In metal work, oxidisation refers to the production of oxides or metallic salts on metals (often referred to as **scale**) when they are heated or subjected to atmospheric conditions. **Corrosion** usually occurs on metals as they break down into oxides or metallic salts. Certain metals (e.g.aluminium, copper and copper alloys), however, require oxidation to prevent the metals from corroding.

Associations
Reduction is the opposite of Oxidation.

See: **kiln, pickle, reduction, firing, solder, dye, stained glass.**

Pronounced: PANT-A-LY (*1st a as in late, 2nd a as in ago, y as in duty*)

Origin

The Swiss art historian Heinrich Wölflinn first used the term at the end of the 19th century to define the masterly use of paint and brush work (rather than linear form) in painting. The German word *malerisch* means the same as painterly and was used originally by Wölflinn, who regarded Rembrandt's paintings as the most superb examples of the malerisch or painterly technique.

Meaning

Painterly is a term related to a style of painting in which masses of colour and tone and light and shade are emphasised, rather than line and contour. The term implies that paint has been applied to a canvas in a skilful, expert manner, especially in expressive brushwork. **Impressionism** is the most painterly of the 19th century art movements and **Neo-Impressionism** is based on a painterly method. Recent painterly artists are Jackson Pollock and Willem de Kooning. The term implies, too, that a painter is more concerned in his or her painting with colour and texture than with the content of the painting and the images produced. **Hard Edge Painting** is a stark contrast to painterly work.

Associations

See: **mass, contour, Tachisme, facture, Expressionism, subjective, style, Fauvism, Neo-Impressionism.**

Titian and Rembrandt are among the most painterly of painters. See the work of Impressionist, Neo-Impressionist, and Expressionist painters and the work of artists who have produced **Action Painting**, such as Jackson Pollock (1912-1956).

Palette

Pronounced: PALAT (*1st a as in mat, 2nd a as in ago*)

Origin

From the French meaning *little spade*. The original painter's palette was in the shape of a spade.

Meaning

A palette is a portable tray or board, made from a variety of materials nowadays (e.g. wood, plastic, plate-glass, masonite) on which an artist carries his or her colours and mixes them. The phrase *an artist's palette* means the artist's choice of colours for a painting. The term also refers to a group of colours characteristic of a style of decoration in ceramics or of a particular ceramist or

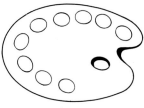

a palette

ceramic factory. Also, it is a tool used in glasswork for shaping the foot of a wine glass (the tool is also called a **battledore**).

Associations

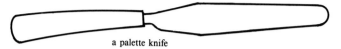

a palette knife

A **palette knife** is a multi-purpose knife with a flexible blade which is used for mixing paints, applying impasto paint to a canvas or scraping paint from a palette.

Panorama

Pronounced: PAN-A-RAMA (*1st a as in ran, 2nd a as in ago,. 3rd a as in far, 4th a as in ago*)

Origin

From the Greek *pan* meaning *all* and *horama* meaning *a view*. Robert Baker (English 1739-1866) invented the first moving panorama by attaching a series of paintings to each other on a moving drum.

Meaning

A panorama is a picture (usually of a landscape) which depicts a very wide view of scenery or of action. It attempts to give a complete survey of a scene. Originally, it was a number of paintings arranged for presentation in a circle which surrounded spectators who stood inside the circle.

Associations

See: **plein air, landscape, water colour, cone of vision**.

Pantograph

Pronounced: PANT-A-GRAF (*1st a as in mat, 2nd a as in ago, 3rd a as in raft*)

Origin

From the Greek *pantos* meaning *all* and *graphe* meaning *writing* or *drawing*. That is a device which is able to draw (copy) all that is in front of the artist. It was invented by a German, Christopher Scheiner, in 1603.

Meaning

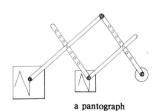

a pantograph

A pantograph is an instrument for making copies of drawings on a different scale from the original drawing; that is enlarging or reducing a drawing. It can also be used to distort the proportions of a picture or design. It is available in different standards from a simple, inexpensive toy to a high-grade, professional precision instrument. It has four hinged sections with a tracing point at one end and a pencil at the other. The hinges can be adjusted to control the scale of the copy.

Associations
See: **squaring, pointing, facsimile, replica, camera obscura.**

Paper

Pronounced: PAPA (*1st a as in late, 2nd a as in ago*)

Origin
From the Greek *papuros* meaning a *reed* and the Latin *papyrus* meaning a reed which grew on the banks of the River Nile in Egypt, from which the writing material *papyrus* was made. Much of the literature of the Ancient Greeks was written on Egyptian papyrus. Paper was invented by the Chinese hundreds of years before the birth of Christ and was used by the Ancient Egyptians, the Romans and the Greeks. The invention of paper using vegetable fibre (that is as we make it) is attributed to Ts'ai Lun, a servant in the court of the Chinese Emperor in A.D. 105. The Chinese also invented the processes of sizing and coating paper. It took about a thousand years for paper to reach Europe, via what we now call the countries of the Middle East. The first paper-mill in Europe was in Spain about 1150, and from there the manufacture of paper spread throughout Europe. All paper was hand-made until the 19th century. The first paper-making machine was invented by a Frenchman, Nicholas-Louis Robert, in 1798 and this machine was developed by Henry and Sealy Fourdrinier in England in 1810. Machines based on the Fourdrinier type of machine are still in use.

Meaning
Paper for printing purposes is made from vegetable fibres (cellulose) which range widely in variety, including wood, esparto grass, cotton, linen, straw, bamboo, bagasse (from sugar cane), and even nettles. Mechanical wood pulp was first used in 1847. The fibres are pulped and added to water and often other materials (e.g. size) and chemicals. The pulp is then drawn through a fine mesh. One fibre or a combination of fibres may be used. The fibres used determine the type of paper produced since different fibres have different characteristics. Some papers used in art, craft and design are: **cartridge paper** (so called because it was originally used for making cartridge bullets), which is a closely-woven, well-sized, fairly heavy paper which is used for drawing, envelopes and some off-set printing work; **calendered paper** (from the Greek *kalindos* which means a *cylinder* or *roller*) is paper which has been pressed through steel rollers (called **calenders**) to produce smooth paper with a glossy surface. The more a paper is **calendered**, the more it is glazed and the better it will take

half-tones; **machine-coated paper** is paper which is coated on both sides mechanically with a mineral, often china clay, which produces a smooth, glazed surface, ideal for fine-screen half-tones and lithographic plates. This paper is also termed **art paper**. **Matt paper** is **art paper** without a glaze. It usually needs a coarser screen than coated paper for half-tones. The best-quality paper is made from cotton rags (not rags from synthetic materials, which are of no use for paper making), but such paper may cost as much as six times the price of paper made from wood. The making of hand-made paper of superb quality in fairly substantial quantities is now to be found only in Japan.

Associations

A **watermark** is a shape which is imprinted into paper, usually near the edge of the paper, both for advertising and security purposes. Most paper dimensions are laid down by the International Organisation for Standardisation (I.S.O.), in order to ensure that the sizes of paper are rationalised from one country to another.

See: **deckle, couch, half-tone**.

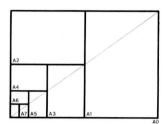

"A" series paper format

	mm		mm
A0	841 x 1189	A4	210 x 297
A1	594 x 841	A5	148 x 210
A2	420 x 594	A6	105 x 148
A3	297 x 420	A7	74 x 105

Papier Collé

Pronounced: PAPI-A (*1st a as in tap, i as in pin, 2nd a as in late*), KOLA (*o as in solid, a as in late*)

Origin

From the French *papier* meaning *paper* and *collé* meaning *pasted* or *glued*. The technique was first used by Georges Braque, a French painter, in 1913, when he used pieces of wallpaper in a still-life painting. The technique was then used by Pablo Picasso and other artists.

Meaning

Papier collé is a **collage** technique in which bits of paper, often of different textures, are glued to a picture to become a significant part of the total composition. It refers, too, to a way of preparing a design for a stained-glass window.

Associations

See the works of Georges Braque (1882-1963) and Jean Arp (1887-1966).

See: **collage, decollage**.

Papier Maché

Pronounced: PAPI-A (*1st a as in tap, i as in pin, 2nd a as in late*), MASH-A (*1st a as in lash, 2nd a as in late*)

Origin

From the French *papier* meaning *paper* and *maché*

papier maché finger puppets
by Chris Burfield

meaning *chewed up*. The craft began in China and spread to Japan, India, Persia and Burma. It became popular in Europe and in England in the 18th century. The term *papier maché* was first used not in France, as one would suppose, but in England in the 18th century, where paper pulp was called *chewed paper*. French emigrés working in England used the French words for chewed paper, which is *papier maché* and the term became popular. It was first made in England by John Baskerville (1706-1775). In 1772, Henry Clay of Birmingham, England patented a method of making papier maché which was so hard that it could be treated as wood. It was superseded by plywood, which was much more flexible.

Meaning

Papier maché is made from torn up paper which is added to water until the paper is thoroughly soaked. An adhesive, such as glue or water paste, is added. Sometimes chalk or sand are added to the mixture to give it strength, bulk or texture. Objects can be constructed by placing

155

soaked strips of pasted paper or papier maché paste to frames or an **armature**. It can be baked to such hardness that it can be drilled, if necessary, and it can be readily sanded and painted. When it has been painted it can be water-proofed with varnish or a fixative. In the past, hundreds of different things were made from it, including furniture, writing desks, and even houses.

Associations

See: **sculpture, armature, size, varnish**

Pastels

Pronounced: PAS-TALS (*a as in cat, a as in ago*)

Origin

From the Italian *pastello* meaning *pasta* or *paste*. Pastels were originally made from paste mixed with pigment and a gum solution. They were first used by artists in the 16th century (e.g. by Hans Holbein).

Meaning

Pastel crayons or chalks are made from dry powder colour mixed with gum. As they contain a minimum of binder, the degree of purity is high. The word pastel also refers to the technique of producing works using pastel paint. Work with pastels is often called **pastel painting** because colour is applied by mass not, as in drawing, by line. Pastel work must be sprayed lightly with a fixative or sealant (e.g. varnish or shellac) on completion as the paint turns to powder as it dries and it tends to smudge when touched. The work is best preserved under glass. Pastels are best used with paper which has a fairly rough-textured surface to which the pastel colours will readily stick. Pastel colours cannot be blended but, as manufacturers produce a wide range of tints for each colour, blending effects can be achieved by the smoothing of tints into each other and also by **cross hatching** and **optical mixing** (See **pointillism**). Oil-based pastels are available which are made from powder colours with an oil binder. Unlike crayon pastels, they blend easily, do not smudge, can be used on all kinds of surfaces (even stone), dry slowly and, like oil paints, can be scraped off and readily altered. They produce surface effects similar to those produced by oil paints.

Associations

One of the masters of the pastel painting technique (a **pastellist**) was the French artist Edgar Degas (1834-1917). See also the work of Maurice-Quentin Latour (1704-1788) and Jean-Baptiste Chardin (1699-1779).

See: **oil paint, cross hatching, medium, vehicle, Pointillism, pigment, mass, optical**.

Pastiche

Pronounced: PA-STEESH (*a as in cat, ee as in see, sh as in ship*)

Origin
From the Italian *pasticcio* meaning *pasta* or *paste*.

Meaning
Pastiche means things pasted together. It is a painting comprising features, motifs or mannerisms taken from the works of other painters and presented as an original work, or acknowledged by the originator as an imitation.

Associations
See: **facture, palette, style, motif.**

Pattern

Pronounced: PAT-AN (*1st a as in cat, 2nd a as in ago*)

Origin
From the Medieval English word *patron* meaning *master* (one who protects). The meaning has changed and now means the master or influential design which stands out in a work by its regular occurrence. Patterns have been used in art from the earliest times. Geometric patterns were made on potteryware in China 6000 years ago.

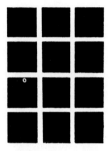

a pattern

Meaning
Pattern refers to the visual forms or motifs which appear regularly in a composition, design or environment in a systematic manner. Also, when elements such as colour, texture, size, volume, direction, shape, position, space are repeated, a pattern is created. Pattern also refers to the term to describe the form of wood or styrofoam which is used to form a mould in sand before molten metal is cast in a **sand casting** process.

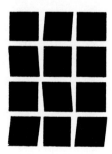

anomaly in a pattern

Associations
Granulation refers to a pattern of tiny balls as decoration on metal.

See: **composition, elements, symmetry, facsimile, replica, gradation, frieze, motif, Art Nouveau, Art Deco, design.**

Perception

Pronounced: PUR-SEP-SHUN (*u as in fur, e as in left, u as in fun*)

Origin
From the Latin *percipio* meaning *to take in* or *grasp with the mind*.

Meaning
Perception is the result of reacting mentally to some sensory stimulation (e.g. a sound, a smell or what is seen

Edgar Rubin's "Reversible Vase", which can be seen as either a vase or the silhouettes of two faces.

or touched). A **concept** is the idea, perception is the mental, physical and emotional result of an action to grasp the idea. Our perceptions are determined to a large extent by our culture and upbringing. For example, the Western World perceives space and depth in paintings in a different way from the Eastern World (e.g. China). Our perception of perspective, where parallel lines appear to converge in the distance, is an aspect of Western culture. When studying the art of other civilisations or cultures, we should take into account their perceptions of reality, which may differ fundamentally from ours.

Associations

Illusion is the perception of an object, involving an understanding or belief which is false. For example, **linear perspective** in a painting is not based on actuality but is an illusion.

See: **plasticity, perspective, illusion, aesthetics, foreshortening, chiaroscuro**.

Periodic Table

Pronounced: PEAR-I-OD-IK (*ea as in fear, i as in pin, o as in rod, i as in brick*), TA-BAL (*1st a as in late, 2nd a as in ago*)

Origin

Periodic is from the Greek *peri* meaning *around* or *about* and *odos* meaning *the way*. That is, literally, *the way around*, a revolution and then a regular occurrence. A periodic table, as a classified arrangement of chemical elements and those elements which have similar characteristics, was part of a *Periodic Law* propounded by Dimitri Ivanovich Mendeleev (1834-1907).

Meaning

A potter's periodic table is adapted from Mendeleev's original table. The table tells a potter what a mineral contains chemically and he can then predict what the separate constituents of a mineral will do (That is the chemical reaction that takes place.) in the mixing, glazing and firing proces when producing potteryware.

Associations

See: **pottery, firing, glaze, pyrometry**.

Perspective

Pronounced: PUR-SPEK-TIV (*u as in fur, e as in neck, i as in ink*)

Origin

From the Latin *per* meaning *by means of* and *spectare* meaning *to look* (Think of *spectator*.) and also *perspectum* meaning *to look or see through*.

The term was first used in the 5th century B.C. by the Athenian painter Agatharcus. Its principles were explained by the Greek mathematician Euclid. The basic rules of perspective, however, were first stated during the Renaissance by Italian artists Filippo Brunelleschi (1377-1446), Leone Battista Alberti (1404-1472), Piero della Francesca (1410-1492) and by Paulo Uccello (1397-1475), who is usually recognised as the author of the formula explaining perspective. The theory and the rules propounded have been developed over the years.

Meaning

Perspective is a man-made concept and technique by which three-dimensional objects or space can be visually represented on a flat (or nearly flat, i.e. a relief carving) surface. The aim of perspective is to create the **illusion** that the objects or people drawn have the same relative positions and sizes as the objects or people have in reality- when viewed from one specific point. To get the three-dimensional illusion, the artist must first draw a series of parallel lines which converge at a single point on the horizon (called the **vanishing point**). Between the lines, objects or people are drawn that gradually diminish in size. The key to perspective is this decreasing in size, which creates the illusion of **depth** and a three-dimensional effect. Early systems of perspective had only a single, central vanishing point (sometimes called **one point perspective**); later systems had two or more vanishing points, in order to attempt to produce greater naturalism. **Linear perspective** describes the system of parallel lines given above. **Aerial perspective** (first used by Leonardo da Vinci), which is also called **atmospheric perspective**, is a system to create the impression of distance and depth by gradually decreasing the clarity and colour brightness and contrast of objects and people, especially making them a hazy blue, as distance from the spectator seems to increase. Mountains in the distance, for example, should appear bluish in a painting. Leonardo da Vinci (1452-1519) advised painters to make the nearest building distinct and its real colour but the most distant buildings much less distinct and bluer. **Textural perspective** creates the illusion of distance and depth by gradually changing the textural appearance of things from sharply defined to hazy and dense. For example, the rough individual bricks in a house near the observer should be seen clearly with their mottled colours; bricks in a house in the distance should fuse into a smooth, one-colour wall.

Most abstract artists defy representation of a third dimension and create their own interpretations of the physical world in an individualistic manner. So, perspective has no importance to them.

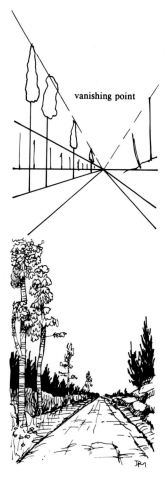

vanishing point

one point perspective

Scenography is the art of drawing in perspective.
Sterography is the art of representing the form of solids on a plane surface.

See: *"The Mill"* by Claude Lorrain (1600-1682), *"Mont Sainte Victoire"* by Paul Cezanne (1839-1906) and *"Christ"* by Andrea Mantegna (1431-1506).

Photogram

Pronounced: FOTO-GRAM (*o's as in go, a as in lamb*)

Origin

From the Greek *photos* meaning *light* and *gramma* meaning *thing written or recorded.* In 1803 two Englishmen, Thomas Wedgwood and the chemist Humphry Davis, produced images of leaves and insect wings by placing them directly on sensitised paper and then exposing them to sunlight. The images, however, were not fixed and disappeared. In 1839, William Henry Fox Talbot, an Englishman, who invented the negative-positive process of photography, placed a piece of lace on a sheet of light-sensitive paper and produced the first photogram. Later, artists among whom were Man Ray (American 1890-1976) and Lazlo Maholy-Nagy (Hungarian 1895-1946), refined and developed the camera-less photographic process. Moholy-Nagy coined the term *photogram* for the process.

Meaning

A photogram is the production of an image, without the use of a camera, by placing objects or making illustrations on transparent paper and then placing the paper on light-sensitive paper in a dark room and exposing it to a beam of light (e.g. from an enlarger, a desk light or a torch). The photographic paper is then developed and printed. Also, printing out paper (also called studio-proof paper), which has a low sensitivity to light, may be used for a design in subdued light and then taken out into sunlight for exposure.

Associations

See: **negative, bromide, monoprint**.

Pickle

Pronounced: PI-KAL (*i as in pin, a as in ago*)

Origin

From the Old English *pekille* or Old Dutch *pekel* meaning *a salt (brine) or vinegar liquid* for preserving meat, fish, vegetables, etc..

Meaning

Pickle refers to an acid solution used in all kinds of metal work, including precious metals. It usually comprises either ten parts of water and one part of sulphuric acid or eight parts of water and one part of nitric acid. It is used to clean metals after an annealing process, before vitreous enamelling to ensure a secure bond between enamel and metal, to clean oxide or flux from silver, and to prepare metals for soldering.

Associations

See: **annealing, solder, vitreous, enamel, oxidation, flux.**

Pigments

Pronounced: PIG-MANTS (*i as in pig, a as in ago*)

Origin

From the Latin *pigmentum* meaning *paint*. The first pigments were made from natural things, such as clays, soot, rocks, insects and plants. The first synthetic pigments were developed by an English Chemist, William Perkin, who discovered the dye **mauveine**.

Meaning

Light is the source of all colour and pigments are substances which reflect, absorb or transmit colour. There are pigment molecules in everything (except transparent substances, such as water, air or pure diamonds) and they vary in form enormously, so some absorb or reflect a certain number of colours of the spectrum, some another number of colours. Daffodils, for example, have in them a pigment of yellow which they reflect and transmit to us. Pigments in art refer to the colouring matter in paints or dyes, which are made from earths, animal and plant tissues, or chemicals. The pigments are usually added to a liquid such as water or oil and mixed to produce paint.

Associations

See: **colour, oxidation, palette, dye.**

Pinch Pot

Pronounced: PINCH (*i as in ink*), POT (*o as in got*)

Origin

From the Old French *pincier* meaning *to squeeze* or *nip*.

Meaning

A pinch pot is a ceramic pot made by the hand-building method of kneading clay and then pinching it with thumb and fingers into the required shape. Simple pinch pots are especially suitable for sawdust, raku and other simple firings.

a pinch pot

Associations

A pinch pot is also called a **thumb pot**.
See: **kneading, raku, coiling, wedging, slabbing**.

Pixelated Images

Pronounced: PIX-I-LA-TAD (*i's as in ink, 1st a as in late, 2nd a as in ago*), IMA-JIS (*i as in ink, a as in ago, i as in is*)

Origin

Pixelated derives from *pixels* which comes from two words, namely *picture elements*, where the common abbreviation of *pix* is used for *picture*.

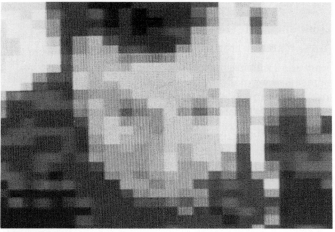

pixelated image of a man's face

Meaning

Pixelated images (pixelisation) are produced by a computer programmed to create graphic material. The process involves the breaking down of an image, or small part of an image, into tiny areas called **pixels** (picture elements), where each pixel can be made one of many hues. A pixel can be 0.1 millimetres, or less, in length. That is 100 pixels to a square millimetre. The images on a screen are abstract in that they comprise thousands of minute squares. The technique is invaluable in restoration work of valuable paintings where small areas of paint have to be analysed. The more pixels there are on a visual display unit, the higher the degree of clarity and **resolution**. Computer graphic displays range, at present, from 320 by 200 pixels (which is a low resolution) up to 1024 by 768 pixels.

Associations

Pixelated is not to be confused with **pixilated**, as the word spelled with an *i* means crazy or drunk!

See: **Graphic Design, Computer Graphics**.

Plane

Pronounced: PLAN (*a as in fame*)

Origin

From the Latin *planus* meaning *a flat and level surface*.

Meaning

A plane is a two-dimensional shape on the surface of a painting which gives no indication of volume, depth or projection but which when combined with other shapes placed beyond the picture plane (particularly when overlapping occurs) can give the illusion of depth and three-dimensional space. Some paintings, particularly landscapes, are arranged with different planes which give the illusion of areas being some distance behind each other. Planes are part of the construction of a composition and are not so much seen as felt. The planes which give direction can be in various positions in a composition, such as horizontal, vertical, diagonal etc.. A plane has been called the **window** through which an artist sees the world.

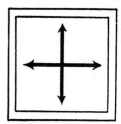

a picture with horizontal and vertical planes

Associations

See: **projection, illusion, composition, landscape, space, elevation**.

Planograph

Pronounced: PLAN-A-GRAF (*1st a as in cat, 2nd as as in ago, 3rd a as in staff*)

Origin

From the Latin *planus* meaning *a flat and level surface* and the Greek *graphe* meaning *writing* or *drawing*.

Meaning

Planograph refers to any method of non-relief printing (i.e. aquatone, collotype, lithograph or silkscreening) from a flat surface. The area of the plate to take ink is on the same level as the areas which stay uninked.

Associations

Intaglio is printing below the surface of a plate; **relief** is printing above the surface of a plate.

See: **printing, lithography, silk screening, aquatone**.

Plastic Arts

Pronounced: PLAS-TIK (*a as in plaster, i as in ink*), ARTS (*a as in far*)

Origin

Plastic is from the Greek *plastikos* meaning *that can be*

moulded or shaped from *plassein* meaning *to mould or shape.*

Meaning

Plastic arts refers to those arts which involve modelling from materials which can be readily carved or moulded into three-dimensional forms (e.g. sculpture and ceramics). The term is also sometimes used generally to distinguish the visual arts from the performing arts, such as music, dance and drama.

Associations

See: **sculpture, glyptic, ceramics.**

Plasticity

Pronounced: PLAS-TIS-ITY (*a as in plaster, i's as in ink, y as in duty*

Origin

From the Greek *plastikos* meaning *that can be moulded or shaped* from *plassein* meaning *to mould* or *shape.* The term was first applied to the analysis of art by Heinrich Wölfflin (1864-1945), who probably more than anyone established descriptive terminology to analyse art.

Meaning

Plasticity refers to the pliability and elasticity of a material which can be pressed, hammered or moulded into a required shape. If, for example, clay is shaped into a long, thin roll around one's finger, it has good plasticity if no cracks appear in the clay. It also refers to an illusion of three-dimensional form on a two-dimensional surface by the use of visual techniques.

Associations

See: **illusion, manipulation, shape, stamp, coil, kneading, sculpture, glyptic.**

Plein Air

Pronounced: PLAN (*a as in care*), AR (*a as in fare*)

Origin

From the French for *open air.* The expression *en plein air* meaning *in the open air* was used during the second half of the 19th century to describe paintings produced outdoors. The outdoor work was probably started by François Desportes in the early 18th century but later became an important part of the Impressionist movement's beliefs.

Meaning

Plein air refers to paintings produced in the open air, rather than in a studio. New techniques were developed and attitudes formed as the artists were influenced by the light, the atmosphere and environment surrounding them. The French artists who worked *en plein air* (e.g. Rousseau, Millet, Diaz, Carot) became known as the **Barbizon School**, after the village of Barbizon near Fontainebleau, where they met to discuss their art. The phrase also refers to landscape paintings produced in a studio but using techniques which have the effect of suggesting that the paintings were produced in the open air.

Associations

See the work of the Impressionist **plein artistes**: Claude Millet (1840-1926), Camille Pissarro (1830-1903), Pierre Auguste Renoir (1841-1919), Alfred Sisley (1839-1899), Jean Carot (1796-1875), Theodore Rousseau (1812-1867).

See: **Impressionism, landscape, water colour, panorama, pastels, pointillism.**

Pointillism

Pronounced: PWAN-TA-LIZM (*1st a as in pan, 2nd a as in ago, i as in pin, zm as sm in prism*)

Origin

From the French *pointillisme* from *pointiller* meaning *to mark with dots or points*. The French art critic Felix Feneon in 1886 used the phrase *peinture au point* meaning *painting by dots* to describe a painting by Georges Seurat. The phrase was abbreviated to *pointillisme* to describe the technique used by the Neo-Impressionist painters

Meaning

The **Impressionist** painters used a technique where they juxtaposed different shades and tones of pure colours, as this produced more brilliant colours for spectators than the mixing of colours or using colours separately. This is termed **optical mixing**. The **Neo-Impressionist** artists developed this technique by applying uniform dots of pure spectral colour or white to a canvas with the point of a brush. As the dots were *divided*, many of the painters referred to the technique as **divisionism** but the term **pointillism** became more popular. Pointillism relies on distance for its effect. Viewed close up, the separate dots can be seen, but from a distance an effect of brilliant, vibrant mixtures of colour are achieved.

Charles Ginner, Great Britain 1878 - 1952 *Battersea Park* oil on canvas 87.0 x 50.0 cm *Art Gallery of South Australia, Adelaide, South Australia*

Associations

Stippled and **dappled** also mean to mark with dots.

See the works of Georges Seurat (1859-1891), Paul Signac (1863-1935), Camille Pissarro (1830-1903).

See: **Neo-Impressionism, juxtaposition, colour, plein air.**

Pointing

Pronounced: POYNT-ING (*oy as in boy*)

Origin

From the French *point* meaning *dot* or *small mark*.

Meaning

Pointing is a process of copying or enlarging a modelled or carved sculpture by marking points on the original work and then marking points on the same scale or an enlarged scale in exactly the same positions on the copy. The measurements and pointings are repeated throughout the operation where a carving is being made to ensure accuracy in the transfer of the details.

Associations

Pointing is the three-dimensional equivalent of **squaring**.

See: **replica, facsimile, proportion**.

Polygon

Pronounced: POLY-GON (*o's as in got, y as in duty*)

Origin

From the Greek *polus* meaning *many* and *gonos* meaning *angle*.

Meaning

A polygon is a geometric figure with many (usually more than four) angles and sides. The following are polygons:

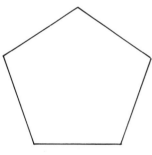

pentagon

tetragon.- a four sided figure which includes the square, rectangle, quadrangle, rhombus and parallelogram;

pentagon - a five sided figure with five equal interior angles. (See the Pentagon Building in Washington, U.S.A.);

hexagon - a six sided, six angled figure; (It is also called a **hexagram**. The star of David which appears on Israel's national flag is a hexagram.)

heptagon - a seven sided, seven angled figure;

octagon - an eight sided, eight angled figure;

nonagon - a nine sided, nine angled figure;

decagon - a ten sided, ten angled figure;

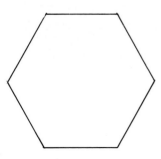

hexagon

dodecagon - a twelve sided, twelve angled figure.

Polyhedron

Pronounced: POLY-HEE-DRAN (*o as in got, y as in duty, ee as in see, a as in ago*)

Origin

From the Greek *polus* meaning *many* and *hedra* meaning *a base*.

Meaning

A polyhedron is a **solid** figure with many bases or faces. The following are polyhedrons:

tetrahedron - with four faces (bases) or triangles;

pentahedron - with five faces;

hexahedron - with six faces (e.g. a cube);

heptahedron - with seven faces;

octahedron - with eight faces;

decahedron - with ten faces;

dodecahedron - with twelve faces;

icosahedron - with twenty faces.

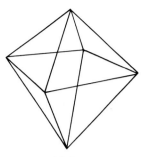

octahedron

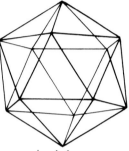
icosahederon

Pop Art

Pronounced: POP (*o as in got*), ART (*a as in far*)

Origin

Pop is the abbreviation of *popular*. Pop Art was a movement, inspired by the *Ready Mades* of the French artist Marcel Duchamp (1887-1968), which began in England in the mid 1950's and was developed in the U.S.A., especially in New york, in the late 1950's and the mid 1960's, when it gave way to Minimalist Art and Hard Edged Painting. The word *pop* was first used by Lawrence Alloway, an English art critic, to describe the art which was based on popular culture. The first exhibition of Pop Art, called "*This is Tomorrow*", took place in London in 1956.

Meaning

Pop Art refers to works of art (paintings, sculptures, silkscreen prints, collages, assemblages, photographs) which use imagery from mass culture (e.g. films, television, comics, advertising, pin-ups, packaging, super-markets, science fiction) and the commercial world. It opposed the acceptable tastes of the conventional, established art world. Artists' sources of inspiration were often things found where the artists lived or socialised, such as magazines, household goods, and take-away food, comic strips from newspapers, commercial art work and manufactured products. It juxtaposed common objects into new relationships, mixed different art mediums (e.g. photography with painting). Often a common object, such as a can of soup was blown up pictorially to gigantic sizes. (See Andy Warhol's huge can of Campbell's soup). The techniques were deliberately "gimmicky" and aimed to appeal to the mass of the public. The artists were sometimes referred to as the *Neo-Realists* or *Neo-Dadaists*.

Associations
See the works of Ray Lichtenstein, Claes Oldenburg, Willem de Kooning, Eduardo Paolozzi, Jasper Johns, Richard Hamilton, Allen Jones, Richard Smith, Peter Blake, Robert Rauschenberg, Andy Warhol, George Segal.

See: **collage, assemblage, objet trouvé, Dadaism.**

Porcelain

Pronounced: POR-SA-LAN (*o as in port, 1st a as in ago, 2nd a as in cane*)

Origin
The true origin of the word is not known. Some say it originated with the Portugese word for cowrie shell, *porcella* (which means *little pig*, because the cowrie shell resembles a little pig), because the portugese explorer and adventurer Marco Polo (1254-1324) thought the inside of the shell resembled the surface of porcelain. Others say the word originated in France, as mention is made of *porcelaine* in French documents in 1360. Recent excavations in China revealed white clay pottery and the earliest types of porcelain (called proto-porcelain), which date from the Sang Dynasty of 16th-11th century B.C.. It was probably imported into Europe in the 14th century. The secrets of its manufacture were not known in Europe until the 18th century. Johann Freiderich Böttger (1685-1719) is usually credited with being the first person to make porcelain in Europe in 1708. On the strength of his discovery, the now famous ceramic factory at Meissen in Germany was opened in 1710.

Meaning
Porcelain is pottery which is fired at 1250°c-1400°c. It is also called *china ware*. It is made from **kaolin**, a white clay made from silicate, aluminium, feldspar and quartz (flint) into vitreous ware. **Hard porcelain** contains 50% kaolin, 25% quartz and 25% feldspar. **Soft porcelain** contains 25% kaolin, 45% quartz and 30% feldspar. Soft porcelain is fired at a lower temperature than hard porcelain and is, therefore, much cheaper to produce. It is very hard, white, scratch-proof, resistant to acid and does not absorb liquids. It is translucent when held to the light and gives a ringing tone when struck with one's finger nail. Porcelain was called *tzu* in Chinese, which can be

Chelsea Derby, Great Britain 1769 - 1784 *Boy and Girl* porcelain Art Gallery of South Australia, Adelaide, South Australia

translated as "that which resonates when it is struck". It can be shaped by moulding, modelling or by being thrown on a wheel and it can be decorated by glazing, sprigging and transfer printing.

Associations

The adjectives to describe porcelain are **porcellanic** and **porcellaneous**.

See: **sprigging, vitreous, kaolin, jigger, jolley, translucent.**

Porosity

Pronounced: POR-OS-ITY (*1st o as in more, 2nd o as in loss, i as in pin, y as in duty*)

Origin

From the Greek *poros* meaning a *passage*. Eventually, it came to mean that an object which had passages in its material along which liquid could flow was *porous* and had *porosity*.

Meaning

Porosity means that an object has pores, like pores in human skin, which are minute holes (*passages*) through which fluids may pass. Porosity is necessary in clay, as if clay is too tightly packed, it cracks as it dries. Porosity is a measure of the number of pores in a specific area of a ware. It indicates the amount of liquid absorption of a ware. Bisque ware has porosity but vitreous ware, such as porcelain, has no porosity. Porosity occurs not only in ceramics but also in shells and in some metals. If pottery is fired below 1000°c, it retains its porosity.

Pinhole porosity refers to a fault in metal casting where small holes appear in metal, owing to to the escape of gas in the metal as it cools and shrinks.

Associations

See: **bisque, vitreous, pinchpot, potteryware.**

Portrait

Pronounced: POR-TRAT (*o as in more, a as in late*)

Origin

From the French *pourtraire* meaning *to draw forth, reveal or portray*. *Portrait* is the French for *a likeness*.
Portraiture (the art of producing portraits) began in Ancient Egyptian civilization, when the portraits were idealised representations of notable people (as they were in Ancient Roman and Greek times and the Medieval period), rather than realistic likenesses. During the Renaissance period, portraits gained much popularity among the wealthy (there was no photography). The

artists problem then and later was whether to portray honestly or tactfully!

Meaning

A portrait is a drawing, painting, modelling or carving, which clearly represents or identifies a sitter-the subject of the portrait. It usually (although not always, as in, for example, Cubism) provides a recognisable likeness of the sitter and also a heightened image in that it evokes a powerful sense of life. It depicts more than photographic realism and should give us some understanding of the character of the person (or animal) portrayed.

Associations

A **portraitist** is someone who produces **portraits** or **portraiture**. **Limning** is an old-fashioned term for painting miniature portraits, which appears to be coming back into common usage to mean **drawing**.

See the works of Leonardo da Vinci, Rembrandt, Hans Holbein, Franz Hals, and Reynolds.

See: **bust, life-drawing, realism, silhouette**.

opposite

Michael van Mierveld, The Nederlands 1567-1641 **George Villier, Duke of Buckingham** *Oil on wood panel 69.5 x 57.5 cm. Art Gallery of South Australia, Adelaide, South Australia Government Grant, 1967*

Positive

Pronounced: POS-A-TIV (*o as in loss, a as in ago, i as in give*)

Origin

From the Latin *positus* meaning *to place firmly* and then *positif* meaning *capable of being affirmed*; that is not negative. It came to mean to place something firmly in place, then to say something affirmatively. The use of *positive* in photography goes back to the invention of photography. Joseph Nicéphore Niépce (1765-1833), a Frenchman, was the first person to fix an image permanently when he made a photograph on a metal plate in 1826. His collaborator Louis-Jacques-Mandé Daguerre (1787-1851) produced the first negative, called a *daguerrotype*, in 1839. This was the first commercially-feasible process of obtaining photographic images on a metal plate. The method produced only one print and it was obsolete by 1860, when the collodion (wet-plate) method was invented which allowed multiple prints to be made from one negative. In 1839, an English mathematician, William Henry Fox Talbot (1800-1877), perfected the callotype process of taking positive prints from negatives produced on glass.

Meaning

Positive refers to a photographic print or plate which shows light and dark values as they occur in the original image being photographed. It means also a model (carved, modelled or cast) from which a mould is made in order

171

to reproduce the model form. It is the opposite of a **negative**.

Associations

See: **negative, half-tone, space**.

Poster designed by Janet Stone, graphic designer, South Australia

Poster

Pronounced: POSTA (*o as in go, a as in ago*)

Origin

A poster was originally a notice or *bill* which was fixed to a *post* to make a public statement.

Meaning

A poster is a placard (or post-bill) which is put up on a wall, using plaster glue, to advertise a product or an event or to inform the general public of something. The purpose of a poster is to attract people, so that they will see the message given on it. A Poster must, therefore, be visually attractive and decorative and also must use language that is not obscure but is readily understood by everybody. It must make instant contact with the viewer it is aimed at. It is the combination of words and visual images which give the poster its unique characteristics. Some posters are works of art in their own right.

Associations

The French for *poster* is *affiche* and a painter of posters in France is called an **affichiste**.

See the works of Alphonse Mucha (Czechoslovak 1860-1939), Henri de Toulouse-Lautrec (French 1864-1901), Frank Pick (British 1878-1941), Privat Livemont (Belgian 1861-1936), Maxfield Parrish (American 1870-1966), Aubrey Beardsley (British 1872-1898), Jean Lurçat (French 1892-1966).

See: **Graphic Design, lithography, Op Art, Pop Art**.

Post-Impressionism

Pronounced: POST (*o as in go*), IM-PRESH-A-NIZM (*i as in limb, e as in fresh, a as in ago, last i as in pin, zm as sm in prism*)

Origin

The term Post Impressionism was first used by an English Art critic called Roger Fry (1866-1936) in 1910 to describe an exhibition which he mounted called "*Manet and the Post-Impressionists*". He used the term as (to use his words) "*the vaguest and most non-commital*" to use. The term was not used during the time the artists in the movement were painting but some time after the event, as the Post-Impressionist period lasted from 1886 up to about 1906 when Paul Cezanne, a leading artist of the time, died.

Meaning

The term Post-Impressionism is used to describe the work of major artists who developed the work of the **Impressionists**. The emphasis of the Impressionists had been on colour and this stress had been developed by the **Neo-Impressionists**. The emphasis of the Post-Impressionists was on form and subject, as well as on colour. Paul Cezanne said, *"Everything in nature is based on the sphere, the cone and the cylinder"*. Painters were more concerned to consider the essential form and basic structure of subjects than their surface appearance. At the same time, they expressed their own personal reactions to a subject. The artists of this relatively brief period were not closely linked in style.

Associations

See the work of Paul Cezanne (French 1839-1906), Vincent Van Gough (Dutch 1853-1890) and Paul Gauguin (French 1848-1903). These artists gave impetus to **Cubism**, **Expressionism** and **Symbolism**.

See: **Impressionism, Neo-Impressionism, form**.

Potter's Wheel

Pronounced: POTAZ (*o as in lot, a as in ago*), WEEL (*ee as in see*)

Origin

The first potter's wheel was probably used in Mesopotamia (now Iraq) in about 4000 B.C.. It first appeared in Ancient Egypt in 2750 B.C., in Greece in 1800 B.C., in Italy in 750 B.C. and in Southern England in 50 B.C.. It was also used in Ancient times in Japan and India.

Meaning

Basically, a potter's wheel comprises a rotating disc onto which a bat of clay is centred and which is then shaped by the potter's hands or with tools. This process is called **throwing** a pot. The device, which is also called a **kick-wheel**, can be rotated either by electrical power or by the potter's foot on a footbar, which activates a fly-wheel. It leaves the potter's hands free to shape a pot. Where a footbar is used, the speed of the rotating disc can be controlled by adjusting the rapidity with which the footbar is pushed. Most wheels today are power-driven. Only symmetrical pots, spherical in shape, can be produced using a wheel; other shapes are made by moulding and handbuilding.

Associations

See: **bat, manipulation, throwing, jolley, symmetrical**.

Pottery

Pronounced: POT-A-RY (*o as in lot, a as in ago, y as in duty*)

Origin

From the Old English *pott* and the Old Dutch *pot* meaning *a rounded vessel of earthenware.* The earliest *fired* clay was produced between 8000 and 7000 B.C. in Jericho, Israel and pottery vessels have been found in Turkey, dating back to 7000 B.C. Painted potteryware with geometric decorative patterns and with contrasting dark and light lines have been excavated in China and date from about 4000 years ago. Pottery has been found in China with marks and signs (probably early writing) which date from about 6000 years ago and which indicates that pottery making had been mastered at that time.

Meaning

Pottery refers to objects, both functional and decorative, made from porous clays (e.g. earthenware, stoneware and raku) which have been fired in a kiln . Pottery fired at less than 1000°c retains its porosity; at temperatures of 1100°c-1300°c, it becomes more compact and is impervious to water. It is then called stoneware. Porcelain is not usually classified as pottery. A **pottery** is a place where potteryware is created.

Associations

Fictile means made of earth or clay and also relates to a potter and pottery.

See the works of Jean Luce (French 1895-1964), Axel Salto (Danish 1889-1961), William H.Grueby (American 1867-1925), Clarice Cliff (English 1899-1972), Keith Murray (New zealand 1892-1981).

See: **clay, kaolin, potter's wheel, bat, kneading, coiling, wedge, greenware, stoneware, earthenware.**

Pre-Raphaelites

Pronounced: PREE-RAF-A-LITS (*ee as in see, 1st a as in cat, 2nd a as in ago, i as in kite*)

Origin

The Pre-Raphaelite Brotherhood (P.R.B.) was formed in 1840 by a group of English artists, among whom were William Holman Hunt, Sir John Everett Millais, and Dante Gabriel Rossetti. The term **Pre-Raphaelite** was chosen by the group, who it seemed did not have a deep knowledge of art before Raphael (1483-1520) but who had a common dislike for Raphael, whom they considered over-rated. In their opinion, his work lacked sincerity.

Meaning

The characteristics of the Pre-Raphaelites are a love of the Medieval period, a Romantic attitude, a desire to tell a story with a lofty moral or with a poetic theme, the combination of elaborate symbolism with detailed realism, the depiction of scenes from the Bible, Arthurian legends, Shakespeare's plays and other great literature. They believed that everything in their pictures should be painted from nature in front of them and not according to rules. They delighted in the use of brilliant colour with an absence of shadows. The Brotherhood was also interested in the **decorative arts** and helped to form the Arts and Craft movement, led by William Morris (1834-1896). The movement is particularly noted for its book illustrations, by means of wood engravings.

William Holman Hunt, Great Britain 1827 - 1910, *The Risen Christ and the Two Marys in the Garden of Joseph of Aramathea* (detail) oil on canvas 117.5 x 94 cm *Art Gallery of South Australia, Adelaide, South Australia*

Associations

See the work of Dante Rossetti (1828-1882), William Holman Hunt (1827-1910), Sir Edward Burne-Jones (1833-1898), William Morris (1834-1896).

See: **Romanticism, symbol, plein air, Decorative Arts, form.**

Priming

Pronounced: PRIM-ING (*i as in kite*)

Origin

From the Latin *primus* meaning *first*. Priming is the first operation in a task.

Meaning

Priming is the process of applying a primer, a first coat of paint, which acts as a ground to a painting.

Associations

See: **ground, gesso, imprimatura, size, porosity.**

Primitive Art

Pronounced: PRIM-A-TIV (*i's as in ink, a as in ago*)

Origin

From the Latin *primus* meaning *first*. *Prim-itive* means associated with the *first things and events*. Primitive art had its beginnings with cave painters of the earliest hunters about 30,000 B.C.

Meaning

Primitive Art refers to the work of self-taught and unsophisticated artists who have had no formal art training. Their paintings are expressed in very simple forms. It is used also to describe the art of people who have not evolved substantially either socially or artistically over a long period, which includes some people who are still living in tribal groups. It has been used by some art critics to refer to the paintings of artists before 1500, especially those whose styles are archaic, but this use makes very little sense nowadays. Many artists have been influenced by Primitive Art, including Paul Gauguin (1848-1903), the Fauvists, the Expressionists and many contemporary artists.

Associations

See the works of Henri Rousseau (1844-1910), Edward Hicks (1780-1849), and Grandma Moses (real name Ann Mary Robertson, 1860-1961).

Print

Pronounced: PRINT (*i as in ink*)

Origin

From an Old French word *priente* meaning *the impression of a seal*, which comes from the French *preint* meaning *pressed*. Printing was probably first started in China about A.D. 740. Books printed from wooden blocks were made in the 9th century. The invention of moveable print is attributed to Pi-Sheng in China in the 11th century. A number of people contributed to the development of printing presses, including a German, Johann Gensfleisch Gutenberg (1397-1468), who perfected a system using moveable lead type. The first book printed in England was by William Caxton (1412-1492), entitled "*The Game and Play of Chesse*".

a brayer

Meaning

A print is an image made by a process where one surface, which holds or transfers ink, (e.g. a printing plate) presses onto another surface which receives the ink (e.g. paper or fabric). It refers, too, to the reproduction of a number of images by a mechanical image-transfer process, such as by

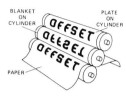

BLANKET ON CYLINDER   PLATE ON CYLINDER

PAPER

off set printing

a letter-press, or by off-set lithography. The main printing processes are: **relief printing** (including letterpress, wood blocks, linocuts), which has a raised printing surface; **intaglio** (including photogravure, engraving, etching and die stamping), which has images below the surface of the plate; **planographic printing** (including off-set lithography and collotype) where the image is on the printing surface; **stencil printing** (including silkscreening and paper stencils), in which stencils prepared by hand or photographically are used.

Associations

Thermography is a printing process where heat is used. **Xerography** is a printing process without the use of ink where an electrically-charged plate is used.

See: **etching, engraving, silkscreen, lino block, printmaking, proof, impression, edition, intaglio, relief, plane, stencil.**

large etching press
*kind permission of
Charles Brand Inc.,
New York*

Lithographic press
*kind permission of
Charles Brand Inc.,
New York*

Printmaking

Pronounced: PRINT-MA-KING (*i's as in ink, a as in late*)

Origin

Printmaking (engraving, etching and woodcuts) began in the Italian Renaissance as a major art form and was helped to develop by the increased availability of paper around 1400. The German artist Albrecht Dürer (1471-1528) and the Dutch artist Hans Holbein (1497-1543) perfected the art of woodcut prints.

Meaning

Printmaking refers to the art of making prints on paper. It is a general term covering engraving, etching, and woodcuts (which date back to the 15th century) lithography (which started in the 18th century) and twentieth century artwork such as lino-cuts and sikscreening (which is invariably referred to as **screenprinting** or **screening** nowadays).

Associations

See: **print, lino-blocks, silksreening, lithography, engraving, etching, drypoint, aquatint, impression, edition, Renaissance, paper.**

Profile

Pronounced: PRO-FIL (*o as in go, i as in mile*)

Origin

From a now obsolete Italian word *profilare* meaning *to draw in outline* and *profilo* meaning *an outline*.

Meaning

A profile is the side view of a person's head and the outline of one side of a form or figure. It is also the form of a moulding in cross section, and a tool or template used in ceramics to shape dishes, cups or bowls, usually as part of a jigger or jolley machine. The profile is the shape of the pottery to be formed.

Associations

See: **silhouette, jigger, portrait, template**

Projection

Pronounced: PRO-JEK-SHUN (*o as in go, e as in let, u as in run*)

Origin

From the Latin *pro* meaning *forward* and *jectum* meaning *thrown*. Thus, to throw ideas forward or to plan or to place something so that it juts out and is conspicuous.

Meaning

A projection, or pictorial view, is the way in which three-dimensional objects are represented on a flat surface, such as on paper. An **orthographic or orthogonal projection** (sometimes called a *working drawing*) is a two-dimensional visual representation of a three-dimensional object, showing separately a plan, a vertical elevation and a section, which have correct scale and positioning, but where there is no convergence of parallel lines. It is probably the most useful projection in that it shows all the information related to shape, dimensions and arrangement of constituent parts. An **isometric projection** is a representation on a flat surface of objects which are arranged in depth but where they are shown in equal scale with no reductions for how they might appear in perspective. Scales of height, width and depth are kept constant. It is useful in that by showing the length, width and thickness of an object it reveals proportion but it does not show the true shape of the object. **Oblique projections** are produced from orthographic flat elevations with the addition and construction of parallel sides drawn at convenient angles, usually 30° or 45°.

Associations

See: **mechanical drawing, plane, perspective, foreshortening, elevation.**

orthographic projection

plan

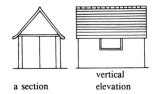

a section

vertical elevation

isometric projection

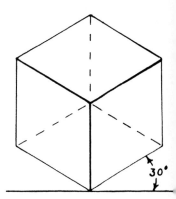

30°

Proof

Pronounced: PROOF (*oo as in roof*)

Origin

From the Old French *prover* meaning *to test* or *approve*.

Meaning

In printing, proof refers to an impression on paper taken from an etching or engraving plate, in order to ascertain the quality of the print and whether the design and medium are satisfactory. It is also another word for a **print**, except that the proof is usually used for revision or experimental purposes. In photography, a proof is a test or trial print. To *pull a proof* is to make a proof. A **pull** is sometimes used for a proof.

Associations

A **counter proof** is a copy proof reproduction of a print, drawing or etching made by the process of damping the work and then pressing it against a clean sheet of paper and then running both through a press. The result is a mirror image of the original. **Touch proof** refers to alterations made to a proof or print by hand. A **maculature** is a faint copy made from a print without the printing plate being re-inked. It is sometimes used as a proof copy.

See: **impression, monoprint, etch, engraving, print**.

Proportion

Pronounced: PRO-POR-SHUN (*1st o as in go, 2nd o as in por, u as in run*)

Origin

From the Old French *portionner* meaning *to share, give a part to*. Since the times if the Ancient Egyptians, artists have attempted to create what appears to the eye to be perfect proportion. The Ancient Greeks studied proportion, as did artists of the Renaissance, such as Leonardo da Vinci.

Meaning

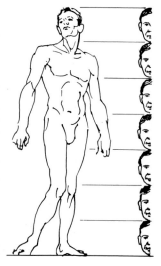

Proportion refers to the relationship of the component parts of a building or of a work of art. Usually the word means that there is a correct relationship or ratio of one thing to another and that each component has been given its appropriate **portion**. It involves a comparison of elements in terms of size, height, width, quality etc.. Proportion may be expressed in comparative terms such as *brighter than*, *twice as large*, etc.. Many artists have given much attention to proportion, particulary to the relationship of different parts of the human body. It has been found that normally the human body is about seven times as high as the length of the head and that the total height is roughly equal to the width of the outstretched arm. The body is divided roughly into eight equal sections. Many artists consider that when proportion is produced a feeling of harmony and balance is achieved. Other artists, however, have felt it necessary to disregard proportion completely and reject all rules in order to express their individual feelings.

Associations

Proportional callipers are used mainly by sculptors. The instrument has a pair of of jaws at each end, one large, one small.A sliding screw allows adjustments, so that proportional settings can be made for reducing or enlarging work.

See: **balance, symmetry, harmony, Golden Section, scale, schema**.

proportional dividers

Pugging

Pronounced: PUG-ING (*u as in rug*)

Origin

The origin of pugging is not known. It may have come from the Latin *pugnus* meaning a *fist*, as clay had to be struck with the fist to expel the air in it. More probably, it comes from a dialect word in English *to pug*, which meant *to pull, tug, kick or knock.*

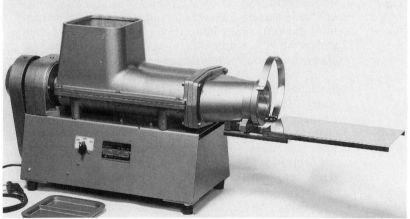

Meaning

Pugging is a term used in pottery meaning to knead loam or clay, in order that all the air bubbles are expelled, so that all the elements in the clay are thoroughly combined. Originally, the pugging of the clay was done by hands and feet; nowadays a mechanical device called a **pugging mill** is usually used in most potteries. The pugging mill consists of a steel cylinder which tapers to a die at one end. Clay is forced through the die by a screw which rotates in the cylinder and the compressed clay is extruded.

a pugging mill
by kind permission of Shimpo Industrial Co., Kyoto, Japan

Associations
See: **wedging, kneading, clay, die**.

181

Pyrometry

Pronounced: PI-ROM-A-TRY (*i as in bite, o as in gone, a as in ago, y as in duty*)

Origin

From the Latin *pyra* from the Greek *pur* meaning *fire*, and the Greek *metron* meaning *measure*.
In 1730, a Dutchman, Petrus Van Muschenbroećk, invented a bar pyrometer. In 1750 , a famous English ceramist, Josiah Wedgwood, invented silica cones for checking furnace temperatures and in 1782 he invented a pyrometer. Throughout the 19th century pyrometers were developed as thermo-electrical knowledge increased.

Meaning

A pyrometer is an instrument for measuring high temperatures (beyond the range of a mercury thermometer) in kilns and furnaces used for ceramics, enamelling, jewellery, glass and metal work. A **photo-electric pyrometer** is a device for measuring the temperature inside a kiln by using electrical currents produced by photo-electric cells. An **optical pyrometer** is a device which focuses on the heated area of a kiln from a safe distance and measures the intensity of light emitted from the kiln, which indicates on a gauge the temperature within the kiln. Kiln temperatures are also measured by **pyroscopes**, which are arrangements of ceramic minerals which melt at different specific temperatures. They are available in the form of cones (e.g. Seger cones), bars or rings. These can be linked to control switches, so that kiln temperatures can be controlled by switching the kiln heating system on and off. **Pyrometric cones** and other forms are made to bend, deform and melt at known temperatures. They do not measure temperature but how much heat-work has been done. Each cone is numbered, according to its melting point. The condition of the pyrometric objects can be seen through a peep-hole in the kiln and temperature adjustments can be made as needed.

Associations

See: **kiln, firing, thermal shock.**

a pyrometer

Raku

Pronounced: RA-KU (*a as in cat, u as in due*)

Origin

From the Japanese word meaning *enjoyment* or *happiness*. The first raku work was produced by a Korean potter, who emigrated to Japan and worked there. His work became famous and in 1598 he was honoured by the Japanese ruler at the time and given a seal, taken from that of the great Tea Master, Semo-no-Rikyu.

the raku symbol

Raku became his family title, and the name of the pottery which he had invented.

Meaning

Raku is groggy, handbuilt earthenware pottery which was traditionally covered with a thick lead glaze, usually with black, red or yellow hues. Nowadays, because of the high toxicity of lead, borax is usually the main flux. A bisque-fired pot is placed in a kiln, using long-handled tongs and fire-proof gloves, where it is fired at a very low temperature of about 750°c-1000°c. The preparation allows it to withstand the thermal shock of over 750°c without having a usual warming-up period. It is usually fired for about 15 to 30 minutes. When it is red-hot, it is removed from the kiln with tongs and then put into leaves or sawdust for reduction before it is thoroughly cooled in cold water. In Japan, the raku process is used to produce small, irregular, handbuilt cups (usually by the pinching or coiling method) which are used in traditional tea ceremonies. Raku is now produced in a variety of shapes with different textures.

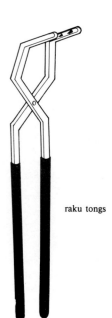

raku tongs

Associations

See: **grog, reduction, glaze, firing, pinch, coil**.

Realism

Pronounced: REE-A-LIZM (*ee as in see, a as in ago, i as in pin, zm as sm in prism*)

Origin

Realism as a movement began in France in about 1840. Gustave Courbet (1819-1877), a French painter, was a leader in the movement. The term *Realism* was first used by a French art critic, Gustave Planche, in 1833 for art which did not use imagination but which involved, as he put it, "*hand-to-hand combat with nature and with truth*".

Meaning

How one interprets **reality** is largely determined by one's culture (including one's education). People interpret reality differently according to their perceptions of experience (see **Perception**). As people of different ages and cultures had different experiences resulting in different thought patterns and attitudes, so the meaning of realism has changed through the ages-and doubtless will continue to change. **Realism** is art which attempts to recreate things precisely as they normally appear in the world, in contrast to things imagined. It refers, too, to a movement of 19th century art, which rejected the idealism of Romanticism, preferring every-day events and the experiences of ordinary people, including poverty and the sordid side of life. It believed that everything should be portrayed objectively, not subjectively or symbolically. Gustave

Courbet, when asked to paint an angel, said, "*What I have not seen, I cannot paint*". He also said when making clear his basic beliefs in 1861, "*I hold that painting is essentially a* **concrete** art and does not consist of anything but the representation of **real** and **existing** things. It is a completely physical language using for words all visible objects. An abstract object, one which is invisible, non-existent, is not of the domain of painting". The development of photography supported the movement. Artists who produce realistic images are said to be **representational** or **figurative** artists.

Associations

Carravaggio (1537-1610) produced paintings more than 200 hundred years before Realism began, yet he was a Realist to some extent in that he included common and "coarse" people in his religious scenes.

See the works of Honoré Daumier (1808-1879), Gustave Courbet (1819-1877), Charles François Daubigny (1817-1878), Jean-Baptiste Carpeaux (1827-1875), Pierre-Etienne-Theodore Rousseau (1812-18670.

See: **objective, subjective, Romanticism, landscape, genre.**

Rectilinear

Pronounced: REK-TI-LIN-I-A (*e as in let, i's as in pin, a as in ago*)

Origin

From the Latin *rectus* meaning *straight* and *linea* meaning *a line.*

Meaning

Rectilinear means in, or forming, a straight line, or bounded by straight lines. Its opposite is **curvilinear.**

Associations

See: **Hard Edged Painting, Absract Art**

Reduction

Pronounced: RI-DUK-SHUN (*i as in bit, u's as in duck*)

Origin

From the Latin *reductum* meaning *lead or drawn back.* Originally, it had the meaning of *to subdue* in the sense of to draw people back into line and subservience. It then came to mean to diminish or lessen, not only people but things.

Meaning

Reduction is a term in ceramics which means to reduce the oxygen in a kiln so that oxides in glazes on ware are starved of oxygen and are forced to give it up to allow combustion. The reduction of oxygen in a kiln creates a smokey atmosphere. The carbon in the smoke draws oxygen from the body of the ware and from the glaze on it. The withdrawal of the oxygen affects the colours of the glazes and the texture of the ware. The reduction process is controlled by adjusting air controls, by the use of dampers and occasionally by the withdrawal of kiln bricks to reduce draught. The opposite of reduction is **oxidation**, where there is ample oxygen in a kiln while firing so that complete combustion takes place and the oxides give specific colours to glazes. Reduction is an important stage in the **raku** process. The reduction technique should not be used in an electric kiln, as it will seriously decrease the life of the kiln elements. The term refers also to proportional reduction of images in graphic work.

Associations
See: **oxidation, raku, kiln, glaze.**

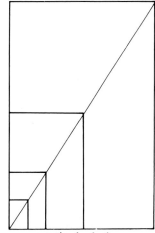

proportional reductions

Refractory

Pronounced: REE-FRAK-TARY (*ee as in see, 1st a as in cat, 2nd a as in ago, y as in duty*)

Origin
From the Latin *refractum* meaning *broken up*. The word came to mean not being part of the unified whole and rebellious, unmanageable and resistant. From there, it came to mean resistant to heat and corrosion.

Meaning
Refractory is a term to describe a material, usually clay, which will not melt or fuse except at an exceptionally-high temperature. That is up to about 1300°c. It is able to withstand not only great heat but also able to tolerate the strain of constantly-changing temperatures without its physical composition **breaking up**. Refractory materials are essential in the building of kilns. As well as clay, there are now other refractory materials, such as fibrous structures with alumina bases.

Associations
See: **kiln, firing, clay, pyrometry, furniture.**

Register

Pronounced: RE-JIST-A (*e as in rest, i as in pin, a as in ago*)

Origin
From the Latin *regesta* meaning *things recorded*. That is things or events put down accurately in documents.

Meaning
Register is a term in printing or design referring to the precise positioning and aligning of images or words next

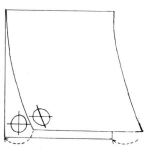

registration marks

to one another or squarely on top of one another, especially the exact positioning of inter-locking shapes and colours to produce a desired colour mix. Colours not registered correctly in a multi-coloured print appear blurred. When printing words in columns, the lines are said to be registered when vertical lines of print are exactly straight and no words or letters stick out from the lines. In painting, when figures are placed on different grounds, they are said to be in different registers.

Associations
Register marks are crosses or other marks put on an original illustration to act as a guide for the making of a printing plate and for colour registration.

See: **ground, print**.

Relief

Pronounced: RI-LEEF (*i as in wrist, ee as in see*)

Origin
From the Italian *relievo* meaning *raised* and the French *relever* meaning *to lift* or *raise* (compare with a *lever* which helps to raise something).

Meaning
Relief refers to a composition which is carved or cut out by some means (e.g. by a tool or by a chemical), so that the sculptural composition, or part of it, is raised and stands out from the background and surface on which it is set. It also refers to the illusion of three-dimensions in a painting. In block printing, relief refers to the area to be printed which receives the ink, leaving the background, which has been cut away uninked. Relief blocks are usually produced by cutting away part of the block but they can be made by building up a composition by adding material cut from wood, cardboard or other materials. Relief can be made on clay by modelling the surface, by adding clay designs (**sprigging**) to the surface of the ware, or by pushing the clay from one side (**repoussé**) or by using relief moulds. **Bas-relief** refers to work on a flat or curved surface, which is in **low-relief**. That is, there is little projection from the surface, as on a coin. This is in contrast to **mezzo-relief** where the projection from the surface shows half the full form of the figure or object, or **alto-relief**, which is **high-relief**, where the sculptured work contacts the surface at only a few points.

relief design on a potato cut

Associations
Torentic refers to carving, chasing or embossing in relief.
Anaglyph refers to a very low-relief sculpture or embossing.

See: **composition, ground, illusion, sprigging, repoussé, chasing, emboss**.

Italian 15th century, *Angel* c. 1450 Florence marble, *Art Gallery of South Australia*, Adelaide, South Australia

Renaissance

Pronounced: RE-NA-SANS (*e as in token, 1st a as in late, 2nd a as in ago*) or RI-NA-SAHNS (*i as in bit, a as in late, ah as in bah*)

Origin

From the French *naissance* meaning *birth* and *re* from the Latin meaning *again*. That is *rebirth* or *revival*. The term was first used by the French historian Michelet to apply to the civilization which succeeded the Middle Ages. While there is no agreement on the precise dates of the Renaissance period, it is generally believed to have begun in Florence in about 1400 and in Flanders and Holland a few years later, in Germany towards the end of the 1400's and in England about 1600. The period lasted until about the middle of the 17th century in Europe and its influence continued in England into the 18th century. The later years of the 16th century are referred to as the **Mannerist** period, because artists tended to imitate the style or *manner* of the three great artists who preceded them: Leonardo da Vinci, Michelangelo and Raphael.

Meaning

The Renaissance period looked towards Ancient Greece and Rome for its inspiration. It renewed the spirit of those times and their concern with human interests and the human race (rather than with supernatural matters) which was expressed in Humanism. It was a period of great change and creativity. Some of the important changes in art during the period were: the introduction of linear and aerial perspective, the perfection of oil painting techniques, the use of chiaroscuro, the start of non-religious portraiture, landscape painting as a genre in its own right, the development of block-printing, engraving and etching, the development of Naturalism (through Giotto 1276-1337), the development of understanding of human anatomy and physiology and its depiction and the develpoment of the notion of an *artist*, as opposed to an artisan (See **Fine Art**).

Associations

Byzantine is a general term to describe art during the Medieval Period that preceded the Renaissance.

See the works of Giotto, Brunelleschi, Masaccio, Boticelli, Bellini, Leonardo da Vinci, Donatello, Michelangelo, Raphael, Buonarroti, Titian, Van Eyck, Bosch, Bruegel, Altodorfer, Fouquet, Velasquez, El Greco, Grunewald.

a Renaissance design

Replica

Pronounced: REP-LI-KA (*e as in met, i as in pin, a as in ago*)

Origin

From the Italian *replicare* meaning *to reply* or *say again*. It then came to mean *do again*.

Meaning

A replica was originally an exact copy of a work of art. Nowadays, it can mean one of a number of versions (duplicates) of a work of art or of a reproduction of any document or illustration.

Associations

See: **facsimile, pantograph, squaring, pointing, camera obscura.**

Repoussé

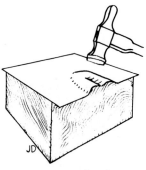

repoussé work

Pronounced: RE-POOZ-A (*e as in return, oo as in moon, a as in late*)

Origin

From the French *pousser* meaning *to push* or *pound* and the prefix *re* meaning *from behind*. *Repousser* means *to push back* or *to push from the back*. Before casting was invented (probably in Egypt about 2300 B.C.) all metal work was produced with a hammer. Decorative metal work, including repoussé work, especially in precious metals, continued to be made with a hammer.

Meaning

Repoussé refers to decoration in relief on metal (i.e. jewellery, silversmithing and goldsmithing), leather or enamelling. It is an alternative term for **embossing**. The metal used must be able to stretch when hammered and should be less than 0.4 mm. thick before it is worked on. Excellent metals to work on are sheet pewter, copper and gold. It is produced by hammering with punches or pressing mainly on the reverse side of the object to raise designs from the surface of the object or material in relief. In metal, the work is mounted on a bowl of pitch, lead or wood to provide the necessary resilience and elasticity for the stretching of the metal. The repoussé work is usually finished off by **chasing**, which defines the repoussé work. In ceramics, it refers to the application of relief decorations to ware.

a repoussé hammer

Associations

Drawing is the term used in metal work for the stretching and shaping of metal by hammering and heating it.

See: **relief, chase, sprigging, decoupage.**

Resist

Pronounced: RI-ZIST (*i's as in wrist*)

Origin

From the Latin *resistere* meaning *to stop.*

Meaning

Resists refers to a material or chemical (e.g. varnish, rubber cement, masking tape, opaque pigment, floor paste, wax, hard ground) which is used to mask or block out part of a work (e.g. in print work, etching, fabric design, air-brush work, jewellery work, potteryware, etc.), so that the covered part does not attract a dye, ink, glaze, slip, paint or chemical that is being used in the process. This is called a **resist technique**. The term applies also where knotting, stitching or tying of fabrics stop dye or paint from penetrating a fabric, as in the tie-dye processes.

Associations

Resist is also referred to as **stopping out**.

See: **ground, tie and dye, batik, blocking, engraving.**

Rococo

Pronounced: RO-KO-KO (*1st o as in rock, 2nd and 3rd o's as in go*)

Origin

From the French *rocaille* meaning *rock work* and *coquille* meaning a *shell.* Originally, the word *rocaille* was used to describe the style but in about 1769 the diminutive form *rococo* was used, invariably in the adversely critical sense. Its frivolity and the fact that it broke Classical rules was criticised, particularly by the Neo-Classical school of artists. The style came into fashion in about 1730, in reaction to the heavier style of *Baroque.* It had its peak of popularity from about 1735 to 1745, during the reign of King Louis XV of France and was adopted, with national modifications, by most European countries between 1740-1760. It then lost popularity in Europe, but it had a revival in England in the 1820's.

Meaning

Rococo is a highly-ornamental style of art and design which found expression in sculpture, precious-metal work, furniture design, ceramics and interior design (especially of walls and ceilings), architecture and painting. Its dainty, pretty, fanciful, delicate forms are characterised by the use of rocks, coral, shells, flowers, foliage, scrolls, asymmetrical motifs, an intermingling of curves and counter-curves and chinoiserie, all in profuse detail. It is strongly associated with the French courts of Louis XV and Louis XV1. The painterly style of the Rococo

rocaille

painters was often called **Rubenism**, as their style resembled the free-flowing brush work of Rubens. A reaction against the extravagances of Rococo style in 1760 led to the development of Neo-Classicism.

Associations
See the works of the following: Painters-François Boucher (1703-1770), Jean Antoine Watteau (1684-1721), Giovanni Battista Tiepolo (1696-1770); sculptors-Etienne-Maurice Falconet (1716-1791), Ignaz Günther (1725-1775); furniture designer-Thomas Chippendale (1718-1779); goldsmith Juste Aurèle Meissonier (1695-1750).

See: **Baroque, asymmetry, Neo-Classical**.

Romanesque

Pronounced: RO-MAN-ESK (*o as in go, a as in man, e as in end*)

Origin
A term coined in the 1920's to refer to a distinct style of art which is neither early Christian nor Gothic. Because the style was influenced by Ancient Roman art, it was called *Romanesque*. The word is now used to refer to European art of the 11th and 12th centuries.

Meaning
Romanesque refers to a style of art which was based on the art of Ancient Rome, especially Roman architecture with its rounded Roman arches and ribbed groined vaults. The style is noted for its emphasis on frescoes, wall paintings, mosaics, manuscript illustrations, monumental sculpture and stained-glass work, but above all for its church architecture. Romanesque art was essentially of and for the Church, especially the many monasteries. The paintings of the style are flat and linear and common is the intermingling of geometric shapes with plant shapes, with some distortion of figures.

Associations
Romanesque is sometimes called **Norman Art** in England.

See: **fresco, stained-glass, mosaics, linearity, distortion**.

Romanticism

Pronounced: RO-MAN-TI-SIZM (*o as in go, a as in man, i as in tin, izm as ism in prism*)

Origin
Romantic is from the Old French *romanz* meaning *a story* of chivalry with incidents remote from everyday life, often involving love affairs. Romanticism was a movement in the arts which began in about 1775 and was strong until the mid 1850's. It has not been totally

superseded, as it is essentially an attitude or way of thinking and feeling which still flourishes to some extent today.

Meaning

Romanticism was a movement which reacted against the formality, exactness and logic of **Classicism**. It is characterised by its recognition of the importance of emotion, imagination and individual freedom of expression. It preferred passion, spontaneity and irregular beauty to rational order, proportion and perfect finish. It emphasised the significance of the force of Nature in life, and in art landscape painting became a favourite mode of personal expression. Picturesque paintings were popular. Artists returned to Medieval themes for inspiration but they also took much interest in contemporary events and the relationship of the individual to a changing world. Some Romantic artists used symbolism and they had an influence on the later Symbolist movement. They tended to have a painterly, **Rubenist** style of painting.

Associations

See the works of J.M.W.Turner (English 1775-1851), Eugène Delacroix (French 1798-1863), Théodore Géricault (French 1791-1824), Caspar David Friedrich (German 1774-1840), William Blake (English 1757-1827), Goya (Spanish 1746-1828), Eugene Von Guerard (Australian 1811-1901).

See: **Classicism, Symbolism, landscape.**

Antoine-Louis Barye, France 1796-1875, **Horse attacked by a tiger** c 1837
bronze 24.3 x 37.2 x 14.8 cm, collection: Australian National Gallery, Canberra. Reproduced by permission of the Australian National Gallery, Canberra.

Saggers (also called Saggars or Seg gars)

Pronounced: SAGAS (*1st a as in sad, 2nd a as in ago*)

Origin

It is thought that *saggar* is a corruption of the word *safeguard*, which means something which guards or protects and keeps safe

Meaning

Saggers are heat-resistant (refractory) fire-clay containers (boxes or oval bowls) in which potteryware can be placed to protect the ware while it is in a kiln from flames and kiln gases. Often saggers are piled on top of each other to form what is called a **bung**. Some saggers have pierced walls at regular intervals into which are placed triangular, tapering pieces of fire-clay called **sagger pins**. These pins, which are about 3 to 8 centimetres long, support and separate ware put in the saggers. Nowadays, as clean fuels or electricity are used in kilns, saggers have been replaced by light pieces of kiln furniture.

Associations

See: **kiln, firing, refractory, furniture**.

Scale

Pronounced: SKAL (*a as in late*)

Origin

From the Latin *scalare* meaning *to climb*. Scale shows how something *climbs* in size. Note the English word *to scale*, which means *to climb*, as in *to scale a wall*.

Meaning

Scale indicates a measurement and shows the relative proportion of one thing to another. Something drawn on a one quarter scale is one quarter of the size of the original. Things designed can readily be reduced or increased in scale.

Associations

See: **proportion, gradation, pantograph, pointing, perspective, drawing, mechanical drawing**.

Schema

Pronounced: SKE-MA (*e as in he, a as in ago*)

Origin

From the Greek *Skhema* meaning *form* or *figure*.

Meaning

A schema is a composition reduced to its simplest forms **diagramatically**. It is an outline showing the essential features of something (sometimes symbolically). A schema can be used in drawing to show proportions of, for example, the human form, by using spheres, cubes and lines to represent parts of the body. A head is often **schematized** as an oval with simple lines indicating the nose, mouth and eyes.

Associations

See: **composition, symbol, proportion.**

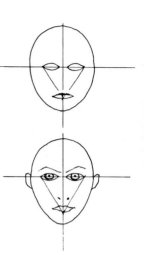

a schematic drawing

Scoring

Pronounced: SKOR-ING (*o as in for*)

Origin

From the Old Norse *skera* or *skur* meaning *to cut* or *shear.*

Meaning

To score is to cut a line or groove with a sharp tool into glass, plastic, jewellery, ceramics, leather or wood, or to make a furrow in paper (usually using a blunt instrument), in order to help in folding the paper without it tearing. Scoring is used in ceramics where two pieces of clay are to be joined (See **luting**).

Associations

A **scorer** is a tool with a rounded end, used in engraving. It used for making thick lines and for removing areas of an engraving plate or wood block.

See: **engrave, aquatint, burin, chasing, lute, lino-block.**

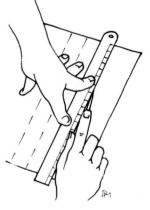

scoring

Scratchboard

Pronounced: SKRATCH (*a as in cat*), BORD (*o as in lord*)

Origin

scratch is from the Old Norse *skrapan* meaning *to scrape.*

Meaning

The terms scratchboard and **scraperboard** mean the same thing. It is a board made of plaster of paris or gypsum (sometimes called **gesso**) and has a smooth, white clay surface. It is usually covered with ink, which, when dry,

"Cat" by H.R.(Ben) Cooke

can be scraped away to reveal the white board and a composition can be created. Black cardboard with an underlayer of white is also used in this way.

Associations

See: **gesso, (s)graffito**.

Sculpture

Pronounced: SKULP-CHA (*u as in bull, cha as ture in picture*)

Origin

From the Latin *sculptura* from *sculpere* meaning *to carve.*

Meaning

Sculpture is the art of producing forms in three dimensions through the elements of volume, space, movement and materials. Until the 20th century, there were two types of sculpture. One is the **subtractive** technique where a material (e.g. stone) is carved (See **glyptic.**) and the material is reduced until the desired

194

form is produced. The other is the **additive** technique where a plastic material (e.g. wax or clay) is built up until a desired form is produced. In the 20th century, artists (e.g. Picasso) have used several mediums to construct forms (See: **assemblage** and **mobile**). The single most important technique in modern sculpture is that of **welding**. Today sculptors use not only stone, clay, wood and metals but also plastics, resins, in fact any materials, including junk and a range of *soft* materials (e.g. rope, latex foam etc.).There are also sculptures in light.

Associations

See the works of Umberto Boccioni (1882-1916), Constantin Brancusi (1876-1957), Jean Arp (1886-1966), Auguste Rodin (1840-1917), Naum Gabo (1890-1977), Alberto Giacometti (1901-1966), Barbara Hepworth (1903-1975), Henry Moore (1898-1986), Jacob Epstein (1880-1959), Marino Marini (1901-1980), Julio Gonzales (1876-1942).

For sculptures in light, see the works of Dan Flavin (1933 -) and Julio Le Parc (1928 -).

See: **armature, kinetic, Constructivists, welding, glyptic.**

Henry Moore, Great Britain 1898-1986, **Seated figure against a wall** *bronze height 55 cm, Art Gallery of South Australia, Adelaide, Morgan Thomas Bequest Fund 1958*

Scumble

Pronounced: SKUM-BAL (*u as in fun, a as in ago. The word rhymes with humble*)

Origin

Probably a derivation of the Old High German *scum* or *skuma* meaning *to cover*.

Meaning

To scumble is to lay on a canvas a very thin layer of light oil paint or acrylic in long, irregular strokes with a fairly dry brush over other layers of a different darker colour, so that the under-layers show through and contrasting colour grounds are blended. An irregular, textured effect is produced. Scumbling is the opposite of **glazing**. **Dry brush** technique is similar to scumbling in some respects but less paint is used.

Associations

See "*Snow Storm*" by William Turner (1775-1851), who used scumbling as much as glazing. See also Edgar Degas (1834-1917), who used scumble to achieve depth of colour. See the work of Titian (1487-1576) and Pierre Bonnard (1876-1947).

See: **ground, oil paint, painterly, glaze.**

Serigraphy

Pronounced: SERIG-RAFY (*e as in let, i as in big, a as in bat, y as in duty*)

Origin

From the Latin *sericum* meaning *silk* and the Greek *graphe* meaning *writing* or *drawing*. The process is said to have been invented by Some-Ya-Yu-Zen in China in the 17th century. The technique was popular in Europe and the United States during the 1960's and 1970's and was exploited by Pop Artists.

Meaning

Serigraphy is a stencilling and silkscreening technique. The same processes are used in serigraphy as are used in silkscreening but in serigraphy **tusche**, in the form of crayon, pencil or liquid, is mainly used, rather than printing-ink stains. The materials under the screen can be textured materials, such as sandpaper or rough wood, so that when the screen is rubbed with tusche (say, with a crayon) a textured print can be created.

Associations

See the work of Richard Hamilton (1922 -) and Michael Andrews (1928 -).

See: **stencil, silkscreen, tusche, registration, resist.**

Sfumato

Pronounced: SFOO-MA-TO (*oo as in food, a as in far, o as in go*)

Origin

From the Italian *sfumare* meaning *to smoke, evaporate* or *fade away and clear like a mist*. It came to mean *to diminish gradually*.

Meaning

Sfumato is a term used in painting or drawing to describe the gradual changes in tone from light to dark. The change is so gradual that it is scarcely noticed. The term refers often to the soft, mellow, hazy, smoked-atmosphere effect in some landscapes and seascapes. In Leonardo da Vinci's notes, he writes that in painting light and shade should blend "*without lines or borders, in the manner of smoke*".

Associations

The works of Leonardo da Vinci and Raphael provide fine examples of sfumato. See Leonardo da Vinci's "*Mona Lisa*".

See: **chiaroscuro, gradation, landscape**.

Shape

Pronounced: SHAP (*a as in late*)

Origin

From the Old English *sceapan* meaning *to form* or *make*.

Meaning

Shape refers to the appearance of an object rather than to its structure. The term is often used for **form**, although to be correct, shape is only one of the elements of form (which includes proportion, scale, mass, volume, structure and texture). Shapes can be three-dimensional (e.g. a person's egg-shaped head) or two-dimensional (e.g. a photograph of a person's oval head). Shapes are associated with human emotions or ideas. For example:

● a circle or tondo suggests something completed or perfect or at rest;

● jagged shapes suggest pain or tension;

● horizontal shapes suggest calm, peacefulness and rest;

● vertical shapes suggest uprightness and nobility,

● diagonal shapes suggest movement and dramatic action;

● pyramid or triangle shapes suggest stability (having a large base) and permanence.

There are hundreds of two and three dimensional shapes and many words to describe shapes, for example:

Torus

Ellipsoid

Pyramid

Prism

furciferous-fork shaped; hamiform-hooked shaped;
helicoid-screw shaped; obconic-pear shaped; palmate-
shaped like a human hand; scutiform-shaped like a shield;
uniform-J shaped; zygal-H shaped; sigmoidal-curved in
two directions; stelliform-shaped like a star; campanulate-
bell shaped; cordate-heart shaped.

Associations
See: **biomorphic, geometric, arabesque, amorphous,
configuration, contour, Cubism, distortion, form, space,
pattern.**

Shrinkage

Pronounced: SHRINK-IJ (*i as in ink, ij as idge in
bridge*)

Origin
From the Old English *scrincan* meaning *to wrinkle* or
shrivel.

Meaning
Shrinkage in ceramics is the decreasing in size of pottery
or porcelain.There are two kinds of shrinkage: that which
occurs as the ware dries, and that caused by firing in a
kiln, where chemical reactions occur. The shrinkage of
ware can be from 2 to 20 per cent, depending on the
chemical composition of the ware. Ceramists are able to
control shrinkage to some extent by changing the
composition of ware, e.g. by mixing clay with grog.
Shrinkage must be taken into account by a potter, as
uneven shrinkage can lead to warping of ware.

Associations
See: **kiln, firing, grog, periodic time-table, warp.**

Silhouette

Pronounced: SIL-OO-ET (*i as in hill, oo as in zoo, e as
in get*)

Origin
The technique of tracing the outline of a shadow cast on
a wall goes back to Ancient Rome and Greece. Cut-paper
silhouettes have been popular in many countries since the
Middle Ages. In the early 1700's in England paper-cut
profiles of people, buildings and animals were popular
under the name of **profiles** or **shades**. The French
Minister of Finance during the reign of King Louis XV of
France, Etienne de Silhouette (1709-1767), had a favourite
pastime during his retirement of making cut-outs from
black paper of the profiles of people's faces. These became
known as **silhouettes** and the word went into common
usage throughout Europe, rather than the English words
profile or shades.

Meaning

A silhouette is an object, person, building or scene drawn or painted entirely in black, showing no internal detail. It is also a portrait in profile painted or drawn in black, or cut out from black paper. This is usually mounted on paper or card of a contrasting colour. It refers, too, to a figure or shape which is projected using a light source to reveal its outlined shadow on a piece of paper or screen on a wall. Sometimes a **pantograph** was used to reduce a copy of the silhouette cast on a wall. The silhouette technique is used in shadow puppetry.

Silk Screen Printing

Pronounced: SILK (*i as in milk*), SKREEN (*ee as in see*), PRINT-ING (*i as in ink*)

Origin

The Jananese and Chinese were probably the first to use silkscreen printing techniques. The Japanese used human hair in a grid of threads to support the unattached parts of their **stencils**. The Chinese also used a thin paper stencil attached to a screen of fine silk threads. Woven silk as a support for stencils was used about 1870. Silkscreen printing was patented by Samuel Simon, an Englishman from Manchester in 1907. The use of a **squeegee** to force ink through the screen mesh was first used in the United States about 1910.

a squeegee

Meaning

Silkscreening (or **screenprinting** as it is more commonly called nowadays) is a printing process in which an image is transferred onto a material (e.g. paper, cardboard, cloth, glass, wood, etc.) by forcing ink through a fine mesh screen (formerly of silk,but now of synthetic materials such as dacron or nylon) onto the material. The screen usually acts as a support for a stencil. However, images can be placed directly onto the mesh and a photograph can be transferred when light-sensitive chemicals or film are placed on the screen. The silkscreen apparatus consists of a screen frame on which the screen is tightly stretched. The frame is attached to a separate printing base by hinges or wooden blocks and there is a locating pin from the screen to the base to ensure the screen is always lowered onto the base, on which it is receiving material, at exactly the same place always, so that there can be **registration**, if required. The parts of the design not to be printed are blocked out by an appropriate **resist** material (e.g. varnish). Ink, paint, lacquer, etc. can be pressed through the screen mesh using a squeegee. Usually only one colour is used at a time. The technique is now widely used as it allows an artist to print on almost any material

simple silkscreen printing frame

a stencil fabric (silk), highly magnified, *kind permission of Swiss Silk Bolting Cloth Mfg Co., Zurich*

of any size or thickness, with a wide variety of colouring materials and in whatever quantity of prints needed.

Associations

Another term for silkscreen printing is **serigraphy**. Screenprinting processes are now widely used in commerce and industry. A number of modern artists have used silkscreen printing techniques.

See the work of Robert Rauschenberg (American 1925 -), Richard Hamilton (English 1922 -), Andy Warhol (American 1928-1986), Roy Lichtenstein (American 1923 -).

See: **stencil, serigraphy, registration, resist.**

Size

Pronounced: SIZ (*i as in rise*)

Origin

From the Middle English *sise* meaning *setting or fixing with a gluey substance.*

Meaning

Size is a gelatinous (i.e. it turns to gelatine or jelly when cold) substance,such as resin, glue or starch. Originally, it was made from the bones or hides of animals. It is put onto a canvas (or other porous material) to seal the pores in it. This prevents the canvas from absorbing paint and consequently deteriorating. The fibres in the canvas do not come into direct contact with the paint. Handmade paper has to be sized before it can be written on (again to close the pores of the material), otherwise the writing ink would penetrate the paper rather than rest on the top of it. Size is also added to most papers to reduce their absorbency. Similarly, fabrics are sized (usually with a chalk-starch filler) to give the fabric strength, called **body**.

Associations

See: **canvas, priming, ground, paper, fabric, porosity.**

Sketch

Pronounced: SKETCH (*e as in let, tch as in stretch*)

Origin

From the greek *schedios* meaning *sudden* and then the Latin *scheduus* meaning *made off-hand.*

Meaning

A sketch is a rough draft or outline of a composition which is made quite rapidly and spontaneously. In drawing, painting or modelling, it is the artist's first effort to put down on paper his or her first impressions. It is a trial run. It is different from a **study**, which provides more detail. The quality of some artists' sketches have been so high (e.g. those by Rubens, Constable or Leger) that they have been recognised as distinguished works.

Associations

The Italian *spezzatura* is an alternative term for sketch.

See: **roughing in, study, schema, cartoon.**

Slab

Pronounced: SLAB (*a as in cat*)

Origin

The origin of slab is not clear. It is probably from the Norwegian word *sleip* meaning *a flat piece of wood cut from a tree* or the Irish and Gaelic word *slaib* meaning *mud.*

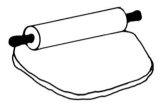

slabbing

Meaning

A slab is a flat, broad and comparatively thick piece of material. To slab in ceramics is to form a pot from sheets of easily-workable clay, which has been rolled out then cut into required size with a length of wire. The edges of the slabs are **scored** to assist their joining when forming square or rectangular shaped pots

Associations

See: **knead, clay, pottery, score.**

Slip

Pronounced: SLIP (*i as in grip*)

Origin

From the Old English *slipa* meaning *slime.* The most primitive pottery was dipped in slip to make it water-proof. Pottery decorated by the use of slip was produced in many Middle East countries before the 9th century.

Meaning

Slip is a creamy solution obtained from finely-ground clay which is mixed with water and then sieved. It is used to coat and give a smooth-textured surface to ware, to decorate it (see **trailling** and **sgraffito**), or to join parts together (e.g the attachment of handles to pots). Other ingredients are often added to the slip, such as colouring oxides, feldspar for strength, flint for hardness and whiteness, fluxes and frits for bonding and vitrification, and a deflocculant to help the mixing process. Slip (with a **deflocculant** added) is also poured into moulds of plaster. Once the slip is dry, it shrinks away from the moulds of plaster and the clay can be removed from the mould. This is called **slip casting.**

slip decoration

Associations

Barbotine and **engobe** are alternative terms for slip. **Slurry**

is a mixture of clay and water which is not sufficiently mixed and sieved to be called slip.

See the work of the English ceramists Bernard Leach and Michael Cardew and that of the American ceramists Mary Louise McLaughlin and Maria Longworth Storer.

See: **feldspar, frit, vitreous, deflocculant, oxidation, flux, cast, (s)graffito, trailing.**

Solder

Pronounced: SOLDA (*o as in old, a as in ago*)

Origin

From the Latin *solidare* meaning *to fasten* or *solidus* meaning *solid.* That is *to make solid and firm.*

Metal workers in the Middle East countries discovered the method of making lead-tin solder (**hard solder**) at about the same time as they discovered **bronze**, about 3500 B.C.. **Hard solder** of gold and silver was known about 2500 B.C.

Meaning

A solder is a mixture of metals (termed an **alloy**), which has the ability when it is in a molten state to stick strongly to other metals. When it cools it sets hard and is able to fuse and bond the edges of metals together. There are various kinds of solder for the different bonding of metals but the most common kind (plumber's solder) consists of equal parts of lead and tin. This melts at a relatively low temperature (about 250°c) and is called a **soft solder.** Solder has a melting point lower than the metals to be joined. **Flux** is always applied to the solder and to the metal to help the solder to flow more readily.

To solder means to join two pieces of metal (which do not themselves melt) together using solder which is heated until it is molten, using a **soldering iron** or a **soldering gun.** Soldering is much used not only in metalwork but also in stained-glass work. In jewellery work, silver solders or gold solders are used which melt at high temperatures (about 700 to 800°c), using a gas torch. This is called **hard solder. Sweating** is a soldering technique where two metals are coated with solder,clamped together and heated, so that the solder melts and the metals are fused.

Acid-core solder is a wire solder which has a core of flux. As the solder melts, the flux removes any oxide film from the metals being joined and so helps to bond the metals.

Associations

Brazing is the joining of two metals, using brass or a similar copper-zinc alloy and a flux to make the joint. The metals are bonded at a temperature above 430°c. As

a soldering iron

acid-core solder

the metal parts are heated, the brazing alloy is drawn into the joint by capillary action. Brazing is often used to join dissimilar metals, such as brass to wrought iron or copper to steel.

See: **pickle, oxidation, appliqué**.

Solvent

Pronounced: SOLV-ENT (*o as in got, e as in token*)

Origin
From the Latin *solvere* meaning *to loosen* or *dissolve*.

Meaning
A solvent is a liquid which can dissolve certain materials, such as water for acids and alkalis, terpentine for oil paint, wax and varnish, acetone for polyester resins. Solvents are often used in solutions of different substances where the solvent will evaporate, leaving just the substance one needs. They are used extensively for cleaning purposes.

Associations
In metalwork and painting a solvent is often called a **thinner**.

Space

Pronounced: SPAS (*a as in late*)

Origin
From the Latin *spatium* meaning *extent, room, open area*.

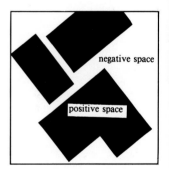

Meaning
Space is a term which is used in art and design to indicate area or shape. Two-dimensional space has height and width; three-dimensional space has height, width and depth. Positive (or occupied) space indicates a filled area or shape; negative (or unoccupied) space indicates an open, blank area or shape, surrounding a positive shape. The illusion of space (and depth and distance) can be created by: overlapping of objects, linear perspective, aerial perspective, differing size relationships, transparency, interpenetration, the contrast of sharp and diminishing detail, advancing and receding of colours, and changes in colour and texture values.

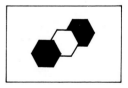

Associations
For an excellent example of the use of positive and negative space see the painting entitled "*The Dance*" by Henri Matisse.

See: **shape, positive, illusion, negative, perspective, colour**.

Specification

Pronounced: SPESI-FIK-A-SHUN (*e as in let, i's as in ink, a as in late, u as in fun*)

Origin

From the Latin *species* meaning *kind* or *sort* and *facere* meaning *to make* (compare with factory). *Specify* came to mean *to make mention of specific kinds of things - that is definite requirements for work to be undertaken.*

Meaning

A specification refers to the written documentation (including drawings and blueprints) which states the materials, the quantities, the forms and methods of construction or manufacture required and the costs involved to ensure that the problems identified in a **design brief** are solved. A specification is only one of the elements in the production of a designed object, which requires:

● consultation between a designer (or design team) and a client (the *project initiation*), where problems are identified;

● a project management schedule, where the design work to be undertaken to complete the *project* is stated, and a time schedule for the work and a schedule of fees are agreed to;

● a design brief, investigating and analysing relevant data and identifying the *design criteria* by which the design problems can be solved;

● a specification;

● the design work, incorporating all aspects mentioned above;

● production of the designed object.

Associations

See: **brief, design, typography, Graphic Design**.

Spectrum

Pronounced: SPEK-TRUM (*e as in let, u as in drum*)

Origin

Spectrum is the Latin for *image, ghost, spectre, phantom.* The term was used into the 17th century for an *apparition* and then was used more for an image than a ghost towards the end of the 17th century. Sir Isaac Newton used the word spectrum in 1671 in his work on the composition of light.

Meaning

The spectrum is the coloured band into which a beam of white light appears after it has been passed through a

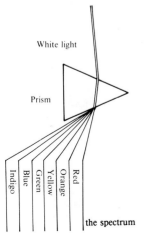

White light

Prism

Indigo
Blue
Green
Yellow
Orange
Red

the spectrum

prism or other source which diffracts (*breaks into pieces*) the light (e.g. a diamond, a water droplet or a soap bubble). The prismatic hues of the spectrum are: red, orange, yellow, green, blue, indigo, violet. You can remember the colours by: *Run off you girls; boys in view,* where the first letter of each word is the first letter of a colour. Each coloured light has a different wave-length. Violet has the shortest and is bent most by the prism; red has the longest and is bent the least.

Associations
Iridescent means displaying the prismatic colours of the rainbow, or flashing with changing colours.

See: **colour, colour-wheel**.

Sprigging

Pronounced: SPRIG-ING (*i as in fig*)

Origin
From the Middle English *sprigge* meaning *the shoot of a plant, a twig,* and *an off-shoot.*

Meaning
Sprigging is the attaching of handles to potteryware or the placing of decorative features in relief on potteryware. The decorative pieces are usually made in moulds and then attached to pots. To ensure a firm joint when sprigging, the clays used should be of the same consistency. With fine clays and pre-formed sprigs, water is usually sufficient to join pieces but with coarse clays slurry or slip must be used to ensure sound **luting**. The separate parts become firmly joined after firing.

Associations
See: **relief, lute, slip, fire**.

sprigging

Squaring Up

Pronounced: SKWAR-ING UP (*a as in fare, u as in cup*)

Origin
From the Latin *exquadrare* meaning *to square (make four sides and four angles)* and *quatuor* meaning *four.* Squaring up was used in wall paintings in Ancient Egypt and may have been used even earlier.

Meaning
Squaring up is a method of transferring a drawing on one scale to a larger scale. The technique is often used where a drawing has to be transferred to a large canvas or to a wall. The technique is to cover the drawing with a grid of numbered squares. The same number of larger squares is

placed, as a grid, on the canvas or wall etc. on which the enlargement will be made. Each square of the drawing is then copied onto the corresponding square of the larger surface.

Associations

Squaring up is also called **graticulation**.

See: **pointing, grid, facsimile, replica, pantograph, scale**.

Stained-Glass

Pronounced: STAND (*a as in late*), GLAS (*a as in fast*)

Origin

Stain is short for *distain* which comes from the Old French *desteindre* meaning *to discolour* or *dye*. The first major glass-producing centre was Alexandria in Egypt about 3000 B.C.. The Ancient Romans and Greeks were also proficient in glass making. Stained-glass windows were developed in the 9th century and the art of stained-glass work improved over the years until the highest form of the art was reached in the stained-glass windows of Gothic cathedrals of the Medieval period (up to the 15th century).

Family Crest by Frans Kat, The Adelaide Stained-Glass Studio.

Meaning

Stained glass, where a colour impregnates the glass, is made by adding metallic oxides to molten glass, so that it is coloured all through. Also, it can be made by fusing together thin layers of coloured glass. Designs in enamel were often fused onto stained glass. Traditionally, stained pieces of glass have been arranged in mosaics or patterns and made into panels which have been joined by lead, copper or zinc strips (called **bandings**). Nowadays, the joining strips can be made from copper foil and expoxy resins, as well as the traditional materials. During the Renaissance, designs and pictorial scenes were painted on clear glass. Sometimes pigments were scraped away to make sections transparent to form highlights. During the Art Nouveau period between 1890-1910, stained-glass techniques were revived and the art form was expanded.

Associations

Grisaille glass is plain yellow or white glass with enamel drawings on it. Sometimes silver stain was added.

See work by Marc Chagall (1887-1971), Georges Rouault (1871-1958), Henri Matisse (1869-1954), Fernand Léger (1881-1955), John La Forge (1846-1920), Louis Comfort Tiffany (1848-1933), Leonard French (1928 -).

See: **enamel, mosaic, oxide, Renaissance, Art Nouveau.**

Stamp

Pronounced: STAMP (*a as in cat*)

Origin

From the Old English *stampian* meaning *to bring down one's foot heavily* and later *to press a mark into something.*

Meaning

To stamp is the process of pressing or embedding an object into a material in order to leave an impression of the object on the material. In **block printing** this is simply cutting a shape on a block (of wood, lino or rubber etc.), inking the block and then pressing the block onto paper or fabric. Patterns can be made on metal by stamping with metal punches. A stamp or **die** can be used to stamp on leather and stamps can be carved in plaster (with the design in reverse) to make patterns on potteryware

Associations

See: **die, potteryware, pattern, impression, symbol, emboss.**

Stencil

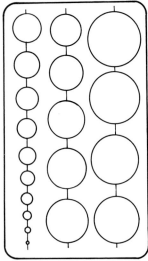

a stencil

Pronounced: STEN-SAL (*e as in pen, a as in ago*)

Origin

From the Middle English *stanselen* meaning *to ornament with sparkling colours or pieces of metal*. The word probably changed from the product to the process to get the product. The device of a stencil originated in China in the 6th century. The stencil was held together by fine strands of hair or silk. Stencils were used to make playing cards in the 15th century and for wallpaper in the 17th century. They were used to decorate walls until the 19th century when the use of wall-paper became a reasonably cheap way of decorating walls. As early as 1775, stencils were made on furniture. They were used extensively in the United States during the 1800's for decorating floor coverings, walls and household fabrics.

Meaning

A stencil is a thin, re-usable sheet of metal, cardboard, paper or plastic in which lettering or a design is cut out. The stencil is placed on paper, card, canvas, fabric or ceramic ware or other material and the cut out parts are painted, shaded, inked or dyed. These areas transfer to the material under the stencil to reproduce the lettering or design on the stencil. The uncut areas act as masks. Stencils are usually used where a repetitive design is needed.

Associations

A stencil is sometimes called a **mask**, because it masks areas of a composition not to be reproduced.

See: **silkscreen, serigraphy, template**.

Still-Life

Pronounced: STIL (*i as in hill*), LIF (*i as in kite*)

Origin

Still is from the Old English *stille* meaning *firm, not moving*. Still-life paintings and drawings did not develop as an independent genre until the 16th century and before then usually appeared as part of a larger composition.

Meaning

Still-life refers to a painting or drawing of inanimate objects which have been arranged by an artist in what is usually an indoor setting. Common subjects for still-life artists were, and still are, : flowers (sometimes in vases), dead animals or birds (often from a hunt), musical instruments, fruit, and domestic utensils. Sometimes the still-life objects had a symbolic meaning. Still-life, as a genre, flourished among Dutch and Flemish painters during the 16th century and has been popular since then. It was a favourite subject of the Impressionist and Post-Impressionist painters.

Associations

See the work of Anthony Van Dyck (1599-1641), Jan Davidsz Heem (1606-1683), Jean-Baptiste Chardin (1699-1779), Vincent Van Gogh (1853-1890), Paul Cezanne (1839-1906).

See: **genre, figurative, Realism, objectivity Impressionism, Post-Impressionism.**

Henri Fantin-Latour, France 1836-1904, **Poppies**
oil on canvas 60 x 53.2 cm, Art Gallery of South Australia, Adelaide, Elder Bequest Fund 1906

Sukhothai Kingdom 1238 - 1419, *Jar*, c. 1400, Ban Ko Noi, stoneware, *Art Gallery of South Australia, Adelaide, South Australia*

Stoneware

Pronounced: STONWAR (*o as in alone, a as in care*)

Origin
Stoneware was developed in the Rhineland, Germany, in the late 14th century and was first introduced into England by John Dwight in the late 17th century.

Meaning
Stoneware is pottery fired at about 1250 ° c, which makes it hard and vitreous and so close-grained it is almost non-porous and therefore water-proof. It is pottery between earthenware and porcelain. The clay is usually brown or greyish, owing to the presence of iron. When it is fired, it is strong but not brittle. Because it vitrifies, it is not necessary to glaze stoneware, but it is often glazed to make it more attractive and increase it uses.

Associations
See: **earthenware, porcelain, vitreous, porosity, glaze, fire.**

Stretcher

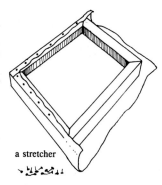

a stretcher

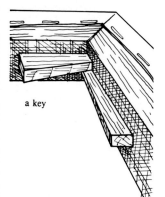

a key

Pronounced: STRETCHA (*e as in let, a as in ago*)

Origin
From the Old English *streccan* meaning *to make straight.*

Meaning
A stretcher is a wooden frame over which canvas (made of flax, cotton, jute or hemp) is stretched to be made as tight as possible. A stretched canvas is less affected by changing weather conditions and is less likely to suffer damage. The canvas is usually held to the frame by metal staples which are attached to the wooden frame, using a compressed-air staple-gun. A **key** or **wedge** is placed at each corner of the stretcher to expand the corners, to ensure the canvas is kept taut. Irish and Belgian linen are generally considered the best materials for an artist's canvas but they are expensive. Cotton duck is a cheaper alternative. Raw canvases should be primed to prevent the possible disintegration of the canvas's fibres. Acrylic paint can be used as a primer on canvases whatever medium is being used.

Associations
See: **canvas, key, wedge, priming, warp.**

Stucco

Pronounced: STUKO (*u as in bonus, o as in go*)

Origin
From the Old German *stukki* meaning *a crust* and from the Italian *stuccare* meaning *to putty* or *plaster.* It is a

plaster material which dries with a crusty surface. Stucco was used extensively in Ancient Egypt and Ancient Greece and during the Renaissance.

Meaning

Stucco is a plaster made from lime, powdered marble and glue, and sometimes animal hair. It was used for decorating buildings, especially walls and ceilings, as it could be readily moulded.

Study

Pronounced: STUDY (*u as in bonus, y as in duty*)

Origin

From the Latin *studium* meaning *zeal* or *affection* and then *applying oneself to something with interest*.

Meaning

A study is a very detailed representation of a part of a composition or design. The artists undertakes a study to ensure he or she gets the parts correct in the total finished work. A portrait artist, for instance, may make a study of the hands or head of a person he or she is painting. It is like a preliminary, practice piece and a rehearsal before the main event. A study is more detailed and carefully prepared than a **sketch**.

Associations

See: **schema, sketch, composition, portrait.**

Style

Pronounced: STIL (*i as in file*)

Origin

From the Latin *stilus* meaning a *stylus*, which is *a pointed instrument for writing or marking*. The word came to mean not the instrument for writing but the manner of writing, and eventually a person's manner of doing something.

Meaning

Style refers to the way one chooses to express oneself when there are several ways of doing so (e.g in brush-work, or use of colour). In art, craft and design, it refers to the personal mannerisms or traits of a particular artist or designer. For instance, El Greco tended to produce people in his paintings with elongated faces; Modigliani's people have oval faces. Style also refers to the characteristics which identify a particular period or school of painting, sculpture or design. Sometimes a painter shows no personal style; sometimes a work has both personal and period or School styles.

Stanley Spencer, Great Britain 1891 - 1959 *Hilda Welcomed* (detail) oil on canvas 141.0 x 94.8 cm *Art Gallery of South Australia, Adelaide, South Australia*

Associations

See: **facture, movement, subjective, painterly, Expressionism**.

Surrealism

Pronounced: SUREE-A-LISM (*u as in pure, ee as in see, a as in ago, ism to rhyme with prism*)

Origin

From the French *surreal* meaning *going beyond the real*. The term surrealism was first used by the poet and art critic Guillaume Apollinaire in 1917. The Surrealist movement, which was originally a literary rather than an artistic movement, was founded by the poet André Breton in France in 1924. It was very much influenced by the growing interest in psychology and psycho-analysis. The first exhibition of Surrealist paintings was in Paris in 1925 and showed the works of Giorgio de Chirico, Paul Klee, Jean Arp, Max Ernst, Joan Miro, and Pablo Picasso. The movement ended about 1966.

James Cant, Australia 1911 - 1982, *The Merchants of Death* (detail) oil on canvas 102 x 122 cm *Art Gallery of South Australia, Adelaide, South Australia*

Meaning

The characteristics of Surrealism are: a liking for juxtaposing things and ideas which do not normally go together to produce an unexpected and startling effect (e.g. in his "*Object*", Meret Oppenheim created a fur-covered cup and saucer with tea spooons); it responded to emotions with little consideration given to reason; it depicted dreams and fantasies and gave free reign to the sub-conscious as a strong source of creativity; it depicted hallucinatory states of mind; it used automatic drawings and created by-chance situations. It introduced **frottage**, **collage**, and **found objects (objet trouvé)** as important elements of its form. The movement was the forerunner of Abstract Expressionism.

Associations

See the works of Max Ernst (German 1891-1976), Yves Tanguy (French 1900-1955), Salvador Dali (Spanish 1904-1985), Jean Arp (Alsatian 1887-1966), André Masson (French 1896-1974), Roberto Matta (Chilean 1912 -), René Magritte (French 1898-1967), and James Ensor (1860-1949).

See: **subjective, Symbolism, allegory, fantasy, illusion**.

Symbol

Pronounced: SIM-BAL (*i as in duty, a as in ago*)

Origin

From the Greek *sumbolon* meaning *mark* or *token*. Symbols are ancient methods of expression by all people.

Meaning

A symbol is an object or drawing which represents or signifies some idea or quality by association in fact or thought, and which gives an instructional message. For example, a white dove is a symbol of purity, love, peace or the Holy Spirit; the lion symbolises courage, the cross Christianity, a heart love, an arrow a direction, a halo holiness. The International Travel Communication Signs are good examples of the importance of symbols in our world. Symbols are used in almost every specialised area, for example in weather signs, mathematics, maritime affairs, etc. A well-designed commercial or industrial symbol (or logo) should be simple and easily identified, easy to produce and photograph in black and white, and should be easily remembered. Colours also had symbolic meanings in the past, and to a lesser extent today, such as white for purity, red for love, green for hope, blue for truth, and yellow for treachery.

Associations

Pictographs are pictures as symbols or signs. An **ideogram** is a letter or character which symbolises an idea.

See: **logo, Symbolism, allegory**.

The tortoise, the Japanese symbol of longevity

Symbolism

Pronounced: SIM-BA-LISM (*i as in dim, a as in ago, ism as in prism*)

Origin

See *symbol*. Symbolism was a movement in Art and Literature from about 1885-1910. In Art, it began as a reaction to **Naturalism** (and a desire to go beyond **Realism**) and to the objective aims of **Impressionism**. The term was coined by the French poet Jean Moréas. The movement began in France, with the French art critic, Albert-George Aurier as one of its main representatives. It spread throughout Europe and became widely influential.

Meaning

Symbolism emphasised subjective rather than objective thinking. It turned away from the representation of external realities and expressed the individual's ideas and feelings through symbols and allegory which were often ambiguous. The subjects of Symbolism were usually related to mythology, religion, art of the Far and Middle East, and the world of fantasy, involving phantoms and the grotesque. It was the forerunner of **Expressionism** and **Abstract Art**.

Associations

In Germany the movement was called **Thought Painting**.
See the works of Odilon Redon (French 1840-1916),

Gustave Moreau (French 1826-1898), James Ensor (Belgian 1860-1949).

See: **subjective, allegory, objective, Realism, Surrealism, Expressionism, Abstract Art, symbol.**

Symmetry

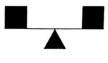

symmetry

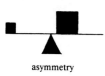

asymmetry

Pronounced: SIM-A-TRY (*i as in limb, a as in ago, y as in duty*)

Origin

From the Greek *syn* meaning *together* and *metron* meaning *measure.*

Meaning

Symmetry is a situation where one part of something (e.g. the human body) is of the same measure or proportion as another part and a harmonious balance of parts results. Usually objects or structures are on different sides of a dividing line (e.g. the columns of an arch) and the sizes, shapes, colours and textures of the objects on both sides are the same and balanced. When symmetry occurs the objects are said to be **symmetrical**

Associations

Asymmetry is the opposite of symmetry and it is when there is no balance or harmony of the objects on the two sides of a dividing line.

See: **Classical, proportion, balance.**

Tachisme

Pronounced: TASH-ISM (*a as in lash, ism as in prism*)

Origin

From the French *tache* meaning *a blot* or *a stain.* The term was used in the early 1950's to describe the technique used in some Abstract Art. *Tachist* painters were popular for about a decade, and the technique reached its peak of popularity in the early 1960's.

Meaning

Tachisme is a technique in painting where an artist throws, splashes or drips paint in blots or stains onto a canvas, or applies it by free gestural brush strokes. It is non-representational and does not use light or shade or perspective. The Tachist artists valued spontaneity and intuition above all else and relied on serendipity (*happy and unexpected discoveries by accident*) for much of their effect. They emphasised the significance of each blot in the painting, whereas **Action Painting**, although using similar techniques, emphasised the total effect of the painting.

Associations

See the works of Kurt Sonderberg (German 1923 -), Henri Michaux (Belgian 1899 -), Jean-Paul Riopelle (Canadian 1922 -), François Arnal (French 1924 -), Gerard Schneider (Swiss 1896 -), Pierre Soulanges (French 1919 -), Georges Matheu (French 1921 -), Bram Van Velde (Dutch 1895 -), Franz Kilne (German 1910-1962), Hans Hartung (German 1904 -).

See: **Action Painting, Abstract Art, facture, Art Brut**.

Tapestry

Pronounced: TAP-A-STRY (*1st a as in lap, 2nd a as in ago, y as in duty*)

Origin

From the Latin *tapete* and the French *tapis* meaning *a carpet*. There is no specific date for the beginning of the art of tapestry weaving but there is evidence to show that it was practised in China, Peru and Egypt in 3000 B.C., and it has existed at primitive or sophisticated levels for thousands of years in all corners of the world. It was probably introduced into Southern Europe by the Arabs in the eighth century. Famous tapestry factories are the Aubusson factory in the South of France (founded 1665) and the Gobelin factory in Paris (founded 1667).

Meaning

Tapestries are hand-woven, decorative fabrics which have distinctive designs. They are woven on a loom. Usually coloured yarns of wool or silk (or both) are used and silver and gold threads were used occasionally to enrich the total effect. A pictorial or abstract design is created by weaving multi-coloured **weft** threads crosswise (which are held on **bobbins**-also called **spools** or **shuttles**) alternately over and under one-colour **warp** threads which run lengthwise. The wefts do not pass from **selvage** (an edge of the fabric so woven that it cannot unravel) to selvage (as in **embroidery**) but only as far as the colour is needed in the design. The fineness of a tapestry is determined by the number of wefts to the centimetre. Coarse tapestries average about eight wefts and the finest Ancient Peruvian tapestries had well over a hundred. Historically, some designs are characteristic of particular countries or areas, such as Arras and Beauvais in France, Brussels in Belgium and Mortlake in England. Formerly, tapestries were used for covering walls and furniture and as curtains and hangings but are now used as hangings for decorative purposes. Modern tapestries are not only pictorial but also abstract in design.

Morris & Company, London, Edward Burne Jones,designer,Great Britain 1833 - 1898 *The Adoration of the Magi* 1887 design (detail), wool tapestry with silk details *Art Gallery of South Australia, Adelaide, South Australia*

Associations

A **cartoon** is a drawing or design to be copied to produce a tapestry.

215

See the work of William Morris (English 1834-1896), François Arnal (French 1924 -), Jean Lurcat (French 1892-1966), Sir Edward Coley Burne-Jones (English 1833-1898).

Technique

Pronounced: TEK-NEEK (*e as in let, ee as in see*)

Origin

From the Greek *tekhnikos* meaning *art* or *craft* and *made by art*. It is related to the Latin *texere* which means *to weave*.

Meaning

Technique refers to a person's manipulative skills and abilities related to a particular activity (e.g. use of brush work, shading or texturing in painting). The term was used originally only in art and craft but now it is used generally for many activities. It refers, too, to any one method of using a material or medium in an art or design process, such as hatching or scumbling.

Tempera

Pronounced: TEMP-A-RA (*e as in temper, a's as in ago*)

Origin

From the Latin *temperare* meaning *to mix in appropriate proportions*. It referred to any **binder** which was mixed with powdered pigments to produce paint. It was used by the Ancient Egyptians and the Ancient Romans and Greeks. It remained the most important medium for painting until it was superseded by the use of oil paint in the 15th century. There was a revival of tempera painting in the 19th century.

Meaning

Tempera is a solution of powdered pigments mixed with a binder to produce paint. Various kinds of binders were used in the past including whites of eggs, milk, glue, gum, and even dandelion juice and sap from fig trees. Tempera is durable, quite water resistant and dries rapidly. It is very difficult to blend tempera colours, so hatching is usually used. The colours are considerably darker when wet than when they have dried. Modern tempera, which is obtainable commercially in tubes, jars and cups or trays, is not water-proof and must be finished with a fixative. The term is used nowadays for opaque, water-based paints which include designer and poster colour paints.

Associations

Tempera is also called **gouache** and **distemper**.

See "*A Miracle of St. Zenobus*" by Domenica Veneziano (birth not known, died 1461), for an example of tempera work before oil painting was developed in the 15th century.

Template (or templet)

Pronounced: TEM-PLAT (*e as in lemon, a as in late*) OR TEM-PLET (*1st e as in lemon, 2nd e as in naked*)

Origin

From the Latin *templum* meaning *an open space marked out for observation of the sky*. The word *tem* became a *marked space* and when joined to *plate*, meaning a *flat shape*, a template became a flat device used for *marking out* things, usually those which needed to be repeated accurately in exactly the same form.

Meaning

A template is a pattern or gauge, usually of thin metal, plastic or cardboard, which is used as a guide to ensure accurate drawing, cutting, drilling or shaping of metal, wood, stone, clay, leather, etc. It is frequently used where a pattern has to be repeated using standard shapes or symbols.

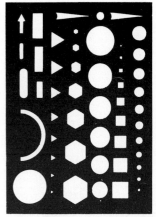

a template

Associations

See: **profile, stencil, mechanical drawing**.

Terra Cotta

Charles Despiau, France 1864-1946, **Tete de Femme**
terra cotta height 37 cm, Art Gallery of South Australia, Adelaide, South Australian Government Grant 1953

217

Pronounced: TERA-KOTA (*e as in let, a's as in ago, .o as in lot*)

Origin

From the Italian *terra* meaning *earth* and *cotta* meaning *cooked* or *baked*.

Meaning

Terra cotta is a hard, unglazed, fired earthenware pottery, which is usually grey or buff but which is fired to a reddish-brown. It was used in the past to build architectural ornaments, statuettes and to make tiles, toys, and domestic ornaments. It refers, too, to a reddish-brown colour, usually associated with brown clays.

Associations

For an example of terra cotta work of the past, see the sculptures of Luca Della Robbia (Italian 1400-1482).

Texture

Pronounced: TEX-TUR (*e as in let, u as in bonus*)

Origin

From the Latin *textura* meaning *weaving*. Originally the word applied to the feel of a woven garment and then was used for the feel of any material or surface.

Meaning

textures

In art, craft and design, texture refers to the nature of the surface of a work (e.g. matt, gloss, smooth, grained, corrugated, etc.). A textured effect can be tactile and felt with one's hand (e.g the roughness of impasto, grog or some clayware) or it can be visual (e.g. the roughness that bark appears to have on a tree in a painting). It is only in relatively recent years that artists have produced real textures (e.g. in collage) in their paintings; previously paintings produced an **illusion** of texture.

Associations

See: **frottage, collage, impasto, contour, illusion, assemblage.**

Thermal Shock

Pronounced: THUR-MAL (*u as in fur, a as in ago*), SHOK (*o as in rock*)

Origin

Thermal is from the Greek *therme* meaning *heat*; *al* is a suffix meaning *forming* or *creating*. Shock is from the French *choquer* meaning *to strike* and *to come into collision with.*

Meaning

Thermal shock refers to the intense strain imposed on

something as a result of being subjected to great heat or acute sudden changes in heat. The term applies mainly to ceramics and glass-making. When there are differences in temperature in different parts of an object (e.g. the inside and outside of potteryware) great strains and pressures can occur as some parts expand more than others. This can lead to cracks in the objects. Sudden heating and cooling need to be avoided and strict thermal control must be made in the heating and cooling of cermics and glass-ware.

Associations

Borosilicate glass is resistant to thermal shock. **Spalling** is the splintering of bricks or tiles caused by thermal shock.

See: **dunt.**

Throwing

Pronounced: THRO-ING (*o as in rope*)

Origin

From the Old English *thrawan* meaning *to twist* or *turn*. Throwing clay on a potter's wheel probably occurred in Egypt and China more than 5000 years ago.

Meaning

Throwing is a technique in pottery of shaping clay into a ceramic object by the use of a potter's wheel. The clay is "*thrown*" on a rotating wheel where it is hollowed, raised and shaped by hand, using water as a lubricant. The technique nowadays is mainly used by studio potters, as the ceramic industry uses machines, such as **jolleys** and **jiggers**.

Associations

See: **jigger, jolley, manipulation, potter's wheel, shape, technique, ware.**

Tie and Dye

Pronounced: TI-and DI (*i's as in bite*)

Origin

Tie is from the Old English *tegan* meaning *to tie*. Dye is from the Old English *deagan* or *deah* meaning *a colour* or *dark colour*. The word *die* rather than *dye* was used until late into the 18th century when dye was more generally used. The craft originated in China thousands of years ago and spread to India, Japan, Malaysia, Java and Thailand. Different countries modified the basic techniques. The craft was also used most artistically by the Ancient Peruvians.

Meaning

Tie and dye is a craft technique where parts of fabrics are knotted or tied with thread to produce a pattern. The fabric which is knotted is protected from the dye when it is immersed in a dye. When the fabric is opened, the undyed parts produce a variety of patterns on the dyed background. This technique is often referred to as **plangi**. **Ikat** is a process where parts of the warp are covered before weaving, so that the fabric can be dyed with the covered parts resisting the dye. This was a common form of weaving in Africa and Malaysia. **Tritik** is a technique of putting running stitches in a material and then pulling the stitches very tightly. The fabric is then dyed and patterns are formed where the dye is excluded.

Associations

Shibori is the traditional Japanese process of resist dyeing,involving tying, folding, stitching, and binding.

See:**batik, resist.**

Tooling

Pronounced: TOO-LING (*oo as in soon*)

Origin

From the Old English *tol* meaning *a tool*.

Meaning

Tooling is the smoothing (also called **dressing**) of stonework, using a chisel. It also means to decorate metalwork, either in relief or intaglio, using tools such as punches, gravers and hammers. This is also called **chasing**. *To tool* also means to decorate leather books with designs, using heated tools which burn into the leather.

Associations

See: **chase, intaglio, relief, sculpture.**

Trailing

Pronounced: TRA-LING (*a as in late*)

Origin

From the Old French *trailler* meaning *to tow (a boat)* or *to haul*, which originated from the Latin *tragula* meaning *a dragnet* and *trahere* meaning *to pull* or *draw*. It came to mean to drag something behind or across something else.

Meaning

Trailing is a method of applying thick **slip** as a decoration to the surface of ceramic ware, usually using an eye-dropper, a syringe or something similar to dispense and control the slip. The term is also used in enamelling when a pointed steel tool is used to trail fine lines of molten enamel across the surface of objects to produce a decoration.

Associations
See: **slip, enamel, ceramics**.

Transfer Type

Pronounced: TRANS-FUR (*a as in fast, u as in fur*), TIP (*i as in ripe*)

Origin
Transfer is from the Latin *trans* meaning *across* and *ferre* meaning *to bear* or *to carry*. That is *to carry across*. Type is from the Greek word *tupo* meaning *to strike* and *tupos* meaning an *impression*.

Meaning
Transfer type and images (which could be called *instant graphics*) refer to commercially-produced sheets of separate type letters (characters) or patterns (e.g. lines, dots, textures, symbols, etc.) which are on sheets of transparent plastic material (called *transfer sheets*). Each transfer sheet usually has an alphabet (in upper and lower cases) of one type-face and also numerals and punctuation marks. Many type faces are available. A letter, line, border, colour mass or image can be placed anywhere on a lay-out by an artist or designer by placing the transfer sheet at a specific point on the art work, pressing the letters or symbols firmly with a **burnisher** and then peeling off the contact paper from the transfer sheet. The letters or symbols transfer directly onto the **lay-out**. A wide range of toning patterns (e.g. Letratone and Instantex), lines (e.g. Letraline) tints, half-tones and cross-hatching are available on self-adhesive film. Often a fixative is applied to the transfers. The largest company producing transfer material throughout the world is *Letraset*.

Associations
See: **cross-hatching, facsimile, gradation, Graphic Design, motif, pattern, stencil**.

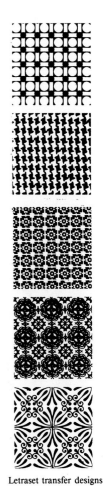

Letraset transfer designs

Trompe L'Oeil

Pronounced: TROMP-LUY (*o as in got, u as in dug, y as in rely. The u and y sounds slide into each other*)

Origin
From the French *tromper* meaning *to deceive, cheat* or *delude* and *l'oeil* meaning *the eye*. It means *deceiving or fooling the eye*. The technique has existed since early Ancient Roman and Greek times.

Meaning

Trompe l'oeil is a technique where an artist attempts to produce the illusion that an object in a work is real. It sets out to *deceive the eye* and one may be fooled into thinking that what is painted is real. A familiar form of trompe l'oeil in painting is the simulation of certain architectural forms, such as columns, mouldings, or pilasters, in realistic perspective. An object can often appear to project beyond the picture. In embroidery, the skilful use of colour and shading can make a work appear three-dimensional. In ceramics, food is sometimes included in the decoration of plates and platters, all of which look real. In decoupage, furniture can be decorated with cut-out paper in such a way that it appears to have real things in or on it.

Associations

Michelangelo's paintings of the prophets and sybils on the ceiling of the Sistine Chapel are good examples of trompe l'oeil achieved by skill in the use of perspective.

See the works of William Harnett (American 1848-1892), Haren Bohrod (American 1907 -), Salvador Dali (Spanish 1904-1986).

See: **illusion**.

three of the many forms of ampersands

Kind permission of Adelaide Apple Bureau.

Typography

Pronounced: TI-POG-RAF-Y (*i as in bite, o as in lot, a as in ago, y as in duty*)

Origin

Typ is from the Greek *tupo* meaning *to strike* and *tupos* meaning *an impression*. That is an impression on a material. *Graphy* is from the Greek *graphos* meaning *writing*. Typography began with the invention of writing and an alphabet was probably invented in the Eastern Mediterranean area about 2000 B.C.. The inventor of moveable type is not certain, but Johannes Gutenberg of Mainz in Germany helped to perfect the system in about 1450.

Meaning

Typography is the art of choosing, arranging, setting and spacing type for printing (called **composition**) in order that printed matter helps the reader to understand as easily as possible the printed content. There are many kinds of **type-faces** (which is the inked part of type), which are described by styles (e.g. Times Roman, Helvetica, etc.) and by size and weight. This book is set mainly in *Times Roman*. Each style has variations, such as light, medium, bold and italics. The size of the type-face is given using a **point system** (invented by Pierre Fournier, 1712-1768, in Paris in 1737). He published a *Table of Type Sizes* which was the first codification and standardisation of type sizes. For example, a 6 point type-face is quite small, a 36 point is large. When working with a manuscript to be printed, a **typographer** must give careful thought to the style and size of the type and also the spaces between the letters and words, and the spaces between lines (called **leading**, as originally lines were separated by strips of lead). Type today is invariably **set** (That is arranged.) by photographic typesetting machines and the process is being increasingly computerised and digitised.

Associations

In typography in early times, the type was contained in cases (like boxes). One holding capital letters was on a high shelf in the *upper case*; the one holding the small letters was on a lower shelf in the *lower case*. Today **upper case** means capital letters; **lower case** means small letters.

The thousands of advertisements in Broadway and Times Square in New York give this area the highest *typographical density* in the world.

See the works of Arthur Morris (English 1889-1967), Arthur Eric Gill (English 1882-1940), Berhold Wolpe (German 1905 -).

6 Point Type
7 Point Type
8 Point Type
9 Point Type
10 Point Type
11 Point Type
12 Point Type
13 Point Type
14 Point Type
15 Point Type
16 Point Type
17 Point Type

type sizes
(set in Megaron Medium)

Varnish

Pronounced: VAR-NISH (*a as in car, i as in dish*)

Origin

From the Middle English *vernisch*, which is from the Latin *veronic* meaning *a fragrant resin*, which was probably sandarac. Varnish was first exported from what is now Bengazi in Libya. Resins and their use to make varnish have been known for hundreds of years. Recipes are given in some early Medieval documents. *Oil varnishes* were common from the 9th to 15th centuries (using mastic, sandarac and linseed oil) and *spirit varnishes* were used from the 16th century. *Synthetic resins* are a product of the 20th century.

Meaning

A varnish is a liquid which is used to give a protective coat to wood, metal and other materials. It dries hard and is usually glossy and transparent, although nowadays there are matt varieties. It is able to protect objects from damp, pollution, grease and corrosive substances. It is easily applied (preferably in warm, dust-free environments), using a brush or spray, and it is readily removed with **solvents**, if necessary. There are two kinds of varnish. One is **oil varnish**, which is made from a combination of a hard, fossil resin (such as copal made from amber) heated with a drying oil, such as linseed oil, and then thinned with a solvent. The other is **spirit varnish**, which is made from a soft, natural resin (such as mastic, sandrac or dammar), which is dissolved in alcohol. Natural resins are secretions from some plants and trees (See **lacquer**). These resins are adhesive, inflammable and insoluble in water. Natural resin varnishes tend to turn yellow with age and become brittle. Consequently, **synthetic varnishes** have been produced which do not have these faults. These consist of synthetic resins (such as bakelite, alkyds and polyurethane) and China Wood oil, with xyol or varnalen as a thinnner. Varnishes are used extensively in art, craft and design, not only as a **fixative** or a **resist agent** but also to provide a gloss or matt glaze to a finished work. **Spar varnish** (so called because of its use on the spars of ships) is a very durable varnish which is resistant to sunlight, heat and rain and is most suitable for use outdoors.

Associations

See: **lacquer, resist, solvent, glaze, matt**.

Vehicle

Pronounced: VEE-I-KAL (*ee as in see, i as in pin, a as in ago*)

Origin

From the French *vehicule* from the Latin *vehere* meaning *to carry* and *vehiculum* meaning *a carriage* or *a means of transport*.

Meaning

In painting, vehicle refers to the medium and binder which hold the pigments in suspension in paint. The function of a vehicle is to make pigments into a liquid or paste form so that the mixture can be spread (that is "*carried*"). For example, linseed oil is a vehicle for oil paint, acrylic emulsion for acrylic paint, and gum arabic for water-colour (gouache). In ceramics, the vehicle is any medium which is used to assist colouring or glazing. The vehicle burns out in firing and does not contribute to the chemical process involved in the firing.

Associations

See: **medium, glaze, acrylic, oil paint, water-colour, gouache**.

Viscosity

Pronounced: VIS-KOS-ITY (*i's as in his, o as in got, y as in duty*)

Origin

From the Latin *viscosus* meaning *full of bird lime and sticky*.

Meaning

Viscosity means the extent to which a thick, sticky liquid will flow when poured. Liquids of high viscosity will pour and move slowly; those of low viscosity will pour and move easily. Generally, the larger the molecule of the substance, the greater is the viscosity.

In ceramics, the viscosity of a glaze is measured in **poise**. A free-flowing glaze will have a **poise-rating** of about 1000; a stiff glaze will have a poise-rating of about 100,000.

The adjective from viscosity is **viscous**. A **reducer** is used to decrease the viscosity of a finishing medium.

Vitreous

Pronounced: VIT-RI-US (*i's as in pin, u as in bonus, s as in sent*)

Origin

From the Latin *vitrum* meaning *glass*.

Meaning

Vitreous refers to the "*glassy*" appearance and character (e.g. hardness) that a ceramic ware has, following some of the ingredients of the body of the ware having fused with a melting glaze at a high temperature. The fusing process is called **vitrification**. When a ware becomes vitreous, its **porosity** decreases almost to nil. **Vitrification** also refers to the degree of hardness of a ware.

Ware

Pronounced: WAR (*a as in rare*)

Origin

From the Dutch *waar* and Old English *waru* meaning *goods* or *commodities*. The word ware was common until the 20th century but is now rarely used except in combination with other words, such as warehouse or stoneware.

Meaning

Ware nowadays refers to pottery in the raw, bisque or glazed state. A descriptive prefix is usually added, e.g. earthenware, potteryware, stoneware, greenware.

Associations

See: **earthenware, greenware, stoneware, bisque, glaze, clay, kaolin, raku, porcelain.**

Warp

Pronounced: WORP (*o as in port*)

Origin

From the Old English *weorpan* meaning *to throw* and also *to twist violently out of shape.*

Meaning

In weaving, **warp** refers to threads on a loom which are stretched lengthwise and comprise the horizontal part of the framework of a fabric to be woven. The other threads are worked vertically through the warp (by means of a shuttle which is "*thrown*") and are called the **weft** or the **woof**. The manner in which the weft crosses the warp decides the pattern in the woven fabric. These terms are also used in **basketry**.

Warp also refers to the twisting and distortion of wood in woodwork and to the buckling of picture frames. To prevent the warping of picture frames, museums and Art galleries maintain an atmosphere in their buildings which has about 55% humidity.

In ceramics, warped describes a pot which becomes distorted because of a number of factors, including uneven drying of the clay, uneven clay walls, rims too thin, poor wedging, the joining of clays of different consistencies, bases and foot rings not level, and a kiln not heating evenly.

Warping also refers to the distortion of a plastic moulding owing to the removal of the plastic from the mould before the plastic is set or cured.

Associations

See: **loom, distortion, shrinkage, wedge, fabric.**

Wash

Pronounced: WOSH (*o as in lot*)

Origin

From the Old English *waescan* meaning *to rinse in water.* Wash drawing techniques were first used in the late 15th century.

Meaning

A wash is an application of dilute water-based paint to form a thin, transparent film of colour on a painting. It is usually applied to give a light tint to a broad area uniformly, such as the sky in a landscape. The expression used is the "*laying of a wash*". A wash drawing is usually made with a brush and coloured ink on paper, often using pen, pencil, charcoal or chalk.

Associations

See the work of painters Claude Lorraine, Nicolas Poussin and Rembrandt.

Water Colour

Pronounced: WATA (*1st a as in war, 2nd a as in ago*),
KULA (*u as in fun, a as in ago*)

Origin

From the Old English *waeter* meaning *water* and the Old
French *color* meaning *colour*. Water colour paints were
used in the Middle Ages (up to the 15th century) and,
after a period when oil paints were invariably used, water
colour paints became popular again in the 18th and early
19th centuries. They were made commercially towards the
end of the 18th century. Moist water colour paints using
glycerin were sold in 1835 and water colours in paste
form in tubes were first introduced about 1900.

Meaning

Water colour is a paint made from water mixed with
high-quality pigment and gum arabic as a binder. The
paint is now sold in cakes, pans, or tubes. It can be
transparent or opaque. It is usually applied in broad
washes using a soft brush, the best being made from the
tail hairs of the Kolinsky red sable. Special paper is
required to produce the best results with water colour.
Usually a light sketch is made before paint is applied,
which must be done relatively rapidly as the paint is
quick-drying. The technique is ideal for small-scale
paintings where an artist can express his or her
spontaneous impressions, especially of an out-door scene.

J.M.W.Turner, Great Britain 1775 -
1851, *Scarborough Town and Castle:
morning: boys catching crabs,*
(detail) watercolour on paper 68.5 x
101.5 cm, *Art Gallery of South Australia,
Adelaide, South Australia*

Associations

Water colour paper is a heavy, thick, absorbent paper
with a clear grain and smooth to rough texture which is
ideal for water colour painting. The best paper is made
not from wood pulp but from linen and cotton rags. Pure
white paper is best as it provides the best ground for the
characteristic luminous quality of water colour painting.
Good quality paper also keeps its shape after several
applications of water colour .

See the works of Albrecht Dürer (German 1471-1528),
Lorraine Claude (French 1600-1682), John Robert Cozens
(English 1752-1797), Thomas Girtin (English 1775-1802),
Joseph Mallord Turner (English 1775-1851), Winslow
Homer (American 1863-1910), Edward Hopper (American
1882-1967).

See: **water colour, pigment, alla prima, aquarelle, gouache,
landscape, medium, opacity, plein air, sketch, typography.**

a watermark dated 1641

Watermark

Pronounced: WATAMARK (*1st a as in war, 2nd a as in ago, 3rd a as in car*)

Origin

Watermarks were introduced into handmade paper during the 13th century by attaching fine wire designs into the sieve into which the paper pulp is poured. All paper was made by hand until the beginning of the 19th century.

Meaning

A watermark is a letter, symbol or motif which is impressed into a sheet of paper and which can be seen only by holding the paper up to the light. It is a form of identification for the paper maker or a means of ensuring the limited use of the paper for security reasons (e.g. as in the use of banknotes).

Associations

See: **paper, symbol, motif, deckle, couch.**

Weave

Pronounced: WEEV (*ee as in see*)

Origin

From the Old English *wefan* and the Dutch *weven* meaning *to move to and fro*. Excavations in China in 1950 revealed evidence that weaving had been *mastered* there 6000 years ago. A horizontal loom operated by a treadle was used for weaving in Europe in the 13th century. Looms underwent little change until the 18th century and mechanised weaving was introduced during the Industrial Revolution in England in the 19th century. The Jacquard loom, which was first exhibited in Paris in 1801 and was introduced into England in 1816, began the automation of the weaving process.

Meaning

Weaving is one of the three processes by which yarn is made into cloth. The others are knitting and knotting. All woven materials have a **warp** and a **weft**. To weave is to make a textile fabric on a loom, or other device for weaving, by interlacing warp (the lengthwise) and weft (the crosswise) threads in a planned and carefully-designed order. The threads, produced by **spinning**, were originally of wool, cotton, linen, or silk but nowadays there are many synthetic fibres which are used, such as nylon, terylene, orlon and courtelle. Computer looms are now available which allow the user to design a woven fabric on the computer, weave the garment and, if necessary, modify the work and then complete the weaving. All this is completed in minutes rather than in hours or days as in the past.

Associations
See: **warp, tapestry, embroidery, loom, fabric**.

Wedging

Pronounced: WEJ-ING (*e as in red*)

Origin

From the Middle English *wegge* meaning *a (wedge-shaped) bread roll or pastry*. The shape was then used to describe a *plough share*.

Meaning

Wedging is the process in pottery of mixing plastic clay by hand in order to get rid of the air bubbles in the clay and so prevent possible **blowing** during firing . The clay is rolled out and cut into a wedge shape which is then repeatedly forced into itself on a **wedging bench**, which is a table strong enough to withstand the force and pressure of the vigorous activity. Usually the heel of the hand is used to bring pressure onto the clay and to thrust the wedge of clay into itself. Wedging is essential, especially where clays are of different consistency or where hard clay has to be mixed with soft clay, or wet with dry. Where large amounts of clay have to be dealt with, it is usual to use a **pugging mill** to mix clay.

A wedge (also called a **key**) is also a triangular piece of wood which is placed in the corners of a stretcher, in order to extend the corners and make a canvas on the stretcher as taut as possible. The tautness helps to reduce the chances of the stretcher frame from warping.

Associations

See: **kneading, key, dunt, warp, stretcher, slab**.

wedging

Weld

Pronounced: WELD (*e as in fell*)

Origin

From the Old English *welled* from the verb *well* meaning *to spring, boil up, rise* and, following the idea of a liquid rising, *to bring metal to a fluid state*.

Hammer or forge welding was practised in Middle East countries before 1350 B.C. and it remained the form of welding until the late 1800s. In 1877, Elihu Thomson, an American engineer, introduced electrical-resistance welding, which is the foundation of modern welding processes. Oxyacetylene welding was developed in France in the early 1900s.

Meaning

Welding is one of the joining processes. The others are

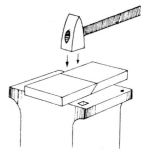

forge welding

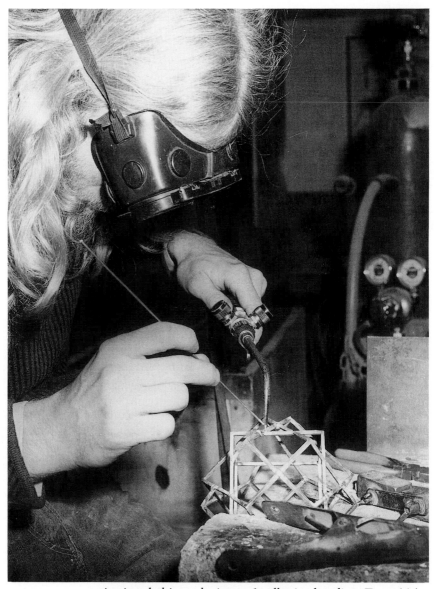

riveting, bolting, glueing and *adhesive bonding*. To weld is
the process of heating two separate pieces of metal until
their edges are molten and then fusing the molten sections
together. This is **fusion welding** and the process is called
coalescence. **Forge welding** is when metal is heated to a
molten state, then the parts to be joined are placed one
on top of each other and then hammered until they fuse.
Gas welding (also called **oxyacetylene welding**) uses an
intense flame (approximately 3000°c) from a mixture of
burning oxygen and acetylene gas (composed of two parts
of carbon and two parts of hydrogen) to heat **welding rods**
which are placed where two pieces of metal are to be

joined. The rods melt and fuse into the two pieces of metal, thus joining them. **Arc welding** is a process where a strong electric current (both direct current and alternating current are used) is passed between a metal to be welded and an electrode or rod held in the welder's hand. Electricity *arcs* between the edges of the metals to be joined, generating sufficient heat for the metals to melt. Additional metal is also melted into the joint and the metals are bonded. In recent years, **electronic-beam welding** and **laser-beam welding** have been developed, and these methods will extend the precision and speed of welding processes.

Associations

Acetylene is a volatile hydrocarbon gas, which is colourless,and has an unpleasant smell. It is used as a fuel for welding, soldering and cutting metals. It produces one of the highest flame temperatures possible. **Welding flux** is a compound used in welding to clean metals and prevent oxidation, to assist metal flow and to assist fusion of metals.

See: **solder, flux, dye**.

Wood Block

Pronounced: WOOD (*oo as in stood*),BLOK (*o as in rock*)

Origin

Woodblocks were used by the Ancient Egyptians and Mesopotamians (now Iraq) to produce designs on their potteryware before 3000 B.C.. The technique of making wood blocks for printing is believed to have first been used in China in the 9th century A.D.. It was a popular technique in some European countries from the 11th to 16th centuries, particularly for the making of playing cards and also religious illustrations. The technique was perfected by the German artist Albrecht Dürer (1471-1528), and the Flemish artist Hans Holbein (1497-1543). The technique lost popularity for a while but there was a revival of interest in it in the 18th and 19th centuries but this declined with the invention of photographic engraving processes.

The term also refers to a natural blue dye used in textiles.

Meaning

A wood block (or **wood cut** as it is also called) is a print taken from a block of wood which is carved in **relief**. Prints are made by inking the block, placing paper or fabric on the block and then putting the two through a press or rubbing the back of the material with a **baren** or a metal spoon. The prints were formerly used to illustrate books, but this is rare nowadays. A separate block is cut for each colour of a multi-coloured print. Wood block prints are made on fabric as well as on smooth-grained printing paper. Wood cuts are still a major art form in Japan.

Associations

See the work of Albrecht Dürer (German 1471-1528), Hans Holbein (German 1497-1543), Lucas Cranach (Austrian 1472-1553), Thomas Bewick (English 1753-1828), Edvard Munch (Norwegian 1863-1944), Emil Nolde (German 1867-1956), Aubrey Beardsley (English 1872-1898).

Xylography is the art of wood engraving and printing from wood blocks.

See: **relief, fabric, registration**.

A woodcut by Albrecht Dürer (1471-1528), entitled *The Knight and the Man-at-Arms*